Natasha grew up in Connemara, in the west of Ireland, and is a native Irish speaker. She's worked with Ireland's national broadcaster, RTÉ, and today runs a successful communications consultancy, *Stillwater Communications*, in Dublin. She is Ireland's leading confidence expert and firmly believes that confidence is at the heart of everything. www.stillwater.ie

⸻sín is Daily Features Editor and Broadcaster at *The Irish Times*. ⸻⸻ writes a popular column in the paper's *Magazine* every ⸻⸻ She lives in Dublin with her partner and six-year-old ⸻ s.

For Mary Troy & Ann Ingle

THE DAUGHTERHOOD

THE GOOD, THE BAD AND THE GUILTY OF MOTHER – DAUGHTER RELATIONSHIPS

NATASHA FENNELL AND RÓISÍN INGLE

SIMON & SCHUSTER

London · New York · Sydney · Toronto · New Delhi

A CBS COMPANY

First published in Great Britain by Simon & Schuster UK Ltd, 2015
This paperback edition first published in Great Britain by Simon & Schuster UK Ltd, 2016
A CBS COMPANY

1 3 5 7 9 10 8 6 4 2

Simon & Schuster UK Ltd
1st Floor
222 Gray's Inn Road
London WC1X 8HB

www.simonandschuster.co.uk

Simon & Schuster Australia, Sydney
Simon & Schuster India, New Delhi

Lyrics from 'Look Mummy No Hands' reproduced by kind
permission © 1986 Sweet n Sour Songs Ltd.
Music by Dillie Keane, lyrics by Adèle Anderson.

A CIP catalogue record for this book
is available from the British Library

Paperback ISBN: 978-1-4711-3531-6
Ebook ISBN: 978-1-4711-3532-3

Typeset in the UK by M Rules
Printed and bound by CPI Group (UK) Ltd, Croydon, CR0 4YY

CONTENTS

One day you will be at the mother of all funerals. Imagine if you could stand at the graveside and have no regrets . . .

1: THE BENCH MOMENT

It's a Tuesday. I'm standing in a hospital on my way to see my mother. The corridor smells of pharmaceuticals and over-boiled vegetables – I'm guessing Brussels sprouts. It's a nose-wrinkling, stomach-flipping cocktail.

I've always been fond of a carefully handled Brussels sprout, thanks to my mother's way with them which involves chestnuts and bacon. She has never overcooked a sprout in her life. If she can smell these sprouts from her hospital bed, I'd say they are momentarily distracting her from the recent diagnosis of lupus, which was handed over to her by Dr Kavanagh.

Ah. Yes. Lupus. What an idiotic name for an illness that causes havoc to the immune system. It sounds so harmless and about as terrifying as a crocus or a snowdrop or any other spring flower you care to mention. But it's that same lupus that has me standing here in front of a lift on my way to Room 41. My mother has it. We just found out. She just found out. Which makes me think that, on balance, she's probably not thinking about Brussels sprouts. I push the button for the lift that seems to be stuck somewhere, above or below. It's in lift limbo. I know how it feels.

Eventually the lift arrives. I get in and a few moments later I get out on the seventh floor. I look left and right in search of Room

41. I am forty-one. I feel more like a two-year-old right now. I was a clingy child. I spent most of the years nought to five attached limpet-like to my mother's legs. I have a flashback to a supermarket in Galway – my mother is trying to reach for a can of beans and I won't let her because it will mean she is detached from me for several milliseconds. It must have been desperately annoying. But she never let on. I can see her smiling at me now while I threaten to topple a display of tins in my determination to Never Let Go Of Her For As Long As I Draw Breath.

Room 41: is this the one? No, not this one, there's a frail-looking old man in it watching *Countdown*. My mother is not frail. I wouldn't even have called my mother old, although I suppose at sixty-nine other people would. I like the word Older much better than plain old Old. Because everyone is older than someone else. The teenagers are older than the toddlers, the octogenarians are older than the fifty-somethings. Old, on the other hand, suggests an ending. You have arrived at Oldstown, your final destination: please make sure you have your luggage and surprising facial hair before departing the bus. Enough. I don't want to think of final destinations at the moment, especially not in terms of my mother.

And now here I am. Room 41. I go in, walking past the woman who tightens her dressing gown around her when she spots me, towards the furthest cubicle on the right by the window. I lean in close to the pink fabric curtain. I take a breath.

'A Mhamaí,' I whisper. 'It's me. Tasha.'

No response.

'A Mhamaí,' I try again. 'It's me.'

Parting the curtain, I see a grey and white head of hair resting against a pile of pillows. She has a tube stuck up her nose and there's an inhaler lying on the bedside locker beside a bottle of water. The oxygen machine on the floor next to the bed is puffing away. Her eyes are shut and her face seems bloated. Her chest moves up and down with every assisted breath. In this unfamiliar scenario, I take comfort in the familiarity of her yellow nightdress, the favourite nightie of my mother, Mary Troy.

I can do nothing except stand there staring, afraid to move in case I wake her although, at the same time, I desperately want her to wake up. I tiptoe to the chair by the locker, put down my bag and the spare nightclothes I brought for her. I sit down on the chair, my eyes fixed on her. She is so still. I look out the window. I am not ready for this.

In my head I tell this woman, the person I love more than any other, what I can't yet say out loud: *This can't be happening. You, Mary Troy, are going nowhere. You have only just stopped working. You're supposed to stay with me this weekend. You said you'd help me pick the tiles for my bathroom and I know that sounds inconsequential in the grand scheme of things, but nobody else I know has your eye for a mosaic tile. We have booked our trip to Egypt and, if I'm not mistaken, you want to see the ice-mountains in the Antarctic one day. Don't you dare even think of leaving. I want to do so much more with you. I need you. We all need you. This is not your time.*

Feeling guilty for giving out to her even in my head, I lean over and stroke her bare arm. Her skin feels soft and loose beneath my fingers. She stirs in the bed and tilts her head towards me, her eyes heavy with sleep. Then she takes the tube from her nose and whispers: 'Oh, hi, love. You're so good to come.'

So good to come? Her politeness is more than I can bear. We talk for a while, neither of us saying anything about how we actually feel. As though by unspoken agreement we keep the conversation on neutral territory. There is talk about a court case in the paper and the mush that passes for hospital food. She confirms that some sprouts did indeed die in vain to create part of the midday meal. There is no reference to the rapid decline of her health or to the sudden shock of her being here or the confusion and helplessness I know we both feel. But we can see it all in each other's eyes, which is one of the reasons I don't hold her gaze for too long.

She doesn't say anything but I can see that she is tired again. I say goodbye, reluctantly, and stumble back down the corridor the way I came, jabbing at the elevator button. 'Oh, bring me down,' I think. 'Let me out of here.' The lift finally arrives. I press G for the ground floor. Where is H for Help? I reach the ground and head for the exit, pushing open doors, moving further away from her as I pass through each one.

I'm outside now. I steady myself on a wall taking greedy gulps of sprout-free air before making my way to a nearby bench. I've never been here before but I suddenly recognise this unremark-able piece of outdoor furniture. This is it. The Bench that marks the first stop on the road to losing someone. A place where we pause before daring to contemplate whatever awfulness might come next. I take a seat, inwardly screaming at all the other people who have done time here before me. Can you all shift over and leave this one to me? Move along please. My turn now. But they are just ghosts and I am alone.

I rummage in my bag for a bottle of water. When I find it, I knock it back as though the liquid holds some kind of cure. I drink too fast and the water splutters back into the bottle. No graces here today. No mercy either. My body bends forward. I clasp my arm across my stomach and I do what I've wanted to do since I first parted that pale pink curtain in Room 41. I cry. I cry and, not for the first time today, I think: *My mother might leave me. But she can't leave me. She's my mother.*

I will never forget that hour outside the hospital. My Bench Moment, I call it. Just thinking about it I can taste the overwhelming panic I felt as I sat there with all those thoughts of what might be to come swirling through my head. I am normally good in a crisis. A fixer by nature. But not this time. Sitting on The Bench I felt inadequate and helpless and out of my depth.

On the one hand I am worried sick about my mother's illness for her sake but, even as I consider the possibility of her being on an oxygen machine for the rest of her life, I am consumed with the prospect of her dying and how her loss will affect me. Me. When I think of my mother dying the tears I cry are two parts grief to one part self-pity. And along with those self-indulgent tears a tidal wave of self-scrutiny crashes in:

Have I been a good enough daughter? Have I told her how much I love her? Does she know how grateful I am for everything she has done for me? In my forty-one years what have I done for her? Is she aware of how I respect and admire her as a woman and as a mother? And, if she doesn't, is there still time left to let her know?

That moment on The Bench was my moment of reckoning. It marks the day I began asking questions about the nature of my relationship with my mother and started looking for ways to cherish what we have. Until that hour outside the hospital, I'd never grappled with the concept that my mother was going to die and that I would be left behind. But there I was on The Bench and that is where this book really begins. It is the place where I first realised the loss I am facing and contemplated how I'm going to deal with that loss. At that point, though, on that dismal Tuesday as I contemplated my first cigarette in twelve months, I didn't have a notion where to start.

My mother contracted lupus five years ago. I first realised something was wrong when we were on holiday in Morocco. One day she noticed her skin was covered in ugly blemishes, which we both assumed were caused by the intense sun. But what we thought were heat rashes turned out to be lupus. It is a disease in which the body's immune system becomes hyperactive and attacks normal, healthy tissue. It comes with a whole range of symptoms including inflammation, swelling and damage to joints, skin, kidneys, blood, the heart and lungs. To complicate things even further, she was diagnosed with pulmonary hypertension and has been on and off oxygen ever since.

Our relationship changed in the early stages of her diagnosis. Suddenly the vivacious and fearless mother I knew was reduced to relying on oxygen and on her children for care when home from hospital. As a family we took it in turns to make sure there was always someone with her and when I couldn't be in Galway, I talked to her on the phone several times a day. I couldn't shake the feeling that compared to what she was going through, my work and everything else in my life was irrelevant. Living and working two and half hours from her in Dublin, where I run a communications consultancy with my brother Cilian, meant I felt constantly guilty about not being around for her when she needed me most.

While I was being educated on the finer points of lupus and the array of medication my mother needed to take each day something else happened.

In an entirely separate and shocking development I started to realise I was sliding into stereotypical middle age.

At the monthly dinner parties I have held for years with my close female friends, a familiar pattern was emerging. We were all getting older and, having left our twenties and thirties behind, at times the conversation would turn to the subject of newly discovered aches and pains. We had started to talk about Our Ailments. As the corks popped, we'd catalogue how somebody's knees had begun to ache when they went upstairs. Somebody else had a weird twinge in their ankle and wondered could they be overdoing it in Pilates. My friend Moira was going through early menopause and we got the blow by blow details of the symptoms over vegetable tempura one memorable night. As she grappled with the awfulness of her first hot flush, I had a flashback to a time when our conversations were exclusively concerned with the latest hot men in our lives.

On top of our various physical complaints, another topic kept creeping across the dinner table: our mothers. The question came as sure as main course followed starter. 'And how is your mother doing?' We'd take it in turns to deliver our mother-related news bulletins. I'd describe in minute detail the latest update on my mother's condition like an expert – I wasn't one – giving a breakdown of the various treatments she was receiving. I talked about her funny illness-related sayings: her oxygen machine was attached to a long tube we kept tripping over – 'Just follow the lead and you'll find me,' she told visitors. I talked about the guilt of kissing her goodbye and taking the train back to my life in Dublin on Sunday evenings.

My friend Nora's father had died a year ago and now her mother had been diagnosed with rheumatoid arthritis so she knew what I was talking about. She was an only child and had to make a four-hour round trip to her mother's house every weekend.

'I'm not sure what's worse. The hassle of the trip or the guilt about how much I resent having to make it,' she said.

Jennifer's mother was in great health and had recently made out a list of Christmas presents she wanted to buy for her grandchildren.

'It's flipping June!' she seethed, the sun splitting the lime green walls in my backyard.

Nora reckoned she could do one better. Her mother was hosting a book club and was insisting on getting the room painted for the occasion. 'I told her nobody was coming to the book club for the paintwork but she has four shades of green on the walls and wants me to choose one,' she groaned. Moaning and laughing about our mothers was what passed for scintillating conversation at my dinner parties these days.

What we were discussing was serious but we always managed to have a good laugh. We couldn't believe how much of our evening was taken up with 'mother talk'. I enjoyed these conversations because, quite simply, I adore my mother. She's an intelligent, warm and wise woman with just the right dose of cynicism. Luckily, we've a lot in common. We are the kind of people who will obsess for weeks over something as inconsequential as the perfect G&T glasses, or chat for hours about a Brian Friel play at the Abbey Theatre. I've always felt lucky to have such a close relationship with my mother but until I started writing this book, I didn't realise exactly how lucky I was.

During one of these dinner parties, I listened as a friend despaired of her mother who, despite having cancer, was insisting on retaining her forty-a-day fag habit. And another who needed to offload about a recent visit by her mother who had spent the entire time criticising her parenting. 'Everything from Sam's hair being too long to the fact that I hadn't started Sarah on music lessons. She just can't help herself.'

As my own mother's health became more of a worry, I looked at the anguish in the faces of my friends and realised our relationships with our mothers were on our minds now more than ever before. We needed to talk about them. We needed to make some kind of sense of our relationships with them before it was too late.

I had an epiphany during one of these dinners: if my friends and I were feeling this way, it seemed likely that most other forty-something women were, for better or worse, spending more time thinking about their own mothers.

This marked the start of my Interrogation Phase – I began asking every woman I met two simple questions:

Firstly – 'Do you have a mother?' And if the nonplussed person I was interrogating answered yes, I then asked, 'Are you worried about her dying?'

At a very basic level I was asking because I wanted to feel less alone in my panic. But I had also become curious about whether other people had ever thought about their mother's death and considered how they would feel when she died. But, even if I didn't realise it then, I know now that it was a curiosity born of self-interest. I needed to know how other people were dealing with this so that I could deal with it better myself.

So, if you were a woman and we were introduced socially, you got asked these questions. I asked them at dinner parties. Art exhibitions. The beauticians. On trains. The reaction was instant. Colour drained from the faces of the person I was asking. Or they rolled their eyes before they could help themselves. Even if they started saying the subject was too personal to discuss, they always ended up telling me about their relationships with their mothers. The good, the bad and the guilt. Always the guilt. Just mentioning the word mother and dying caused an emotional earthquake in the faces of the women I spoke to. In one case I had a memorable conversation on a plane from New York to Dublin with a woman who answered my question about her mother by saying:

'I can't bear to be in the same room with her, if you must know. We fight most of the time. And yet, even when we're fighting, I have this quiet dread about when she is gone. It comes over me at the oddest moments. I don't even want to think about it.' She was still talking two hours later.

These conversations showed me that whatever their relationship, women my age had an awful lot to say about their mothers.

Other questions I started asking were: Do you think you are a good daughter? Could you be a better daughter than the one you are now? When I look back now, this was the beginning of my preparation. I could see a treacherous cliff edge looming in front of me. I wanted to be ready when life came up and pushed me off. I wanted to prepare for the time when my mother wouldn't be around any more.

But how to prepare? Well, for me it was about casting a forensic eye over my relationship with my mother. For the past five years the dread of losing her has been occupying my thoughts so much that I decided to write this book. It is a book not just about my fears and my relationship with my mother, but about daughters in general and our attempts to negotiate the most complex, infuriating, joyous, messy, enduring relationship of our lives.

The shelves and online bookstores are heaving with baby manuals but there are hardly any about making life with your mother as rewarding and life enhancing as it can be. The more I thought about it, the more I felt there was a need for a book to help daughters reflect on the relationship they have with their mothers and to help them consciously work to make that relationship the best it could be, particularly in those final years. A book to help them navigate the last years of their relationship. A book about the person many of us will always yearn for and turn to when times are hard – the woman with the ability to nurture, comfort and annoy you more than any other on the planet. One woman. For better or for worse. Your mother.

Ever since The Bench I've been on a mission and by reading this book this mission is also yours, should you choose to accept it. Imagine if you could stand at your mother's graveside and have no regrets. Well, let's be realistic, hardly any regrets. Imagine if when you stood there you could be confident, even in the midst of grief, that you had done the best you could, particularly in the final chapter of your lives together.

That is what this book is about. It's about doing things with and for our mothers that will enhance our time and our relationship with them as they age. It's about bringing pleasure to our mothers, whether you think they deserve it or not. This will come naturally to some of us and be more challenging for others. It is also about acknowledging that there might not be anything to do, apart from accepting that the relationship is as far away from the Hollywood version of mother–daughter relationships as it's possible to be. The Hallmark crowd don't make Mother's Day cards for daughters who don't get on with their mothers. But daughters who don't like their mothers still send them. It's just that they are usually blank inside, with no flowery message.

Here's what I found from talking to daughters: we are mad about our mothers. Mad with our mothers. And in many cases we are driven mad by the guilt that our mother–daughter relationships just aren't good enough. We need to get to grips with all of this before it's too late.

The original title for this book, the one I knew probably wouldn't end up on the cover, was *Ten Things to Do with Your Mother Before She Dies*. It had a macabre sense of urgency about it because what we are trying to do here is urgent in every sense. There is no nice way to put this – your mother is going to die. Most likely she is going to pop her clogs, or in my mother's case her round-toed, leather slip-ons, well before you do. If you felt the need to buy this book or if someone gave it to you as a gift, I am making an educated guess that the longest, most complex relationship of your life is now in its twilight years. In footballing terms, we are in the dwindling moments of extra time.

Parts of this book may not be easy to read, especially if your relationship with your mother isn't in good shape. Some of the ideas may seem unthinkable. One of my suggestions is that you help your mother plan her funeral. For many people that might be hard to consider. The things we are going to explore in this book are simple, straightforward and, in most cases, blindingly obvious. But that doesn't mean they are easy.

If you are one of the lucky ones whose relationship with their mother is in need of nothing more than a daughterly MOT, then this book is your chance to make something already really positive even better. For others, reading this book might just be about finding ways to make a bad relationship bearable. Or finding ways to accept that the bad relationship, the kind not generally described on Mother's Day cards, will never change. Or finding ways to forgive. Most of all, though, this book is about asking questions. Questions like:

How do we make sure that when she goes we are at peace with the way we behaved towards her when she was here?

And:

How will we feel when she dies if we leave things exactly as they are?

The answers will be different for everyone. The fact that you are reading this book suggests that, whatever your circumstances, we are all in the same boat, scanning a similar horizon. The scenery may be different but the destination is the same. One day we will be standing at a grave or in front of a crematorium curtain or reading a eulogy at the mother of all funerals. And we are going to have regrets. What we're trying to do is minimise those regrets. Not tomorrow, not next week, but now. While we still can.

2: A COLLABORATOR

I set off on this mother-centric odyssey – I have banned the word 'journey' from this book, blame *X Factor* – feeling pretty confident that I could help others make the most of their relationships with their mothers. I had a clear mission: to pour a little healing oil on troubled daughters. I had done my research, talked to a wide cross-section of concerned women and had my own experience to fall back on. However, I am the first to admit that I was naive about the extent of the difficulties daughters were experiencing. As I said earlier, I am lucky. I've always had a great relationship with my mother. It's not perfect, we have our challenges, but Mary Troy and I are good together. I talk to her on the phone every day. I genuinely enjoy her company. I seek her advice when I'm in tricky situations and she makes me laugh. The pleasure I get from my relationship with my mother is one of the great joys in my life. But having 'interrogated' so many other daughters, I knew that if I relied solely on my own experience this book wouldn't accurately reflect the complexities of mother–daughter relationships.

I had also begun to appreciate that I might need a bit of help. A collaboration started to seem even more attractive when I contemplated the pressures of running a company and writing a book at the same time. I also wanted a second opinion, a springboard for ideas, a brainstorming partner, someone who would bring fresh perspective to the tricky matter of mothers and daughters.

I'd been reading Róisín Ingle's column in *The Irish Times* for years. It's one of those personal columns, the kind that aren't everyone's cup of tea. They are mine, though. I like her style. I've always found her funny, thought-provoking and, more than anything else, fearlessly honest, sometimes painfully so. I had noticed her mother provided lots of material for her weekly musings. She seemed brimful of love for her mother but she also wrote about taking her mother for granted and being too needy a daughter. So I called her, left a message which I hoped was intriguing but not off-putting. And I waited.

Take a guess as to my whereabouts when I, Róisín, listened back to Natasha's voice message? Exactly. I was sitting in my mother's house, at her kitchen table, drinking pots of her excellent coffee. I'd like to be able to tell you my being there was a serendipitous, fateful happening. The truth is, at the time, if I wasn't in my own house or at work, I was pretty much hanging around my mum's. I was on another health kick and, since I didn't have weighing scales in my house, she was keeping track of the logistical side of things for me. This was not an entirely straightforward arrangement. My mother lives with my younger sister and I wasn't keen for her to know that I was enlisting our mother as some kind of WeightWatcher's leader. So I had my mother hide a blackboard behind her telly where she could surreptitiously record my progress in white chalk.

When Natasha left that message I was in my mother's house for my weekly weigh-in. I was also eating a plate of my mother's fried mushrooms on toast. It wasn't just the lure of the blackboard that had me round there so much. I'll tell you later on about how wonderful she is but that is only part of the reason why I like spending time with my mother. See, apart from myself, there is nobody in the world as interested in me as she is. Mothers are, in a lot of cases, aren't they? I wouldn't have said it at the time but, since I met Natasha and started thinking about all of this, I've realised that her interest in me is one of the things I love most about her.

She knows me – every particle of me – and, more importantly, she accepts the whole messed-up kit and caboodle of me. She sees all the stuff I try to keep hidden and loves me anyway. When I first learned and understood the phrase 'unconditional love' I thought of her. She is it. You know how boring it is listening to people's dreams? Well, I could tell my mother every dream I'd ever had and, not only would she not want to kill me, she'd ask me for more details.

I didn't recognise the number when Natasha called so I let it ring and carried on talking to my mother about how hard it was to jog for two and a half minutes without stopping. And when I'd finished she told me about the latest short story she'd written in which she'd imagined Booker-winning novelist Ian McEwan listening to Desert Island Discs and seething with jealousy because he'd never been asked on the programme. Then she read it out to me in her best posh stage voice. I probably should have been in work but, what with the mushrooms and McEwan, we were having a rare old time and I figured five more minutes at her kitchen table wouldn't hurt.

A short while later I listened to the voice message. This Natasha person was very cagey on the phone. She said she wanted to talk to me face to face about some idea or other she had. When I finished listening to the message I got off the phone and told my mother. 'Ring her and arrange to meet,' said my mum. 'It could be something good.' So I did.

My mother is sometimes wrong but not often, and she was right this time. It was something good. I knew it as soon as I walked into Natasha's office and she said, 'I've an idea for a book with the working title *Ten Things to Do with Your Mother Before She Dies*.' She didn't need to say another word. Help her write the book? I wanted to read that book. One recent trip with my mother to London goes some way towards explaining why.

When I travel with my mother I know that, as well as her sleep-apnoea machine, she has to pack a suitcase of anxiety related to years of having to deal with my various losses and travel mishaps. I lose passports. I mislay boarding cards. I turn up late for flights. I am, to put it mildly, a bit of a liability. So it's no wonder that on this latest trip to London my mother looked at me and saw all that potential for travel-related chaos.

I get highly irritated by this, obviously. 'I'm not a five-year-old,' I mutter when she asks for the third time if I have my passport. Even when she's not asking me, I know she's thinking about asking me. 'What a total head wreck,' my inner thirteen-year-old silently moans. I'm clearly a responsible adult. I have twin five-year-old daughters. Having managed to keep Joya and Priya alive for five years, I think I know a thing or two about being respon-sible. I only put jalapeños instead of gherkins in their lunchbox that ONE time. Give a mother a break.

We accidentally lose each other at the scanning machines. When we find each other again there's a man waving a boarding pass he has found on the ground.

'Did you lose your boarding pass?' she asks. I stare up at the screen to check for our gate number, pretending not to hear. Eventually she stops asking. We carry on to the gate. When I produce my boarding pass I see a familiar look in her eyes: relief.

I can't blame her for this constant fuss but, of course, I do because she's my mother. She is remarkably restrained in London, I notice. I nearly lose my phone twice and she manages not to tell me to be more careful. I can see it in her face, though: the care, the concern, the worry. (Infuriating, obviously.) But she mostly doesn't turn the concern into words, for which I'm grateful.

Still, there are other ways she manages to make me feel like that hard-done-by thirteen-year-old. I buy some bone-handled knives in a charity shop but she vetoes the purchase of two cups because she doesn't like the look of them. And just before we go downstairs for my sister-in-law's fortieth birthday party, she wonders – tentatively, I'll give her that – whether I might be going to brush my hair. The icy stare I summon up is enough to send her scuttling out of the room.

Of course I was going to brush my bloody hair, I think, getting the hairbrush out and making it look slightly less Worzel Gummidge. I don't need my mother to tell me I have hair issues.

Anyway it's a great party. My brother Peter makes a wonderful speech that annoys all the men in the room who say he's raised the bar too high. Everyone loves the food and Nigella's Guinness cake. Even my generous offer to sing 'The Mountains of Mourne' at 1am – with too much Prosecco on board I'm convinced it will have deep resonances for all these smart London folk – doesn't spoil things.

'People are happy, it's a good party,' Peter says kindly. The subtext is clear: Percy French, no harm to him and his Mountains of Mourne, will take a wrecking ball to the ambience.

It's a flying visit for me but my mother is staying on. We've barely woken up the next morning when she's asking what time my flight is. '10pm,' I tell her through gritted teeth. 'Are you sure?' she asks.

I check the time on my phone just to keep her quiet and discover, through my hangover, that I'm wrong. 'It's 6pm,' I tell her. She manages not to gloat.

Before I leave she wonders whether it might be wise for me to take the bone-handled knives out of my hand luggage and give them to her to bring back in a suitcase. How annoying and at the same time how massive-security-incident-avoiding of her.

When I get to the airport the flight is closed. Because, as the woman on the airline desk tells me, the flight is not at 6pm; it was at 4.45pm and it's on the tarmac about to take off. I have to buy a new ticket for the next flight which costs twice as much as the one I bought to come over.

When I ring my mother, distraught, she says she'll book it on her Visa and that it's only money and she knows I'll pay her back. Then she says she feels bad because she should have checked up on me regarding the time of the flight but, you know, she didn't want to treat me like a child.

Later I sit in the airport and cry. Over my stupidity and over the fact that, when my mother goes, there will be nobody else in the world who will care about me as much as she does. I make a promise I know I'll break: that I'll never again react negatively to her concerns, whatever my inner thirteen-year-old might think. Because – and you'd think I'd know this by now, you really, really would – she ain't heavy, she's my mother.

I love this idea of Natasha's. The notion that we can be more conscious of our mothers while they are still alive, rather than regretting what we did and more importantly what we didn't do when they die. There's lots I still want to do in my life. I want to learn another language. I want to get fitter. I want to play at least three songs well on the guitar. I want to run for an hour without stopping. And I want to be a better daughter. It's as simple as that. Or not. We shall see.

3: FINDING THE DAUGHTERS

The day after comedian and actor Robin Williams died, I – Natasha – listened to an interview he did at home that was broadcast in his memory. During the podcast, between the glorious comedy riffs, candid stories of drug addiction and revelations about the fear that followed him constantly, the man who was Mork talked about his mother. He had heard something once that struck a chord: 'Mothers know how to press your buttons. They know because they installed them.'

Our mothers install our buttons during our childhood and they spend the rest of their lives pushing them. Accidentally sometimes. And sometimes by design. That, in a way, is their job. With all the argy-bargy and ructions between mothers and daughters, it's a wonder we survive them at all, never mind get to know each other woman to woman. Since we met and decided to start working on this book, Róisín and I had begun to look more closely into the world of mothers and daughters. In one book we read as part of our research, a frustrated daughter exclaimed: 'If she wasn't my mother I'd divorce her.' But, by and large, mothers and daughters don't divorce each other. The relationships, even the difficult ones, endure longer than any others in our lives.

A book like this wouldn't have worked fifty years ago. Not

because there wasn't a need to discuss mother–daughter issues, but because the mother–daughter relationship didn't last long enough to warrant quite so much examination. We twenty-first-century daughters are spending longer with our mothers than any other daughters in history. Life expectancy since the 1900s has doubled. Women are generally outliving men. The fact that past the age of seventy women are often living alone has obvious repercussions when it comes to the intensity of their relationships with their children, particularly their female children. As they move into late middle age, daughters begin to worry more about their mothers. And, as they age, mothers become more concerned with their children who will be left behind, and about what will happen to them when they go.

In her excellent research study *Mothers and Their Adult Daughters*, Karen L. Fingerman Ph.D. points out that, apart from this new longevity, the uniquely enduring nature of the mother–daughter relationship is down to certain psychological and social factors. 'Their shared femaleness contributes to the nature of their ties,' she writes. 'Women share a disadvantaged status in society. Poverty, educational deprivation and poor health-care forge ties between mothers and daughters. Women are more likely to require assistance with daily tasks, emotional problems and financial needs than are men; they often receive this assistance from their mothers or their daughters. Yet . . . even women who are well-off retain strong bonds to their mothers.'

Fingerman talks about the fact that, throughout life – although this is changing as fathers become more involved in child rearing – mothers have tended to be more invested in their children than men. 'Older women were socialised from an early age to view themselves as mothers and the maternal identity enhances their investment in their children.' And, meanwhile, daughters were, in many cases, brought up to invest in generations above and below them. 'From childhood on, girls are taught to remain close to their mothers, while boys are encouraged to establish independence from their parents.'

There is a common arc to the mother–daughter relationship. It starts out mirroring many of the characteristics of an intense love affair. Róisín told me once how her twins lie in bed with her sometimes, early in the morning, when as a general rule she is not looking or feeling her best. They see miles past her matted hair and morning breath and last night's make-up. They see something else, something she can't see. They tell her she is beautiful. 'Mummy is so pretty,' they say, appraising her, heads to one side, as though she is some kind of work of art. Róisín's instinct is to tell them to stop talking rubbish but instead she smiles and soaks it in. They really mean what they say so she honours that and lets the purest love she's ever known wash over her. Then she brushes her teeth.

Every day she sees the joy on their faces when she praises them for writing a word or pouring milk into their cereal without slopping it all over the place or saying please and thank you. She also sees the dark, bleak expressions when she has to be sterner with them. Being a mother has given her direct experience of how from the very beginning, mothers have the power to influence how daughters feel about themselves, good, bad and indifferent.

As teenagers, in many cases we rebel and reject the intense bond, as we start negotiating the world on our own terms. We get older, we experience more of life, we may have children and our view of our mother expands. The ideal is that we begin to see our mothers as individuals in their own right. Women with needs and feelings and desires. We begin to respond to them in a more equal way. This development can take longer in some than others. I know from talking to Róisín that she feels she hasn't moved in this direction enough.

Another study by Fingerman shows that, while many aspects of the relationship change as daughters become middle-aged, certain emotional qualities remain constant. 'Mothers continue to influence the way their daughters feel about themselves. Years after daughters are grown, daughters feel guilty and ashamed when their mothers criticise them and feel happy when their mothers are proud of them.'

Our research gave weight to what we had already learned anecdotally and from our own experience: an in-depth conversation about daughters and their mothers was well worth having. So we decided to cast the interrogation net a bit wider. If we were really going to get under the guilt-gnarled fingernails of daughterhood, we needed to find out what other daughters were feeling and see if they were willing to share their stories. It was Róisín who suggested putting out a call to the daughters of ageing mothers across Ireland. It was one way to take the temperature of the nation's mothers and daughters. The worst that could happen was that nobody would reply and I'd have to face the fact that nobody was interested in talking about their mothers after all. So I told her to go for it.

This is what I – Róisín – wrote at the bottom of my newspaper column: *If you are a woman and you would like to improve your relationship with your mother before it's too late then send an email to* . . .

The response was immediate and forceful. It seemed we had

apped into decades of daughter-related strife. We received nearly 100 emails from women all over Ireland, some of them pages long. Many were speaking about their mothers for the first time, which made us think about all the other daughters struggling with the same issues but afraid even to put their thoughts down in an email for fear of voicing what might be considered 'undaughterly' emotions.

The emails dripped with guilt and resentment and worry and bitterness and regret and joy and sadness. Natasha and I sat at her kitchen table one night, a glass of wine by our sides, reading through them. We laughed. We cried. We got a bit drunk. We sobered up. When we had finished reading, we were overwhelmed with compassion for these women who had spilled out their innermost thoughts about their mothers. Many women wrote about the difficulty of being a dutiful daughter to a difficult mother, especially when there was illness, whether mental or physical. The stories were different but what they all had in common was various levels of angst about the relationship and a desire, in most cases, to make it better before it was too late.

We felt like we were reading the outpourings of an under-ground, long-silenced and desperately vulnerable community. Most of these women mentioned the taboo nature of what they were saying, especially where the relationships with their mothers was at breaking point. When we put out the call, we never imag-ned we would be tapping into that level of heartache and anguish. It made us think again about what we were trying to do.

Not long afterwards, we were back in Natasha's kitchen reading through the emails again. We had developed an easy friendship from the start and these nights, sitting around talking about our mothers, didn't feel like work. My book club was on the follow-ing night and so I had half an eye on my laptop and the other on

the doorstopper of a book I hadn't yet finished reading. As
flicked through Donna Tartt's *The Goldfinch*, I told Natasha abou
how without membership of the book club, I'd find it hard to ge
around to reading any books at all.

'The book club forces me to read at least one book a month,'
said. 'I have to find the time to do it because I know at some poin
I'm going to have to turn up in somebody's house and talk abou
it. I also know from bitter experience that it's very hard to bluf
about a book you haven't read, even if you have skim-read a bool
called *How to Talk About Books You Haven't Read* by Pierre Bayard
Natasha thought I was joking about the book but I wasn't. On
mischievous member chose it for our book club last year
Obviously, most of us didn't bother to read it and that gathering
turned out to be one of the most stimulating meetings in bool
club history.

I put down *The Goldfinch* to read out a particularly heart-
breaking email from a daughter who was considering severing al
ties with her mother.

'Imagine,' said Natasha when I was finished. 'Imagine if ther
was a club where instead of discussing books, daughters sat aroun
discussing their problems with their mothers.' It was a joke, really
But, as soon as she said it, we both knew she had hit on something

When we thought about it, we realised most of the women w
knew were members of themed clubs. We all had diaries fille
with weekly or monthly appointments where we gathered t
drink or eat but mostly to talk. If some self-improvement happened along the way, all the better. Book clubs. Cake clubs. Suppe
clubs. Running clubs. Wine-tasting clubs. Clothes-swapping clubs

What about a daughters' club? What better way to figure ou
how to improve our relationships with our mothers than with .

bunch of women toiling away at the coalface of daughterly life? I suppose, to all intents and purposes, Natasha and I were already in a sort of daughters' club. A very small one. We talked about little else these days.

A daughters' club? It seemed almost too obvious but I – Natasha – knew that now the idea had been put on the table we would have to at least have a go at setting one up. Every club needs members and the first task was to persuade some daughters to get on board with the idea. We arranged to meet with a few of the women who had responded to Róisín's column. We wanted to find out a bit more about them and see if they'd actually be interested in membership of our club. A lot of them were. Although we probably shouldn't have been, having had such a positive response to the column, we were still surprised that there was such an appetite for sharing mother stories. We had long conversations with the women on the phone. We arranged to meet some of them in cafés, some in my office and, in one instance, in a train station when Róisín was on her way to Belfast for work.

Most of the daughters we spoke to really liked the idea of a support group but we would be asking for quite a lot from them. Reading a book a month is one thing, opening up to a bunch of strangers about the cracks in a relationship that society says should be the most joyful in your life was something else. With monthly meetings as our structure, we were asking for a serious time commitment before you even got into the nitty gritty of working on mother–daughter relations. It was a commitment that some women simply couldn't give.

These reluctant daughters varied from Jane, whose mother was so critical and negative towards her that she stopped going home for weekends, to Molly, whose mother kept constant tabs on her even though she had left home years earlier. And then there was Sally. Her story stuck with me. She and her two young children had returned from living abroad. They had temporarily moved in with Sally's mother while the family got settled. Sally had separated from her husband and her mother seemed to blame Sally for the breakdown of the marriage. At forty-two she felt that she was capable of knowing why her marriage hadn't worked out without her mother interfering in the way that she did.

'My mother made me feel terrible about leaving Ireland and I felt guilty about taking the children as I knew she'd miss them,' she told me. 'Now that I'm home and have separated from my husband she makes me feel even worse. She keeps saying she is concerned about the children but I think she is slightly ashamed that her daughter has separated. She and Dad were married for forty years and marriage is for life, as far as she is concerned. It is going to take me a very long time to convince her that this is better for everyone.' Just when Sally needed her mother's support the most, her mother seemed incapable of giving it.

I had huge sympathy for Sally, as she was stuck in a situation where she had to rely on her mother whilst sensing her disapproval on a daily basis. When I phoned her after she had eventually moved into her own house, she told me she had only seen her mother once in the last three weeks. In a way, she needed a daughter's club more than anyone, but she was conflicted about being part of a daughter experiment.

Meanwhile, Jane was the youngest of five and had been sent away to boarding school at the age of twelve. She came to me as a client to be trained for an important presentation she was giving to her board of directors. She told me she lacked confidence when it came to speaking in public and I reassured her that this was the case for most of the world's population. We got talking about where her lack of self-belief came from and out came her Motherstory.

'My mother thought I was useless at everything when I was a child, so she sent me to boarding school in the hope it would sort me out,' she told me. 'I was constantly compared to my two older and more intelligent brothers and I began to believe that I wasn't as smart or as worthwhile as them. My mother's negativity would drain your blood. I have worked very hard to get to where I am in my career but she never ever praises me or tells me that I'm doing well. And here I am at thirty-six still seeking her approval. I have confronted her on numerous occasions about it and it always ends up in a row.'

Jane had recently started seeing a counsellor in the hope of resolving the conflict with her mother. I told her about our project and asked whether she thought it would help her. At first she said she would love to be a part of such a gathering. A week later she told me, with regret, she didn't think she could commit. She was too scared her mother would find out.

This was one of the main obstacles preventing many of the women we met from joining our group. They felt disloyal talking about their relationship with their mothers, even in cases where mothers had clearly failed their daughters. We were learning more and more all the time about the depth and complexity of the mother–daughter relationship. If any other person treated these women the way they were being treated by their mothers they would have walked away. But the mother relationship was not something they felt they could walk away from. They didn't feel it was an option, even though the relationship was causing them pain.

While lots of the women were happy to talk about their mothers at length, most were not prepared to go on the record using their real names. 'I don't even talk about this to my best friends,' was a common response. So we decided the daughters would have to be anonymous. But even when we told them their identities would be disguised, many were still reluctant. The daughters with difficult relationships were not surprisingly the most wary of committing but those were the daughters that we knew we needed to hear from most.

Thankfully for every woman who felt they couldn't make the commitment, there were many others who were keen to get involved. By the end of our search we could have set up three groups but we decided, being amateurs, to keep it to one. The women who came on board for the first group were enthusiastic, if a little nervous, about sharing the trials of wanting to be a better daughter.

Our plan was to swap stories from the trenches and motivate each other to greater daughterly heights. This was our question:

What would happen when a group of daughters set out to fix, improve and challenge a relationship that had been left to its own devices for years?

We weren't sure but we guessed there would be as much laughter as there were tears. And wine. There would definitely be wine.

4: THE DAUGHTERHOOD

I – Natasha – am a candle person. I light them at breakfast, which shows you how devoted I am to a little flicker on my table. Róisín knows the drill when she comes round to mine now. The candles have to happen before the conversation can flow. I lit more than usual the night we gathered for our first meeting of daughters. We had decided on a name for our group. Mothers have a widely used description for their status – motherhood. According to my dictionary, 'Motherhood is the state or experience of having and raising a child. Giving birth to and raising a child is an example of motherhood.' So, Daughterhood is the state or experience of being a daughter, a female child. And that state is exactly what we had come together to explore. We had started The Daughterhood and now the first members were about to walk through my door.

There was chilli warming in the oven and wine on the table. Part of me was excited but another part of me was terrified. I didn't know these women. What if it turned out to be a terrible idea? I remember calming myself down by thinking about all the other people, strangers, who were meeting in the city that night and the reasons they were all getting together – Bridge clubs. Zumba classes. Yogalates (whatever that was).

And while it was true that there might not be another meeting of daughters who wanted to talk about their mothers going on anywhere else, that didn't matter. When we have a passion or a problem, I reassured myself, it's natural to want to spend time with other people with whom we have that thing in common. I thought about all the AA meetings happening around the city that night. This felt like D A. Daughters Anonymous. The doorbell went. I lit another candle for luck, took a breath and opened the door.

Part of my day job involves running confidence courses but I felt quite anxious that evening. As the women arrived, they looked shyly at each other, sat at my kitchen table, and waited for something to happen. I tried not to think about the fact that we had no guarantee anything would.

There were seven of us, including Róisín and myself, at the beginning. In time this would grow to nine. Two women came to join us in unexpected ways and you'll hear about them later. That night, though, I looked around my table and tried to exude the air of somebody who knew exactly what they were doing. Dark-haired Maeve said no to the wine, and I remember Lily, in her bright red jumper, looked pale as a ghost. I could see how anxious she was. Sophie, with her jet-black hair and lapis lazuli necklace, was very still and quiet and I wondered if she was contemplating a dash to the door. Róisín was chatting to Grace who was all red lipstick and smiles and banter and, if you looked more closely, a bit teary eyed. Cathy, who looked obviously nervous, took another gulp of red wine. I was the facilitator, managing the proceedings, like a conductor trying to organise an orchestra at their first rehearsal. We were a rookie orchestra, of course. We didn't know the notes to play but we were willing to give it a try and that was the main thing.

We were seven very different women with, it might have

seemed on the surface, not much in common. Here in my kitchen our differences didn't seem so obvious. We wanted to talk about our mothers. We wanted to listen to other daughters talking about their mothers. And so the evening began. As the rain lashed and wind howled outside, we went around the table listening to each other tell their Motherstories in the glow of the candles. It felt natural. I was so relieved.

I started the ball rolling by introducing the concept of The Daughterhood and what I hoped it would achieve. I told the daughters about my own mother and how her illness led to a period of self-scrutiny about myself as a daughter. I told them how Róisín had come on board. I told them that The Daughterhood was all about improving our relationships with our mothers before it was too late. I asked them to commit to six meetings over six months. I said I didn't have a magic wand but if only one positive thing came out of the six meetings in terms of their mother relationships then that would be a success.

I started to dish out the chilli and I placed a Dictaphone on the table in front of me. We had decided we were going to record the meetings so that we could get the stories transcribed for the book. When I listened back to the transcription of my introduction I could hear how emotional I was talking about my own mother and about what we were embarking on:

'I know it might feel a bit weird to talk about our mothers as a group like this but I hope we will get used to it; I'm used to it already because I've been thinking about this for a long time. The intent is important. And the commitment. We are all here because we want to do something with our mothers and to think more consciously about our relationships. Nothing is right and nothing is wrong and that's the whole point about it. And if there's only one thing you get at the end of all of this for yourselves and for your mothers that one thing will be worth it. Some of it might not be easy for us and we need to be prepared for that, too. We will meet every month for six months. That's all I'm asking. A commitment of six months and whatever comes out of it will be good enough.'

After I spoke, each daughter took their turn and that became the structure for all the meetings that followed. Maeve was funny about wanting more intimacy with her mother and yet keeping her at arm's length. From Sophie we heard the story of her mother's mental illness and from Lily we learned about what it was like to have a narcissistic mother. Cathy told us about her fear of becoming her mother; Grace about her mother who had Alzheimer's. Róisín described how close she was to her mother but was honest about her daughterly failings. 'I keep promising myself I won't talk too much about myself when I meet my mother, but I always do. I find myself endlessly fascinating in her company,' she said with a laugh.

After everyone had spoken and the plates were cleared, I passed around a list of 'things' that people might like to do with their mothers over the course of the six months we were planning to meet. Listen more. Be patient. Bite your tongue. Travel with her. Stop being her doctor. That kind of thing. We were all talk at the beginning, thinking it would simply be a matter of ticking off dinner parties and lunch dates, iPad lessons and shopping trips. We talked about what we needed to do and doubts were expressed about whether we would come up to scratch in The Daughterhood stakes. We laughed and groaned as we ticked the boxes that seemed most appropriate to our situation.

We had shared so much with each other that by the time the

women got up to leave they no longer felt like strangers. Some of the daughters had told the stories of their mothers for the first time. There were damp scrunched-up pieces of kitchen paper dotted about the table, the evidence of the tears that had been shed. I made a mental note to provide a box of proper tissues at our next meeting.

Róisín and I had a post mortem after the first Daughterhood meeting. It was the first of many post mortems. It was clear that, as daughters, we all had very different back stories and challenges. There are many types of daughters, just as there are many types of mothers, and that first meeting had thrown this variety into sharp relief.

As we got to know each other better over the next couple of meetings, we figured out each of our biggest challenges and began to understand how we saw ourselves as daughters. We came up with titles for us all, for the kind of daughters we were, at this time in our lives anyway. Clearly, being master multi-taskers, we daughters have the ability to switch from one daughter label to another depending on what stage we are at and what is going on in our lives. As you will see, there's a little a bit of each daughter in all of us.

5: MEET THE DAUGHTERS

MAEVE: THE BUSY DAUGHTER

My mother has a pink, almost disco neon coat. She wears it through winter and summer. It's water resistant and has a fleece lining which is attached by a zip, so you can remove it depending on the weather. 'A coat for all seasons,' she says. 'You know me, Maeve, frugal fanny.' And she IS a frugal fanny. It's one of the things I really like about her. She pickles things in the summer, cucumbers, say, or baby beetroot, and fills up her old dilapidated walk-in larder with jars. In the winter, you can't leave her house without at least three of the jars rattling about in your handbag. My mother is constantly prepared for a nuclear emergency. When The End comes you want to be in my mother's house. In my mother's larder, specifically, which smells of vanilla and vinegar and pickles of every shape, provenance and size.

She never thinks anything she makes is good enough, though. She'll shout after you, 'They're probably awful but you could give them to the cat.' This is something that infuriates me about my mother. This idea that what she makes, potentially prize-winning grub, if you ask me, isn't up to scratch. She's kind of lived her life like that. Apologising for her existence. It drives me mad.

I like her pink coat. I like it because it's bright and therefore visible through my glass door from about twenty paces. If I miss the clang, scrape and squeak of my rusty old gate, which I could easily do being engrossed in some software bug or other, some tricky techie conundrum, I won't miss the flash of pink through my glass front door. And when I see the flash of pink I have two choices.

Option A: Answer the door to my mother and give up precious hours of my day to chat about the minutiae of my life and hers, when I should be earning a crust. (I should point out that I answer the door quite a lot in these situations. I'm not a complete monster.)

And then there's Option B: Hide. (Sometimes I hide.)

It's interesting, I think, that the morning I read the notice in *The Irish Times* I was hiding. My mother had long gone, leaving, I was to discover later, a Kilner jar of pickled red peppers on the doorstep, but I was sitting behind my sofa feeling guilty. I was having my usual conversation with myself after I've hidden from my mother. 'Would it have killed you to answer the door and just have a chat with her? Could you not have had a coffee break? What are you doing hiding from your mother?' In the time I spent giving out to myself about hiding from my mother I could have had two cups of coffee with her and discussed the entire plot of *The Archers* and/or *Coronation Street*.

The magazine was on the floor beside me, and I'd picked it up, just flicking through, and the thing at the bottom of the column on page three caught my eye. *If you would like to improve your relationship with your mother before it's too late, then send an email to . . .* I can't say I thought that deeply about it at the time. Later, though, at dinner with Tony my husband, it must have come back into my mind because I asked him what he thought of my relationship with my mother. He laughed, which I remember thinking was interesting. 'Well, you're not as close as some daughters are to their mothers. You are not in each other's pockets,' he said after thinking about it for a few minutes. 'But it's hardly a relationship that needs saving.' Tony didn't want to talk about it much beyond that. I think there was football on the telly and I was pulling an all-nighter for work. But it got me thinking. And that night I sent Róisín an email:

Dear Róisín

About my mother. The main thing is I hide from her when she calls to my house but it's not my fault it's hers. She knows I'm busy working and that I'm self-employed but she still calls around without prior arrangement at the drop of a hat. It doesn't matter how many times I've told her not to do it, she still does. She sometimes brings food. It's only when I'm writing this that I see how ludicrous it sounds. My mother calls around with nutritious vittles and I hide from her. Of course, this is not the whole story. There is more, if you want to hear it. It's only when reading the bit at the bottom of your column that I realised that while we are close and spend a lot of time together my relationship with my mother isn't what I'd like it to be. For various reasons. And that I would like to improve it. I'm not sure if you need more dramatic stories than this one but if you think it would help I'd like to get involved with whatever it is you are organising.

Yours truly and feeling a tiny bit silly,

Maeve

I left my mobile phone number at the bottom of the mail but I didn't expect to hear back. Anyway, just the act of sending the email and naming something I had spent years shying away from was liberating. There was a lot more I could have said but I held back. I resolved to carry on happily ignoring the 'problem'. I had to put it in inverted commas because I wasn't even sure it was a 'problem'. I remember idly wondering if anybody else had answered the email and what kinds of stories other daughters had to tell. And then I forgot all about it. Until I got the call from Róisín. I listened to her talk about mothers and daughters and I remember laughing a bit. I felt understood, or something. But I didn't say yes right away. I told her I'd think about it. I needed to think about it.

I'm thirteen. My father is working abroad in Singapore and my two younger brothers, my mum and I are in Dublin. We don't see my dad much. We used to travel with him everywhere. Dubai. Singapore. Australia. New Zealand. He was a salesman. Technology mostly. Gadgets and gizmos, he used to call it. I ended up in pretty much the same game.

We moved back to Dublin because my mum wanted to mind her mother. My nana, who lived on her own, had been 'failing', as my mother put it, for years. It made me think about living as a kind of failing. Every day failing a little bit more. Death being the ultimate failure. Cheery, eh?

So I'm thirteen and I'm standing in the hall, trying to get my little brother, Ciaran, to put on his football boots. It's a sunny day and Mum wants us to go outside where there's a patch of green and a makeshift football pitch. The posts have graffiti on them. 'Timmo fancies Sinead', 'U2 Foreva', 'Slug was here', that kind of thing. Ciaran is not playing ball in terms of putting on his boots. So I'm shouting at him when the phone rings. My mum shushes me.

The thing about being the eldest is you are always 'in charge'. You have to do the right thing at all times. People expect stuff from you. You're to act older and wiser than you are and you're not to mind. I feel a bit resentful of this. These are my mother's children, not mine. Why isn't she putting on his boots? I'd like to go out to the patch of grass myself and hang around with Timmo and see if he might fancy me instead of Sinead but, no, I'm wrestling with my little brother while my mum shushes me on the phone.

'Keep it down,' she hisses, and I look at her and I know something's wrong. Under normal circumstances she's got ruddy cheeks, the cheeks of a farmer, I always think. Her dad was a cattle farmer; her mother milked cows and kept hens. She has the cheeks of a farmer's daughter, I suppose. But they were pale then as she stood there on the phone, her apron splashed with red bits from the strawberry jam she was making.

'What? When? Who was with him?' she is saying. She has the phone, one of those old, black, sturdy-looking things with a coiled lead attached, in her right hand and she puts the other hand up to her face, to her mouth, as she listens. When she takes the hand away all you can see is a bright red jam patch. And when she puts down the phone to tell me Dad has had a brain haemorrhage in a restaurant on the twentieth floor of some big hotel and he's dead, all I can think about is that smear of jam.

I'm sad. I think so anyway. I don't exactly miss him because I haven't seen him for three and a half months. I think what I miss is something I don't know yet that is lost. His body is flown back. He is buried in the cemetery I walk past on the way to school. My mother makes mountains of sandwiches which she tells everyone who crams into our tiny kitchen are 'awful, terrible, the worst I've ever made'. They are delicious. I take six – they are tiny – and go up to my room with the Atari my dad sent me for Christmas and I play Pong until I fall asleep. I wake up with an imprint from the keyboard on my face. In my dream I was in a vat of strawberry jam, trying to escape but never getting my head above the sweet-smelling gunk. I haven't eaten strawberry jam since.

I grow up. It happens in a blur of housework and homework and child-minding. And my relationship with my mother becomes workmanlike. We are in business together. We are in the business of running a household together. There is no man of the house. He is not coming back.

Snapshots: I'm thirteen and a half and bringing my two brothers to school every day while my mother grieves for her mother who died two months after my dad. I'm fourteen and, since my nana has died, my mother says she feels so alone and wonders whether death is stalking our family. I'm fifteen and helping my mother decide whether to paint the garden shed or knock it down. We take an axe to it and make a sandpit for the boys. I'm sixteen and my mother and I have family meetings, with yellow legal pads where we write things down, finances, holidays, as though my mother and I are co-parents, co-workers, not mother and daughter.

No, scratch that, we aren't co-workers. We aren't co-anything. My mother is the boss. A strict boss. With high expectations of her most senior employee. Me. And I love her, I do, but sometimes I don't feel connected to her the way I imagine a daughter should. I'm seventeen and I cannot wait to get out of the house. My mother is constantly trying to keep up appearances. She worries all the time. Where are us children going? Who with? When will we be back? Death is still stalking us, she imagines. That's what it seems like anyway but I don't ask her because, although we live

together, we are on separate continents in terms of our understanding of each other. She makes gourmet dinners but takes the
joy out of it by telling us how she could have done it so much
better. She wonders about night classes, even going so far as to
circle the ads in the newspaper. She never goes to a night class,
though. Her life is small. Our lives are small. But one day I will be
older and I will live a big life and I cannot wait.

And now I'm grown up, living a medium-sized life. I'm married.
And sometimes I hide from my mother and her superior pickles
and preserves. But I want more than this. She is only sixty. I am
only thirty-seven. We still have so much time left together, I hope.

I want, I suppose, more intimacy and the kind of deep connection I know is possible. Being older, I can see that we are more
alike in personality than I ever thought we were. We laugh at the
same things, even if I can't admit to my friends I love *Mrs Brown's
Boys*. We get stressed over the same kinds of issues (from choosing
furniture to form filling) and we have the same almost scary perfectionist streak. Hers is about pickles and mine about my work.
I enjoy her company and the time we spend together is easy and
enriching. For both of us, I think.

And yet, I don't have a completely authentic relationship with
my mother. Even when I'm not hiding from her there are times
when I don't let her in. She wants to know more about my relationship with Tony; she'd love to hear about my issues with work.
I don't want to tell her because, when I do, she gets unduly worried.

I think this need for more connection and intimacy, and wanting to make more time for her, is the reason why, suddenly, here I
am agreeing to meet up with other daughters who want to

improve their relationships with their mothers. 'Strangers,' I can hear my mother's voice in my head. 'What would you want to do that for?' As she often does, the woman in my head has a point.

But I go to that first meeting. I remember it because it was lashing rain. And freezing, even for a February night. If you were the kind of person who looked for signs in the weather it would have felt ominous, but as soon as I stepped into Natasha's house with the candles and the smell of good food and the smiling, nervous-looking faces of the other daughters, I felt like it would be fine. Grand. Everyone at The Daughterhood says it, we kind of marvel about it, but that first night, although I was nervous, too, was a revelation. That feeling of everyone being there with their very different stories but wanting the same thing. I think someone joked about it a few meetings later in a corny way, calling it a 'circle of belonging', but it definitely had that vibe.

That night I talked about my mother for longer than I ever had before. We all did, I think. We ate, and some of us drank and smoked. We circled our 'things' on Natasha's list. I seemed to circle everything. But one thing stood out for me – travel with her. Every time I had been away with my mother before, it had ended in disaster. If she irritated me at home, that irritation seemed to multiply when we travelled to foreign shores. I wanted to go away with my mother and for it not to be a holiday from hell. I put that at the top of the list as, punch drunk from hearing what everyone had to say, we stumbled out into the still-freezing, rain-soaked night. I don't know what everyone else was thinking but this is what I thought:

Who would have thought that a good night out could be had just chatting about our mothers?

But it happened. Apart from anything else, it was a bloody great night out. I was less keen on the thought of what I had to do now – focusing on my relationship, getting my hands dirty with my mother, as Natasha put it. But I'd signed up to this Daughterhood now and so, apparently, I had work to do.

Reflections on the Busy Daughter

When I – Natasha – get a call from my mother, a picture pops up on my mobile phone of her on a moped. This photo was taken on a family holiday in Portugal. We hired this little moped, well it's not really a moped, it's one of those mobile things that people use to get around from A to B when they can't walk that far. We hired it for her so she could come down the hilly path to the beach with us for swims. 'I can't believe you put that photo on your phone,' she says to me when I show it to her; 'my hair looks wild and I look so old.' But I don't care; I love it.

That little vehicle was her saviour on holiday as it conserved her energy for a swim. She was very weak at the time but determined to swim every day. The waves could be fierce depending on the winds and I would link one arm through hers and my eighty-year-old aunt, her sister Margaret, would link hers through my other arm and the three of us would head for the water. Like my mother Margaret is a great swimmer but these waves were so strong they could knock you over. We stood in the water as I balanced both of them on either arm and laughed and screamed like children as the force of the waves swept towards us. The moped was then revved up and my mother scooted back up the hill again.

So Mary Troy perched on that moped is the image that pops up on my screen when she rings. 'Sorry to ring you at work, love,

know you're very busy but I just wanted to ask you something . . .'
I nearly always answer the phone to my mother, particularly since
she got sick. I answer unless I'm training, on a phone call or in the
middle of a really important meeting. She doesn't ring just for the
sake of it and when she rings it's normally for a reason. We talk
every day, usually midmorning, around 11am, and then at some
stage in the evening. Sometimes if she rings me at work and I'm
on a deadline, I'm conscious that I'm pushing her off the phone.
'Sorry, but I can't talk to you now, is everything all right?' 'Yes, just
wanted to ask you . . .' and before she gets to the end of her sentence she has been cut off by me at 90 miles an hour,
'CallyoubackassoonasIcan!' She doesn't stand a chance. Later I do
call her back, 'Sorry I was too busy to talk to you . . .' and we carry
on as normal. The last time I got annoyed was when I had to re-
order her mobile oxygen machine for our trip to the Arctic. There
seemed like five million phone calls to make to get it sorted – the
hire company, her doctor, the heart doctor, the health insurer, the
delivery company, the airline to give them the model number. On
and on they went. I needed a spreadsheet to manage all the different forms and various tasks that it took to finally hire it for a
week. I expressed my frustration to her when she rang me for the
umpteenth time to tell me, 'And don't forget you also have to ring
the something or other.' 'This is a total pain in the head,' I blurted
down the phone. 'It's only a bloody machine and we only need it
for a week.' I was totally exasperated.

'But my mother is totally out of sync with my life, especially at
work,' a friend said to me recently. 'She rings me at the most
awkward times. She knows I'm busy and when I tell her I can't
talk to her because I'm busy, she then asks me what I'm doing that
has me so busy? It's so annoying.'

Mothers don't stand a chance with their daughters in our busyness. In talking to our daughters at the monthly meetings, it became clear that outside of those relationships where mental illness or dementia played a part, mothers in later life simply have more time to invest in their daughters than their daughters have to invest in them. This fact alone is a common cause of tension and severe button pushing. Janice, a friend of mine, has regular minor set-tos with her mother, usually on the phone, when Janice feels her mother is being far too curious and concerned about the minutiae of her and her daughter's life.

'So, where are you going for lunch tomorrow?' she'll enquire. Or 'Do you think you better send that form back for the girl's music lessons?' Innocuous comments like this set Janice ridiculously on edge; it's the mother equivalent of the sound of scraped fingernails across a chalk board. 'I veer constantly between annoyance that my mother is keeping tabs on me, to gratitude that my mother could be bothered to mention these things. I mean, who else, apart from her, would really care?' Janice told me. Newsflash: our mothers tend to be motherly. They can't help it. And yet we can often resent this expression of something that is as natural to them as their morning cup of tea.

Too often they are up against the clock from the moment they get a ring tone or knock on our door to say hello. The skill involved in them getting the words out quickly before we cut them off is an art in itself. They are in a race against time – and it gets worse, so often the conversation starts with an apology.

'Sorry, hope you don't mind me calling you …' 'Hi, love, is it OK if I call in – I won't stay long …' And so on. Let's face it, with our busy lives, our mothers are often terrified of encroaching on us. Often I'll be with a friend when the phone rings and is left unanswered. I'll say, 'Take that if you have to.' 'No, it's OK, it's only my mother,' is the regular response. 'I'll ring her later.' 'Only my mother' – I often wonder how do so many mothers get to that *only* status? How does it happen that they end up there? In our early years, it is us ringing them – we are the ones coming home for the home-cooked food, getting our laundry done, and the support that comes with it. As the years pass, we gradually ring less and visit less, as we carve out our own place in the world. And then, finally, they are reduced to 'It's only my mother'? Are our mothers really so annoying that our reactions are justified, or are we really so busy that we just can't take that call?

Of course there are mothers who drive their daughters crazy and ring and call in at the most inappropriate times, and, of course, there are many others who don't listen to their daughters when they tell them that the best time to ring or visit is at lunchtime or weekends or when the children are in bed. But most of us don't tell them, we don't give them a steer or even a hint of what might work better because we are afraid of offending them. Instead we get annoyed or cut them short and we let them keep doing it again and again. The cycle continues. From talking with daughters, I've found that setting acceptable boundaries between them and their mothers is a constant frustration.

But how to stop ourselves from feeling guilty when we are simply too tired to answer the phone to our own mothers? School runs, days at the office, making dinners, getting children to their various after-school activities and meeting deadlines: the last thing I need is a call from my mother.

To change a recurring situation which only makes you feel bad needs a solution. I'm a great believer in strategies – they set clear objectives, they have desired outcomes and there are steps set out to achieve those outcomes. Yes, I know this sounds drastic but there is no reason why we can't apply a strategy to our personal lives and, in this case, to our relationships with our mother.

Let's say the overall objective is to make sure you and your mother are clear on when it is most suitable for her to call or visit. And you would like to achieve this objective without you feeling guilty or your mother feeling dismissed or brushed aside. How do you do this? Tell her. Simply tell her and agree a solution that works for you both. Have the conversation.

Describe the situation to her – 'Mum, you know when you ring me at work or call into the house unexpectedly . . .' What does it do to you? – 'It puts me under pressure and . . .' What are the consequences? – 'It means that I fall behind in my work . . .' or 'I spend the rest of the day catching up with what I need to do in the house.' What's the solution? – 'How about we agree a time that it would be suitable to call and you agree to phone to set up a time for a visit?' While this may sound harsh or business-like, it is in fact about protecting your mother, so that when she does call or visit, you have time to be with her and she does not feel rushed or dismissed.

I've used this technique in both my work and with my mother. Soon after she became sick and after a few weeks of increasingly regular phone calls from her, I realised that I was snapping at her when she called. The moped that I used to love popping up on my phone became a source of anxiety. In our busy lives, full of work, home, friends, commitments, children and lovers, somehow the room for our mothers gradually decreases until we reach a point where we have to make a conscious decision to make time for her. In order to protect her from feeling bruised and to manage my own stress, I realised that it was in both of our interests to sit down and talk about what would work best for us with regards to our daily phone calls.

Busy daughters I've spoken to who have navigated this tricky territory successfully say that setting some ground rules in a gentle, compassionate way can often result in less frequent impromptu visits or calls, and ease the pressure on both parties. It's also worth remembering that daughters are not the only ones with full lives – mothers are busy people, too.

SOPHIE: THE DAUGHTER OF MADNESS

I'm not a person who writes to newspapers. I'm a person who keeps herself to herself. I would describe myself as a private person. Discreet. Self-sufficient. I have a small circle of friends and we don't sit up all night baring our souls to each other. We meet for lunch. We go hiking in the Dublin mountains. My friends are people who, when bad things happen, get on with life. They are stoic. I am stoic. Or at least I try to be.

I don't talk with my friends about my mother. I have two women who are my closest friends. One of their mothers has been dead for a long time. The other gets on incredibly well with hers. So that's not what we talk about when we meet up. I'd feel I would be boring people, even my close friends, by going on about my mother. People don't know how to respond when I tell them about her. I've learnt to give carefully prepared, ambiguous responses over the years. So I just don't talk about it. I like to talk to my friends about positive things. Plans we are making. Happy events that have happened. The kind of things I'd be saying about my mother would be a total buzzkill. My teenage daughter Jo taught me that word. But that's exactly what it would be – buzzkill.

I don't know why I wrote in about my mother. It was one of those things that you do sometimes, without thinking. If I had given it much thought I would have stopped myself. I dashed off the email quickly and I didn't expect to hear anything back. I think now I did it as a sort of mark in the sand. A little flag planted in the world to say, 'I'm here' and my Motherstory has made me sad my whole life and I think it always will.

This is the email I sent:

Hi Róisín

I read your note with interest. I have never been close to my mother. I am now in my early thirties and the mother of a fifteen-year-old. My mother is in her mid-seventies and suffers with depression. There have always been issues throughout my childhood. She had a difficult life. Our lack of relationship has deeply affected how I feel about myself and saddens me greatly at times.

I have learned to accept that you can't change what went before. It has taken me a long time to get to that point. But before it is too late I would like to see if we can make amends to each other in some way.

I think it would help us both so I would be keen to be involved in this research study. I'm a single mother and I run a small architect's firm in Clontarf. I think being involved would help my daughter, too, as she picks up on my sadness. I am willing to try anything that might help us heal a bit and show each other what we don't seem to be able to show: that we love each other, deep down, underneath it all.

As I grow older I am reflecting on my life more. And I can't help comparing my healthy, loving relationship with my own daughter. It makes me think what a shame it is that things couldn't be different between me and my mother.

Sophie

I planted the flag, made my mark in the sand and I forgot about it. I can't even say I felt a sense of unburdening. It was just something I did and, if anything, it was a little embarrassing. I went on with my life.

I don't know why I agreed to this. I'm sitting around a table with a group of admittedly friendly-looking strangers. There is chilli and some sort of roulade and lots of wine. I think I can smell garlic bread. Possibly home made. I had thought it was an academic paper of some kind that was being researched. But no. It's a book. My life is going to be material for a book. Or at least a version of my life. How can the full story of anyone's life ever be told?

I'm going to try to stop resisting. The woman called Maeve who talks about hiding from her mother makes me laugh but the happy ease of some of the daughters' connections with their mothers gives me a yearning in my heart that I don't like. Listening to them is difficult. It's a reminder of everything that has been missing from my life. I take a big sip of wine to get rid of the feeling, a sensation like indigestion or heartburn. The wine doesn't work. I feel isolated and alone and like I don't belong. But then another woman begins to talk about her mother with a distinct absence of affection in her voice. She makes no apology for the cold way she talks about the woman who reared her. I recognise this mother. I can relax now. This is my world.

When it's my turn, and I try to start my story, I can't speak. This is a shock to me. The women are patient; I can see in their eyes that they know this is a painful experience. I try using a whisper instead. That works. Whispering helps me get the first words out. For so long when I was younger I was mortified about my family situation: the constant embarrassment that comes with having a mother who has manic depression. The phone calls from people saying your mother is wandering around the main street and can you come and get her? Calls from the hospital saying she has just been admitted and can you bring in her things? Eventually I get beyond the whisper; I get through the embarrassment barrier. I start to speak.

The first thing I tell this group of strangers is that my mother is not a bad person. I need them to know that at the outset. My mother is kind and my mother is good and the reason I am here is not because she is a horrible, mean figure, but because she is a person who lacks any capacity for motherhood. As a child I would go to other people's houses and be amazed by the bog-standard, common-or-garden mothering being carried out there. I saw my friends from school being fussed over and smiled at and told off. I saw heads being ruffled affectionately and help being given with homework. I witnessed classic childhood rows about eating your greens and sneaky hugs being given by mothers to children who pretended to resist before melting into their marshmallow embraces.

I saw all this and I'd go home wondering why I didn't have a mother like that. A mother with treats in her apron pocket and funny pet names for her children. I'd wonder why something as seemingly straightforward as a hug (it was hardly rocket science – I witnessed hundreds of hugs being given and received in other people's homes) was in short supply where I lived. I spent my childhood wondering. It was years before I found out.

I know my mother didn't have a good relationship with her own mother. My grandmother was full of charisma, by all accounts, but she was also mean and controlling. Sometimes my mother would tell me stories about Gran and they were never loving or affectionate. My mother escaped the house she grew up in and married a man who was full of charisma, everybody said it, but who was also mean and controlling. The pattern of my mother's life continued. He was an entrepreneur who got rich with one investment before losing it all on another. The cycle continued for years and gave us children (I have two older sisters) a rollercoaster kind of life. We moved a lot. My mother and father fought a lot. They had what I know now was a toxic relationship. My mother had a lot to put up with.

When I was eleven my father moved away very suddenly to England. He still lives between there and Ireland. My older sisters were put into boarding school and I was left in the house with a mother who wasn't really a mother. I know that now. I had a mother who didn't know how to give a hug. I mean, she actually couldn't put her arms in a hug shape. She just couldn't do it. We laugh about it now. I had a mother who wandered around the house in her swimming togs saying, 'Are you happy, darling? Oh, it's so wonderful to be happy' while in floods of tears. I had a mother who was prone to becoming strange and unresponsive and when that happened I had to ring an ambulance and I didn't know when she was coming back and if she did come back God knows what kind of state she'd be in.

By the time I was a teenager I remember thinking it was odd and probably not normal and that, perhaps, I shouldn't have been left in that situation on my own. One night in particular stands out in my memory. I was fourteen. My mother was in bed, catatonic, although I didn't know the word for the state she was in then. She kept saying she wanted to die. That her life was not worth living. I didn't know what to do, so I just kept talking to her:

'It will be all right, Mum. You have everything to live for. We need you; we love you. What about us?' I spent the night on the bed beside her, afraid to sleep in case she was gone when I woke up.

There were people I could have called but some kind of family code told me not to involve anybody and to keep this to our-selves. The next day some relatives arrived unannounced and insisted on going upstairs to see her.

My mother was crying. She had soiled herself in the bed. They stood at her bedroom door looking in, talking about what had happened as though she wasn't there. It was the indignity of it, I remember feeling. She didn't even like those relatives. And what use was I as a daughter when I had not been able to protect her from this.

'Are you happy, darling?'

No.

I'm fourteen and lost and happiness doesn't come into it, if any-body really wants to know.

Later I found out that my mother had depression. Much later. But for years I didn't have a clue. And her depression has since been rebranded. She now has what the doctors call a bipolar condition. It means that she has spent years in and out of psychiatric institu-tions, a revolving door of medication and not much more, as far as I can see. And I have my own daughter, my sweet Jo, to think of now. I feel the responsibility of motherhood so keenly that I can't understand the lack of it in my own mother.

There is something to be grateful for, perhaps. My own child-hood has shaped the kind of mother I am now. In a good way.

At every stage of motherhood I ask myself questions: 'What would I have wanted at that age?' 'What would I have needed?' And the big answer, the one that has guided me always, is the need for a mother who made me feel secure, who made me feel cherished and nurtured. What I craved as a child was a mother who would have killed for me. I never felt that security growing up, or anything close to it. I never knew what it was to be protected and championed. And yet somehow I broke the cycle and Jo, my daughter, knows and enjoys and often takes for granted the kind of security I never had. And that's how it should be.

The counsellor I see now talks about looking at life through the rear-view mirror, as though driving a car and watching your life pass by, reeling past the scenes and moments and images. The idea of this exercise is to look back on life, all that pain and confusion and dysfunction, and then decide to move forward. I don't ever wish to be glib about what happened, or minimise it, but it's about acknowledging the past and then putting the foot on the accelerator. It's about moving on.

When I'd confessed about my mother – being the daughter of madness still feels shameful no matter how much you know it shouldn't – I told the group about my As Good As It Gets moments. I had one a few weeks ago. My mother shares the same birthday as my daughter, who had just turned fifteen. I decided to organise a family outing. My father couldn't come and I didn't push it. So it was just us three women out in a fancy restaurant, chatting, laughing, enjoying being waited on. It felt like something approaching a normal family event. As Good As It Gets, you see. I remember thinking, as my daughter laughed at something my mother had said, that, yes, my mother is a bit of a daisy, she's not the mother I might have wanted or needed, but sitting here now looking at my mother and daughter smiling at each other, this is something good. I cling to these moments. I want to create more of them. My plan is to build a memory bank for my daughter that is not all sadness and hurt, because even though I worked hard to give my daughter what I never had, I know Jo has picked up on my pain and anxiety over the years.

Lately I have been able to step back and look at my mother more clearly. I see a tormented person who is never at peace. A woman wracked with anxiety and guilt. A woman who can't hug. When the mood between us is less fraught, more peaceable, I will sometimes put my arms around my mother and her arms will stay limply by her sides as they always do. And I'll attempt a joke. Hey, you know what a hug is? It's when you put your arms around another person. Bears do it a lot. And toddlers. And on good days my mother might smile back at me and I think of that as her hugging me with her mouth.

Then things deteriorated. The last time I saw her I could see something was off kilter. I asked her, 'Hey, Mam, what's wrong?' She seemed a little bit dull. Her energy was low. She said she hadn't slept and said she'd run out of sleeping tablets but the chemist wouldn't give her any. She was confused.

And then she had a nervous breakdown, which was a mental manifestation of the depression but, because of her age, it was physical, too. And it took five days to get her in for treatment. In those five days she was catatonic. I'd call over and she'd be sitting on the steps in her nightdress. She'd have been there for hours. The house was cold and she was walking around half dressed. And when this happens, you are beyond being upset or even crying about it any more. Seeing anybody in that state is distressing but when it's your mother, it is unbearable. I'd speak to her, even though she wasn't listening, or couldn't listen. I'd say, 'Come on, Mam, let's try and get you dressed.' And then I'd help her get dressed and she'd lose control of her bodily functions and suddenly she's going to the loo on the stairs.

My father, home again from England and reluctantly minding her, couldn't cope. One night he got so frustrated that he put my mother into the car and called over to my house. 'Your mother's in the car,' he said. And I told him my daughter was there, in the house, curled up on the sofa with a cup of tea watching *Friends*. 'What do you want me to do? I don't want her to see her granny like this. I don't want her to be exposed to what I was exposed to through all my childhood.'

I had to tell my daughter to go upstairs and I brought my mother into the house, she could barely walk, and I was just saying, 'You're not well, are you, Mam?'

But the strangest thing is that, because we are not terribly close, because we've never had that mother–daughter bond, I didn't feel like the person I was coaxing into the sitting room was my mother. I was looking at her and I was thinking, 'You poor person. You poor stranger.'

I know this is going to sound cold but I find it so difficult to access a sense that she is anything to do with me. Don't get me wrong, I care. But I care in a way that I'd care for any vulnerable, hurting person. Eventually, we got her into a home. My sisters came over from Australia and London, and I let them do as much as they could for her. They were great. It gave me a break from the feelings of responsibility. In the home, they have family meetings, sort of interventions, and it was a relief that they were there. The consultant sat beside my mother explaining what was going on. 'Your family are here,' he said, talking about me and my sisters, 'and they really care for you.' And at the end of the consultant's spiel my mother said: 'Care for me? I don't really know about that.' I sat there with my sisters and I said, 'Oh my God, where do you go with that?' And the consultant said, 'You go nowhere.'

Because they don't talk about any of this stuff. They just make sure the drugs are topped up so they can send her back out in the world again.

I went for a coffee with my mum after that incident, down to the miserable café where people are visiting the inmates and sitting not really talking or having awkward conversations. 'Jesus,' I said. 'Mam, why did you say that?' And she just smiled and said, 'Oh, I don't know. . .' I told her how hurtful it was. The idea that she would think we don't care about her. I got the impression that on one level she does think that and she's not able to see the love that's there. It goes back to her not being able to hug. She doesn't have it in her.

They asked me at The Daughterhood meeting about her dying. Someone, I think it was Natasha, said, 'If your mother was going to die in thirty days and you were asking yourself, "What do I need to do before she dies?", what would you do?'

My answer? I think I'd just try to accept her. Accept this woman who is a nice woman, but who hasn't been a great parent. She is kind and in her own way she has always done her best. I would keep in touch with her more. Maybe phone her every day. At the moment I don't see either of my parents for weeks on end, they are just not part of my life. I don't think there will be any final closure with her. There is no wrapping things up in a neat bow. I get the feeling she is always suspicious of me in some way, that she questions my motives. That's the feeling I get and it is so hurtful. What did I do to deserve that? What did I do?

I've tried to talk to my mother. I have said, 'Mam, I know you did the best you could at the time.' I say this more for myself than for her. When I first went to counselling seven years ago it was through fear. The fear that I wouldn't be able parent my daughter properly. That I would fail to mother her because I had not been mothered. I was scared that the pattern would be repeated. That I would not be able to love my daughter as fiercely as a child needs to be loved. But somehow I figured out how to be a mother. I broke the cycle. I am sitting here at this table of strangers not as a betrayal of my mother but as another step on the road to acceptance and forgiveness. And somewhere in all of that, there is love.

Reflections on the Daughter of Madness

When I – Róisín – put the call out for daughters who wanted to improve their relationships with their mothers, I expected to hear stories about all kinds of mother–daughter dilemmas. What Natasha and I found most devastating in the responses, though, was the amount of women with mothers who had suffered for decades through some kind of mental illness. These daughters wrote long, detailed emails full of despair, anger and frustration. 'She has spent her entire life hurting me and, while I have adopted different strategies to overcome this, she still has the power to hurt me like no other human can,' wrote one woman. 'This will end when she dies.'

The emails from daughters with mentally ill mothers spoke of the emotional carnage wreaked on families: 'I never realised how much of an impact a mental illness has on the whole family. Even my father's family and her own sisters do not speak to her, due to her behaviour,' one woman wrote.

'I had no relationship with my mother growing up,' wrote another. 'I found out when my father died that she is bipolar and always has been, which explains the "absent mother" of my childhood and the difficulties I have connecting with her now.'

One woman explained the challenge of caring for or about a mother who, because of her mental condition, gave the impression all her life of not caring for her very much at all: 'I will be denied the opportunity to grieve for my mother because I never felt I had one.'

What all these women had in common was a feeling of not fitting in, compared to their friends who all appeared to have 'normal' mothers, who did 'normal mother things'. They also spoke of their reluctance to talk openly about their mothers because of the way people tended to respond. In her book from 2007, *Daughters of Madness: Growing Up and Older with a Mentally Ill Mother*, psychotherapist Susan Nathiel explored this. 'Telling someone that there's a mental illness in your family and watching the reaction is not for the fainthearted,' she wrote. 'Telling them that it is your mother who is mentally ill certainly ups the ante.'

As the daughter of a father with schizophrenia I have some understanding of this; although, as I was eight when he died, my exposure to his illness was minimal. For years I used my father's illness as a way to mark me out as different. It was a weapon I threw into conversations, before anybody could find out or use his mental instability against me. I pretended for a long time that I didn't care how he had died or what kind of mental state he was in. It was immaturity, I think, and the fact that, as a family, we hadn't really collectively grieved my father. We got on with things. We had to.

As an older and slightly more mature person, when I've confided details of my father's illness – the electric shock therapy, his long stays in institutions, his suicide attempts – I have often been asked: is it genetic? And being someone who has experience of self-destructive behaviour with both alcohol and food as a coping mechanism for darker emotional undercurrents, you can't help sometimes wondering yourself. There is a shadow cast by mental illness in a family and the daughters who wrote in told us all about the dark nature of that shadow.

Natasha and I embarked on this project because we wanted to help daughters improve their relationships with their mothers by telling our stories and theirs. Neither of us is an expert in the area of mental health, so the following astute assessment by psychotherapist Susan Nathiel, who *is* an expert in that area and has personal experience of growing up with a mentally ill mother, is worth including here:

'No mother is perfect, obviously,' she told an interviewer once. 'But a child's sense of the world and her place in it, and her place in her own body and mind, is formed in the web of interaction with the mother, hour to hour and day to day and year to year.

'For a young child, "how mother is" and "how women are" can be one and the same. So, if mother is volatile, mean, depressed or neglectful, this can be confusing to the daughter. Being a woman may seem to be a bad thing, so a girl may do her best to be not-like-her-mother. Many women I interviewed said they didn't really know how to be a "woman" – they didn't admire their mother, or want to be anything like her. It was very hard to separate what was the illness, what was the person, and what was the woman. So if a girl doesn't want to be anything like her mother, where does she find a role model? "Being a woman" is something we learn most easily by identifying with a woman we want to emulate – it's not something we naturally know how to be.'

There is more discussion now than ever before about mental health, more articles being written and more celebrities 'coming out' about their own struggles. And yet, for women with mothers who are different and who are unable to mother properly because of their mental condition, the stigma is still all-pervasive.

A daughter looks for a role model in her mother, a way to make sense of herself and of the world and, when that is absent, what's left for daughters like Sophie are a lot of unanswered questions. Susan Nathiel describes in her book the kinds of questions that gnaw at women of mentally ill mothers as they grow up:

Is it my fault? Will she ever be able to love me? And is this going to happen to me?

Women in their forties and fifties grew up at a time when that stigma was far worse than it is now – an era when mental illness was not discussed on radio shows and in newspaper articles. Like Sophie, these women were often alone in trying to answer these questions and figure out the puzzle of their very different mothers.

LILY: THE DAUGHTER OF NARCISSISM

I don't buy the newspaper every day but I buy it on Saturdays. It feels like a bit of a luxury, a weekend treat. I buy *The Irish Times* and the *Guardian* and I'll flick through them all week. That Saturday morning I was in the sitting room with the papers. The place needed a good tidy up but I wasn't in the mood. My friends with children are always talking about not having time to sit and read a newspaper from cover to cover, so I really appreciate the fact that I can. It's one of the perks of being child-free. I hate the term child*less*. It sounds somehow lacking. Child-free suits me better. I feel free. I am, I think, happy. At least, I'm more contented than I have been in a long time, despite everything.

My husband Rob was out playing golf, I think, and my black cat Billy was curled up at the other end of my green sofa. It was a sunny day – I remember because I'd just put washing out on the line and I was using a pink peg as a clip to keep the hair out of my eyes as I read.

For the past three years I had been in counselling with regard to my mother. So when I read that bit about 'improving your relationship with your mother' it struck a chord. I knew immediately that the improving part wouldn't apply to me. My relationship was not going to be improved. All the counselling I'd undertaken was about accepting that. I had read two books about narcissism by that stage. I knew exactly, as much as anyone can, what I was dealing with when it came to my mother. I also knew my Motherstory was not going to have a happy ending.

We venerate mothers not just in Ireland but all over the world. And I think that's right, I really do. But when you have a mother who doesn't live up to that saintly ideal, who doesn't even come close, you can end up feeling very alone. Not all mothers are benevolent beings. I've lived with the loneliness of that knowledge for years. Not just the feeling of having a mother who wasn't quite right but of being what my mother made me feel, the wrong kind of daughter.

I spent decades wondering what was wrong with me. Wondering why nothing I ever did was right. Beating myself up, hearing my mother's negative voice in my head: 'You are too fat. You are stupid. You will never find a man to marry you. You are a bad daughter.'

The counselling helped a lot. Realising, with my counsellor's help, that my mother was not well, that she was a narcissist, and that she has suffered with it all her life. Or rather, I have suffered with it. And my father. I realised that it was not my fault and that realisation changed my life. But it doesn't mean I can forgive.

I find it difficult to develop compassion for my mother, even though I know all that she's lost because of her condition. She lost me, her only child. She lost out on the joy of a loving relationship instead of the controlling one she had with my father. She lost out on friends and fun and the simple joy of being alive. But maybe she doesn't know any of this and maybe her ignorance is a kind of bliss.

I feel lucky that I got help but I had always thought there must be other people like me, who felt as alone in this as I did. So when I saw the call for daughters who wanted to explore their relationship with their mothers, I wasn't just thinking of myself. I was thinking of other lonely daughters and how my story might help them to feel less alone.

My friends say I ramble and I probably rambled in the email I sent to Natasha and Róisín but it spilled out of me. Here it is:

Dear Róisín

All my life I've had a tortured relationship with my mother. She has narcissistic personality disorder but I only realised this as a result of three years of counselling. It gave me some of the skills I needed to deal with her. We'd had no proper contact since my dad died two years ago. Now I'm in touch with her sporadically.

For a long time I felt so alone with all of this; I felt that somehow I deserved what happened to me in my relationship with my mother. I felt I'd been a bad daughter. I felt I'd disappointed my parents. Counselling helped me to understand and reading other stories (albeit American ones) helped me to realise I wasn't alone in what I had previously thought was a unique situation. I'm writing to you because I'm hoping someone might read my story and recognise they are not alone.

For a long time, I was scared even to contemplate becoming a mother myself. I was scared I would turn out like her. Because not every mother is made to be a mother. I know that from bitter experience.

I'm trying to rebuild my relationship with her. I will try any suggestions you may have. Will we ever be friends, a proper mother and daughter, love each other as we should? I don't believe so. A lot has happened in our lives to damage the love and respect and trust we should have in each other. I'm not suggesting we're a lost cause – therefore not suitable for your project – but I am being realistic.

Thank you for doing this. It's a taboo subject to consider our mothers anything but perfect. We joke about it. We say 'nobody can do guilt like an Irish mother' and joking is fine but sometimes it's not. Some daughters suffer physical abuse and others, like me, are mentally and emotionally abused. Either way, it's very hard for us to recover and become happy people again. I've come a long way down this road. But the myth needs to be broken.

Lily

It always seems to be lashing when I go to Natasha's house. That first night I was a bag of nerves. I got there early; I wanted to settle in before everyone else came. Natasha and Róisín were there, and I felt welcome and warm coming in out of the rain. But I was uncomfortable, too. I felt I knew Róisín through her writing but I didn't really know her, if you know what I mean, and I'd only spoken to Natasha on the phone. The others started to arrive. Maeve and Sophie, Cathy and Grace. Somebody joked it was like AA or WeightWatchers, or something, and I didn't take offence, although I could have. My weight was always an issue with me and my mother.

They were calling it The Daughterhood. And that night I did feel a bit like I was at my first AA meeting. I was able to stand up and tell the truth about something I had struggled with my whole life. 'Hi, I'm Lily and my mother was no good at being a mother.'

The Daughterhood. Like a kind of secret society. I liked that. I lived with a strange kind of secret for most of my life. I don't love my mother. I don't even like her. Now here I was about to say it and explain why and I wondered what all these women would think. I wished I was drinking but I had the car outside so I just sipped my water and listened. Then it was my turn. 'Just tell us your story,' Natasha said. So I did.

I have one good memory. There was one time when I felt like a daughter and she felt like my mother. A moment where I got a glimpse of what it was I saw my friends had. They would laugh with their mothers. They seemed close. I have just one memory of closeness. Sometimes I think that can't be right but then I close my eyes and take a leap across the years with my mother. There are presents at birthdays and Christmas. There are Sunday dinners when I sit at our long dining table chewing beef and looking out the window at the garden. I'm not saying it's a bad childhood. But it is an empty childhood. Something important is missing but I am only small and I don't know that yet.

We're having a picnic on the beach. There are boiled eggs in Tupperware boxes and the lettuce is cold and crispy. My mother has made brown soda bread, and has put some mayonnaise in a small jar. We have a flask of tea. My dad is back at our restaurant working in the kitchen. It's just Mum and me. I'm eleven or maybe twelve. I'm an only child. My mother starts to talk about the kind of man I might like to marry one day. It's an obsession with her – that I will find a man and settle down and that's the most important thing as far as she's concerned. I remember flinching, worrying that she was going to start talking about the swell around my bottom and hips and tummy again. I've read in a magazine that this is called puppy fat but my mother doesn't believe in puppy fat. 'You're getting to be the size of a house and no man wants to look at that,' is what she'd say. But this time, she doesn't go there. 'What kind of man would you like to marry?' she is asking and there's something new, some kind of twinkle in her eye. 'He'd have to make me laugh,' I tell her. And then my mother laughs. And we sit smiling, thinking about this funny man who will one day come into my life. In my memory the sun is shining. The moment is light and fresh and full of promise. It feels like a new beginning. But now I see it as an ending. It was the only time I felt close to her. I suppose I should go back to the beginning. The parts I have pieced together. The view from where I stand now.

My parents owned a restaurant. My mother and father were much older than the average new parents when I came along. She was forty-four and my dad was forty-eight. I only found this out later. I found out a lot of things later.

Apparently, I was carried by my dad into the restaurant like a trophy, surprising all the customers in the middle of their lunch, held over his head in triumph, *Lion King*-style, when I arrived. I always had a good relationship with my father. When he was dying a few years ago and my mother was giving me her worst in the hospital, he gave me a big wink as if to say, 'You and I know what she is saying is not true, don't mind her, love.' That was as much as he could do for me when I was growing up but it meant everything. I know he loved me.

And I know I was a desperately wanted baby. But because I've never been able to have a straightforward conversation with my mother about it, I can only speculate about that desperation. Keeping up appearances was everything to my mother. She saw herself and my father as pillars of the community; people 'of good standing', as she always used to say. Being married but not having a child constituted a failure of some sort. It just didn't look right. My mother was always saying 'people will talk' and I suspect she knew 'people were talking' about the fact that the Bradys didn't have a child yet. The way she treated me all my life makes me think that my mother wasn't maternal and yet she must have felt a social pressure to have a child. I was a box to be ticked. That's what I think now anyway.

Growing up I always felt different. And one day at school when I was about seven, a girl, I don't remember her name, threw some words at me, the way girls do sometimes. 'You're adopted,' she said. It sounded like an accusation. But I didn't even know what the word meant. She might as well have said, 'You're a tomato.'

But I did go home to my mother and tell her what had been said. Her response was to take me on a trip to London. The thrill of it! Nobody we knew had been to London. I see now it was supposed to be a distraction. And it worked. It was only a few years later, in biology class, that I got to wondering why I had blue eyes and my parents both had brown eyes. It didn't make sense. I tried to bring it up with my mother but she would never allow the conversation to happen.

So all through my childhood there was this undercurrent of not knowing. All I did know was that I was to be a good girl because 'people will talk' and we were 'people of standing' and every single thing I did reflected on my mother. If I was bad, that would look bad for her. So I was a good girl and I never rebelled and it was a relief to be sent to boarding school where the pressure was off and I could just be my anonymous self instead of having to deal with the expectations of my mother.

After school I moved to Dublin and got a job in an ad agency. I felt free. I was learning about who I was without the pressure to be the woman my mother wanted me to be. I'd go home every weekend to help out in the restaurant, though. It was expected of me. The Good Daughter.

Then my father became ill. He had a knee operation and my mother demanded I tell my new boss that I needed three months off to come and be with the family. It shows the kind of hold she had on me that I did go to my boss and ask for three months' leave. He laughed at me. And then he said no. I was relieved. The thought of going home was like going backwards into a life I was desperate to escape.

My life moved on. I stopped going home as regularly. I had a couple of relationships, even moved in with one man. My mother got in touch with him behind my back, told him that he was to ask me to marry him or forget about the relationship. I was mortified. A 27-year-old woman whose mother was trying to pull the strings of her life. I can laugh about it now. That relationship didn't work out but not because of my mother. And then I met Rob. The man I'd described at that mother–daughter picnic, the one who could make me laugh. The man I wanted to marry. I didn't want or seek my mother's approval. I was stronger by then. Rob made me see that I was good enough as I was. I felt like a whole person for once, not damaged goods.

I found out the truth about myself while sorting out the paperwork for my wedding ten years ago. I had to apply for my full birth certificate but it was taking longer than I expected. The registrar rang to ask whether there was any chance I might have been adopted. I remembered the accusation from the girl in school and the puzzle of my blue eyes in biology class and the unexpected treat of a trip to London and I said, 'I might be.'

Then there was the letter that turned up one day, an ordinary-looking piece of post. It was my adoption records. I felt sort of unhinged that morning. It was an out-of-body experience. But the overwhelming feeling was relief. I realised that undercurrent of not knowing was not in my imagination. It was confirmation of how dysfunctional and off kilter my upbringing was.

Realising that the mother I had was an accident, not of birth, but of papers signed in a room in a convent away from prying eyes, shifted something in me. She could have taken any baby, is what I imagine. Any child. But she chose me. An accident. I was the casualty. Of course I confronted my mother. It was a damp squib of a confrontation. I asked her why she had never told me I was adopted and she replied that she thought I had always known. She said, and I remember being too astonished to respond, 'I don't know what you are making such a fuss about.'

I tracked her down, my birth mother, as soon as I could. It didn't take long. She had her own family now, three children, but she said she'd be happy to meet. I was busy with the wedding preparations, though, and it felt like the beginning of the rest of my life. After a few letters, the correspondence with my birth mother fizzled out.

In the meantime, I was growing closer to my husband's mother. We are even closer now. She knows that I like a cup of tea straight after my dinner and which biscuits I prefer. (Fig rolls, if you're asking.) She can sense when I'm down and offers just the right amount of support without being intrusive. I imagine this is what a normal mother–daughter relationship is. Finally, I can see what all the fuss is about. Sometimes, when my mother-in-law is preparing a tray with her scones and tea, making sure it's just the way I like it, I drift off in a daydream where my mother-in-law is really my mother and there was just some document that went missing. A computer error. I only need to reboot and everything will be fine.

My mother was cruel to me growing up. Always criticising my weight and my appearance. I remember watching *The Help* and understanding when Aibileen says: 'Not a good road if Mama don't think child is pretty.' As a child, I knew never to step out of line with her. I remember knowing what I had to do to gain her approval. And if I did step out of line, kicking a stone along the pavement in her presence once, she would withdraw from me for days. I grew up in fear, desperately craving her love.

As I became a young woman, I put on more weight and it's been an issue ever since. I rebelled against her by not caring about what shape I was. I felt as long as I wasn't conforming to her idea of beautiful, I was somehow more in control.

A couple of years into my counselling, I had a clearer understanding that my mother was just not cut out for motherhood. As I began to understand, my contact with her became more intermittent. After my father died, I would barely see her. She got in touch about the blessing of the graves, an old custom carried out where we live and I went down but it was a fraught meeting. And now? I don't know where she is. She sold the family home without telling me. Packed everything into a van and left. Well, nearly everything. A neighbour let me know and I went down with Rob, not believing. I peered through the windows and saw everything gone. A pile of my childhood toys was discarded by the mantelpiece. An old rag doll called Dottie. A battered wooden cot.

I don't know where my mother went. An old family friend knows. On his deathbed my father, knowing my mother's difficulties and that our relationship was so fractured, asked him to look out for her. My father knew that I was OK, married, with someone looking out for me. But he worried that my mother, who had alienated so many people, would be left alone. He still cared.

This family friend, Peter, he keeps in touch with me. He says my mother has sworn him to secrecy. He says he can't tell me where she is but he did say she is living in sheltered housing. And that she is being tested for dementia. And that late at night the staff have reported back on nightmares she's been having. 'Lily, Lily,' she calls out into the night. 'Let me go, let me go. Don't hurt me.' And so, even though I don't know where she is and I have no contact with her, she still manages to spread her poison and her lies. My aunt, my mother's sister, told me recently that in despair she once begged my mother to find it in her heart to treat me the way a mother should. 'Lily's your only daughter,' she told her. 'A beautiful girl. You know you should be loving her you should be telling her every day that she's great.' And my mother said to my aunt, 'Oh, Lily? She has just been one big disappointment to me.'

The women of The Daughterhood listen to my story. They ask me, tentatively, about the possibility of washing my hands of my mother. Whether this is now an option. Or was that too wicked a thought for any daughter to have? But I have had more wicked thoughts than that. The wickedest is that I wish she were dead. So that I could be free of her for ever.

Yes, I know I have people who do love me – my friends, my husband, my mother-in-law – but I think there's a motherchip in your brain and it doesn't matter how many people tell you they love you, it's just not the same. If your mother doesn't love you then you feel unlovable.

And yet, walking away feels like a defeat. It feels like the final acceptance that I don't really have a mother. A big part of me doesn't want to accept that. I think I feel the rejection more keenly because I'm adopted. It's an abusive relationship that I keep going back to. I want validation from her.

Reflections on the Daughter of Narcissism

I – Natasha – don't know where I would be if my mother hadn't accepted me for who I was from the very start. The late Maya

Angelou wrote a lot about her own mother over the years and about the ballast she provided in her life. 'She had my back, supported me,' she once wrote. 'This is the role of the mother . . . a mother is really important. Not just because she feeds and also loves and cuddles and even mollycoddles a child, but because in an interesting and maybe an eerie and unworldly way, she stands in the gap. She stands between the unknown and the known.'

My mother always stood in that gap. As a child, I had many challenges. I was different from my siblings, in a way I'll explain when I come to tell you my own story, but as I grew up she accepted me on so many other levels, too. She accepted the choices I've made with regard to my career, my love life and how I live my life. I'm confident that she approves most of the time and when she doubts me or doesn't think much of something, she'll hint at it. To be honest, all my big life decisions get thrashed out with her at some stage or another. I value her opinion. She doesn't try and influence me but she does let me know what she thinks.

We can feel accepted and loved by our mothers but it's often the small things that affect us most. They stick; we carry them around with us. Why did she have to say that? What did she really mean? According to Deborah Tannens, author of *You're Wearing What? Conversations Between Mothers and Daughters*, it's the big three – hair, clothes and weight – that we critique each other most on while, at the same time, looking for approval and understanding.

When I ask my mother, 'How do I look?' and she says, 'You look fine, grand', I know there's something she's not sure about. 'Is that top a little loud?' or 'I prefer your hair back from your face.' She is right. I've asked for her opinion and I want an honest answer. I don't always like it and I don't always take her advice, but the truth is I feel so much happier when she approves.

I recently saw an interview with Whoopi Goldberg. She was talking about her mother. After her mother died she realised that she would never get a hug from anyone else who loved her as much as her mother had. A mother's hug is the queen of hugs. Unconditional love is hard to compete with. It's a forgiving kind of love. It lets you forget about the 'Don't like her' bits. It is the purest kind of love. A love with no limitations, and with no terms or conditions attached. Isn't that what a mother's love is supposed to be?

But if only life were that simple. If only all mothers could have that instinct for maternal, unconditional love. As I'm discovering more and more through The Daughterhood, some mothers are just not cut out for that work.

Many of the women who wrote to us had stories that talked about 'narcissistic' mothers who treated them cruelly, in a manner that couldn't be further from what society expects from a universally loving, nurturing and protective mother. Examples of narcissistic mothers can be found in the most familiar fairytales, from Snow White to Hansel and Gretel. But the fact they are mostly *stepmothers* in these stories and not mothers, suggests the possibility of psychological cruelty by biological mothers towards their children was taboo at the time the stories were written. That kind of cruelty and neglect had to be explored through stories about stepmothers not mothers. It turns out, not much has changed in that regard since Hans Christian Andersen was in business.

Lily told us at the first Daughterhood meeting about a book that had been something of a lifeline for her: *Will I Ever Be Good*

Enough? Healing the Daughters of Narcissistic Mothers by Karys McBride. The author writes: 'Narcissistic mothers tell their daughters that love is not unconditional. That it is given only when they behave in accordance with material expectation and whims. As adults these daughters have difficulty overcoming feelings of inadequacy, disappointment, emotional emptiness and sadness.' It is a subtle kind of emotional neglect that was mentioned by many of the women who wrote into us.

Róisín is Daily Features Editor of *The Irish Times* and part of her job involves editing an advice column written by Trish Murphy, a psychologist. While we were writing this book, a woman wrote into the column with a question that resonated with The Daughterhood.

Q. I have just become aware of a document about narcissistic mothers that describes my mother perfectly. I am fifty, and it took me all these years to work out why I felt so bad about myself and how I kept self-punishing. I would have appreciated it if someone had pointed this out to me a long time ago.

After my first marriage split up, someone very close tried to point it out to me, but I couldn't quite get my head around it at the time because I was too confused by my mother's crazy behaviour. Plus, I suppose there was a reluctance to believe that your primary carer could behave like that.

My mother continually puts me down. She has favourites in the family and always took credit for any of my successes. She insinuates that I am unstable, oversensitive and ridiculous when I try to confront her about her behaviour. She is envious of me and has always criticised how I look and interfered in all my relationships, and she twists what I do and say into something undermining. My mother is selfish and self-absorbed to the extent that she will ruin any party or event to do with me and make it all about her.

If I try to address any of this with her, she flies into a rage or gets upset or sick, so that I look like the cruel one.

I could list endlessly the ways she has ruined my life. An article on this subject might help others who have had their lives dominated by a personality disorder that isn't even their own.

Trish Murphy replied:

A mother-child relationship is one of such fundamental importance that to have a mother who does not put you before her own life is tragic. A mother's love is the closest most people get to experiencing unconditional regard, and it is often the safety net that allows us to go out and tackle the world, knowing that we can return no matter how difficult our experience has been. Not having this fundamental stability in your life can be a life-long affliction, but the starting point for healing is full awareness and acceptance of the reality of the relationship.

When we are born, we have not developed any defence mechanisms, so we love whoever is our primary caregiver.

That the caregiver might not be worthy of our love or is actually harming us may take years to recognise, and much of our youth can be spent trying to mould ourselves into something that will meet their approval. The result can be a wariness, cautiousness and lack of spontaneity that cripples our natural expression and development.

On top of this we usually hide this bad relationship from other people as we are both embarrassed and fearful that it is our fault that we are unlovable. The result is isolation and loneliness, and the hope of another reasonable adult intervening recedes into oblivion.

When our primary experience of love is so damaging, it is difficult to form later relationships that are based on trust and dependence. We may have developed an innate fear and self-protection that can create a distance from our partners, and find ourselves repeating patterns that we loathed in our parents.

This is the real tragedy, but it does not have to be a foregone conclusion: once we are aware of it, we have the power to stop it becoming a generational pattern. However, it may take immense courage and support.

You need to accept and see your mother for who she is: a very sad person who no longer has any power to hurt you unless you grant it. She has denied herself the best of what life has to offer: the enduring love of a child for her whole life.

It is not up to you to fix this for her, and your energy should be reserved for your own needs. Your challenge will be to see yourself as worthy and lovable, and to take the risk of truly depending on another human being. You will have to let go of emotional barriers while trusting your intelligence to let you know who is worth taking a risk for.

When acclaimed Irish writer Colm Tóibín was interviewed last year about his latest novel, he spoke of his challenging relationship with his mother. As an adult he had refrained from bringing up the difficulties and traumas of the past: 'I think you have a duty to be immensely polite to your parents, especially when they're getting older and you're getting older and you won't have them forever,' he said. It's a sentiment that could earn him honorary life membership of The Daughterhood. But Lily and other daughters of narcissism have moved way beyond politeness. As Trish Murphy says, their energy must be reserved for their own needs.

CATHY: THE BECOMING-MY-MOTHER DAUGHTER

I'm a cynical person. I don't mind admitting that. I can't walk through the self-help section of a book shop without smirking at the titles and feeling smug that I've managed to get through life without adding to the bank balance of any of those authors. I have never been to counselling. I'm a big believer in my inner resources. I sort things out myself. I don't ask for help.

It's not that I don't have struggles. The past few years have been challenging in that clichéd middle-aged kind of way. My marriage is sometimes a struggle; nothing too dramatic, just the usual irritants and frustrations of your typical long-term relationship. We are bored with each other, I think, but too polite to say so. I love Graham still and it's all very civilised, but sometimes I find myself looking at him, trying to remember the person I fell in love with. I catch him looking at me the same way sometimes. Of course, it's never mentioned. We have so much of everything else – a lovely home, good jobs, holidays twice a year – it would seem churlish to bring it up and, anyway, I believe these things go in cycles. I fully expect to fall madly in love with him again one day, perhaps when the children have left home.

On top of the marriage issue, which is a cause of occasional low-level anxiety, I have a troublesome teenage son who communicates only in grunts and spends most of his time locked in his bedroom attached to various electronic devices. I have another son and daughter, both under the age of nine. My plate is pretty full at the moment but my cup does not runneth over. My glass? It's half empty, you might have guessed.

Lately it seems as though a lot of this angst comes up when I'm around my mother. I'm beginning to remind myself of her, and I'm not taking this well. After I read the bit at the end of Róisín's column, I began thinking about how much I have taken on of my mother almost by osmosis. My children tease me about my sayings, my little verbal quirks, personal foibles I thought were my own but, when I look more closely, I see they are things my mother used to say to me growing up. When I thought more about it I realised that a lot of the values I was instilling in my children and the methods I have of dealing with challenges were not ideas I had thought up on my own.

I'm not one of these hands-off mothers. My own mother wasn't either. She was the original helicopter parent. She had an opinion on every decision I made, from the colour of my hair to the man I married. I can hear my mother's voice now when I'm telling Jack what subjects he should pick in school. Sometimes I don't tune in to what he actually needs. I think more about what I'd like him to do. It's usually about what would be best for him in *my* opinion. My mother was wonderful in so many ways but she did that. And now I do it, too.

I remember sitting in my house last year and musing, like your woman from *Sex and the City* except I was gazing out at a Cork skyline instead of over Manhattan: 'I couldn't help but wonder – am I morphing into my mother?' And if I am becoming my mother, is there something wrong with that? Or is it a good thing? Reading Róisín's mother–daughter call to action in the paper, I had this urge to explore that.

I think what motivated me the most was wanting to explore how the future might look in terms of my relationship with my own daughter Jenny and my sons. Could I stop myself becoming the worst aspects of my mother? Could I take the good bits, the parts that would be beneficial for my children, and train myself to discard the rest?

So sending the email was very unlike me. But the content *was* very like me: short and to the point.

Dear Róisín

I think I'm becoming my mother. This might be a good thing but I'm not sure. I'd like to figure it out.

Cathy

When I heard back about The Daughterhood, and Natasha explained what she and Róisín were doing, I recoiled at the idea at first. It sounded like a cultish kind of gathering. I wondered whether there'd be secret handshakes and women who swished out their cloaks before sitting down to utter incantations. *Spiritum, sanctum, motherum.* But since my oldest sister Lorraine had fallen ill, my mother had been on my mind so much that it felt opportune. I felt she needed me now and neediness is not a quality I'd ever associated with her. Her vulnerability in the face of Lorraine's illness was a side I hadn't seen before. Or perhaps I hadn't been looking closely enough.

I don't believe in fate but I do think that in my middle age I'm getting braver. I am more confident in myself and less worried what people might think. Ten years ago I would have felt stupid sending off that email but now I felt I didn't have anything to lose. And sure, what harm? What's the worst that could happen? Sending that email had been a practical, pragmatic decision. Like going to the dentist when your tooth aches.

*

I remember thinking when the meeting started in Natasha's house and the stories began spilling out of these women, that talking about your mother might be one of the most difficult things you could do in a group setting like this.

In a way, all this Mothertalk felt more exposing than any exploration of marital relationships. It was deeply personal in a way I couldn't quite put my finger on. Talking about our mothers seemed to go to the heart of who we were as women. I held back at first, not out of shyness but because I was conscious of my brother and sister and the story they might have told if they were sitting around this table. My Motherstory is mine alone and I was aware that the other daughters around the table might read things into what I was saying that weren't there. I was concerned that my mother be misrepresented, that people might go away from the evening thinking of her in a negative way. I heard myself stressing over and over to the women that my mother was a great person. They probably thought I was protesting too much.

I thought about my own children, particularly my daughter. How would I feel if they were attending a meeting where I was the main topic of their conversation? Would I like it? Probably not. So that felt strange. And somehow disloyal.

When Lily started talking about her mother, I sat there nursing a feeling that was bordering on smug. At least, I felt, there were things that could be done in terms of my relationship with my mother. Lily seemed to be at the point of no recovery. I admired the fact that she could talk about it; I was blown away by that actually. And it made me grateful that my relationship with my mother was so redeemable, if it even needed to be redeemed. Listening to Lily, and Sophie to an extent, gave me real insight into the fact that there were loads of things I could do, in terms of my mother, to make things better, which these women hadn't a hope in hell of ever doing. I felt sad listening to them. And hopeful for myself at the same time. When it was my turn, I just told it as it was and as it had been.

I grew up in County Clare, in a small village in the west of Ireland. In our house my mother made it her life's mission to ensure there was No Place Like Home. There was always a pot of something delicious on the stove, a roaring fire in the grate, several board games on the go and at the heart of all this was my mother. The ultimate matriarch. On bad weather days, when the wind rattled the roof tiles, if any of us children suggested we might head off to a friend's house, my mother would bat away the suggestion as ridiculous. Go? Leave here? But where could be better at this very moment with your family around you? So the idea was dropped, the crazy person who had momentarily abandoned their place at the fire or the Monopoly board sat down again. Peace and familial harmony was restored.

You see, you didn't need to visit anybody's house because everything you needed was at home. My mother organised it that way. Friends came to visit us in droves and my mother's tea brack was famous all over Co. Clare. My mother was the typical Irish Mammy and that wasn't some kind of slur. She would have recognised that as the ideal version of motherhood and she was determined to live up to it.

We were a close family growing up but sometimes too close. We always offered each other advice, whether about clothes, relationships or finances, but it sometimes bordered on pure interference. Busybodying, meddling, sticking your nose in someone else's business, whatever you want to call it. My brother used to voluntarily throw out ridiculous advice on my boyfriend troubles and I can remember thinking how much better it would be if everyone else in the family sorted out their own stuff before poking around in mine. But of course I was guilty of it too.

Verbalising that thought, telling someone off for being interfering, would have been almost sacrilegious in our family. Giving too much advice is almost a way of life for all of us. It still is. It's there when I catch myself telling my teenage son to put on a nice shirt instead of a T-shirt if he's heading out with friends. Sometimes when I hear myself talking to my children I see my mother standing in the doorway of my childhood bedroom about to show me the best way to store socks in my bottom drawer. In my memory, I turn away from her and raise my eyes to heaven, the way my son does when I'm blabbing on about the importance of looking smart in front of your friends. It's true, you know. I am becoming my mother.

As young children, my brother and sister ran everything past my mother. My dad was away a lot and she was the person you went to. But I was more of a Daddy's girl. I always looked to him for advice. I was also more independent. Rebellious, my mother would have said. My siblings were much closer to my mother than I was. Our relationship didn't have the same depth that they seemed to enjoy. Now I live further away from her than they do. I'd never thought about this before but perhaps it means something.

And yet I always loved coming home. Especially when it all became too much. One summer, during college, I headed off to Barcelona in search of the famous Spanish fiesta. I was only there two weeks when my apartment was broken into and all my money was stolen. I remember making that phone call home and sobbing down the phone. And of course my mother knew exactly what to do. The next day she wired money over to me and I got the next flight home – my Spanish fiesta had come to an abrupt end. When I got home my bed had been made up with fresh sheets, there was hot water for a bath and of course there was tea brack in the oven. So when I think of my mother, I think of this nurturing spirit, this safe harbour. I have a lot of memories like that.

But as I get older I worry that I'm not the best daughter I could be. My mother had a knee operation a few years ago but she refuses to use the stair lift that we installed in her house. I wouldn't mind, but it cost us a bloody fortune! I do appreciate that she doesn't want to see herself as old and I should be more understanding about this. But I'm not. It irritates me and I don't always hide the irritation. I feel bad about it. I make dutiful phone calls but I don't always listen to what my mother has to say. I interrupt. I make pronouncements about how she should live her life and how she should feel.

When I went to Natasha's house that first night, I found the atmosphere stilted and awkward. It wasn't a natural situation. But then, after Sophie and Lily told their stories, I was overcome with gratitude for my own mother. I felt that I owed it to them and to daughters like them to do whatever needed to be done to improve my own mother–daughter relationship. After all, I knew there were loads of little things that I could do. I remember feeling sad about their stories but hopeful and grateful when it came to mine.

Life is so unexpected – that's hardly a profound or original thought, but sitting in that room with all those women it really struck me. We were honoured to be able to witness each other's lives and the different stages we were at with our mothers.

I was here because I had an inkling I was turning into my mother but I was also here because I sensed there were ways I could be a better daughter and that I could do better at accepting the things about my mother I cannot change. Talking it through at the meetings gave me clarity about what I needed to do. I realised that I don't listen to my mother as much as I should. I am so busy telling her what she should do that I forget to really tune in to what it is she might need.

I've caught the 'meddling bug' but it doesn't mean there's no cure. When I weigh in on my teenage son's life – he's eighteen, old enough to know his own mind about a lot of things – he doesn't even listen. He's become immune to my meddling. I don't want to be known as Cathy the interfering Mammy, who can't help but put her oar in. Most importantly I don't want to be that person with my 79-year-old mother who has decades more experience in this living business than I have. I want to listen more and inter-rupt less. And I want to learn to be more patient and less intolerant. Listening to the other women had motivated me and made me appreciate the time I have left with the most important woman in my life. And it had made me wonder – in Carrie Bradshaw mode again: 'Was becoming my mother the worst thing I could do?'

Reflections on the Becoming-My-Mother Daughter

I – Róisín – think of my mother as my hero. The wind beneath my wings. My moon, my stars. My north, my south. She's basically 'my everything', as my fourteen-year-old niece Hannah would say. Now Hannah says this about everything from salt and vinegar Pringles to *The Fault in our Stars,* so it's not as potent as it might seem. But that's how I feel about my mother. And it's corny and it's clichéd but it's the truth. That great Dubliner Oscar Wilde once said, 'Most women turn into their mothers; that is their tragedy. No man does. That is his.' Well, Oscar, my fear is not that I will turn into my mother; my fear is that I will not.

I read somewhere recently that the experience of being a mother and a daughter at the same time is quite a privileged one. I'd never thought about it like that; the idea that to experience both of these states – daughterhood and motherhood – simultaneously is something to be cherished. It scares me a bit. As my daughters grow I find myself worrying that I won't be for them everything my mother has been for me. That I won't be their 'everything'. It's a silly worry. I know I am doing my best. But this worry is the curse of having a mother as brilliant as mine.

Sometimes I cheer myself up by listing the ways I am like her. There are a lot but these are the top five – and some of them are more tenuous than the others:

1. We are optimistic people. I'm much grumpier than she is, but if there's a glass there in front of us, chances are it's half full. Of white wine, hopefully.

2. We get incapacitated when we laugh. I am talking weak. A couple of Christmases ago, my mother walked in the door wearing a jolly-hued flowery number. My siblings, their partners and children usually come over to my house on Christmas morning. This Christmas my mother looked more than unusually pleased with herself. She sort of danced across my kitchen tiles in this dress I'd never seen before. It was her Christmas dress, I deduced.

'I love your dress,' I said, when what I really meant was '*What* is the story with your dress?'

'It's really comfortable,' she said. It had been a present from my brother Michael and his wife Rukhsana, so she thought she'd wear it for Christmas day. She wanted them to see her in it. After a while everyone headed back home to their own Christmas dinners. My mother was staying with us for hers. That dress distracted me all through the turkey. And even through her award-winning trifle and the turkey sandwiches with Branston Pickle, which I only eat once a year. And I was still distracted by something I couldn't quite put my finger on about the dress when the *Royle Family Christmas Special* came on. Eventually I had to ask her what I had been wondering all day long. Was it at all possible that the dress she had been given might actually be a nightie?

Apparently, this had crossed her mind but she'd dismissed the idea because when Rukhsana gave it to her she said, 'I thought they were your colours.' And so my mother thought it couldn't be nightwear because who cares what colours you wore in bed?

I looked at the label. Then I did a bit of Googling and found a pair of pyjama bottoms in the same jolly-hued flower print. By the time I found the 'dress' which was actually a 'chemise de nuit' I was rolling on the floor, incapacitated with the laughing and the fact that she'd spent all Christmas day in a nightdress. When she got over the shock she joined in. We were laughing so hard at one point I actually thought we were going to have to trouble the ambulance service for a few minutes on Christmas night. On the plus side, she didn't have to change going to bed that night.

3. We are quite fond of our food. After the first Daughterhood meeting I had signed up to talk less and listen to my mother more. I took her to lunch the other day to do a bit of quality listening.

We ended up in a restaurant called Cleaver East. It's a restaurant where you have to order several tapas-sized tasting dishes and they come in the order the kitchen decides. There are no starters or main courses. You order your tiny dishes and you take your chances.

I'm not exaggerating when I say that my mother and I sat in that restaurant for twenty minutes deciding whether to stay or leave. Our dilemma? Would we be left hungry after our lunch? The idea was unbearable. When they said ravioli, how many ravioli did they mean? When the menu said deconstructed hake and chips, how big a piece of hake did the chef have in mind? We had the waitress demented. In the end we stayed. I can highly recommend it. We were stuffed.

4. We love Barry Manilow. And Gilbert O'Sullivan. (What? What's your point? Legends, both of them. End of.) Gilbert O'Sullivan, singer of such classics as 'Alone Again Naturally', is a great Irishman from Waterford. When I was a teenager Mum took me to see him once. He was starring in the musical story of his life in the Gaiety Theatre in Dublin. Afterwards she bought me a book with the sheet music and lyrics of his most famous songs and we queued down a little lane to get backstage so that he could sign the book. When we got there I was shaking. Gilbert was lovely to me. I sang his songs all the way home. Years later I would write a column about him, when he brought out an album called *The Berry Vest*. It was a pun on the Very Best. Gilbert loves puns. Anyway, I wrote this column saying there should be a statue commemorating him in his home town of Waterford and how everyone should stop trying to be so cool pretending to like Radiohead and just go out and buy *The Berry Vest* immediately.

My mother wrote Gilbert O'Sullivan a letter enclosing the

column. Except she didn't know his address so she just wrote Gilbert O'Sullivan, Jersey Island, the way children just write Santa, The North Pole. Sure enough a few weeks later I got a beautiful letter from Gilbert responding to my column. When I wrote a book he sent flowers to the launch. And every time he comes to Ireland to play, he gives me tickets. All thanks to my mother.

5. I wish I didn't have this in common with her but we both dye our hair. One abiding childhood memory I have of my mother is her walking around the house with a see-through plastic bag, like something you'd carry sandwiches in, on her head. Underneath the clear plastic, her hair was plastered with an unnatural-looking shade of brown gunk, which would sometimes splash on to her cheeks, giving her a sort of mad scientist appearance. It was Clairol's Nice 'n' Easy and she was covering up the grey that had begun to creep in during her early thirties. She got the stuff in McAuliffe's, the local chemist. I remember as a child how the women on the packets of hair dye always looked so happy. As someone who regularly gets unnatural gunk put on her own hair to cover up the grey, I now recognise the true nature of those delirious facial expressions: relief. I grew my grey roots out for a while recently, just to see how far I could go. I even began to like it a bit. I felt – and I know it's ridiculous – brave. I've got roots and you're gonna hear them roar, or something. But I knew it was time to take action when I noticed my aforementioned teenage niece staring at the space just above my forehead. 'Are you looking at my grey roots?' I asked. 'Might be,' she said. Luckily I had an appointment that afternoon to stem the advancing grey tide.

'When did you stop dyeing your hair?' I asked my mother the other day. She was surprisingly specific in her answer. She stopped applying her own Clairol at the age of fifty-four because a woman she met complimented her hair, admiring 'that purple tinge'. From then on she let Christian, her hairdresser, take care of it. At around age sixty-five she asked Christian to leave a sort of transitional streak of grey at the front, which she thought looked cool at the time, but when she looks back at photos now she's not so sure. And then, at age seventy, she decided to stop playing the dyeing game altogether. 'By that stage I reckoned there was no use pretending. Everybody knew I was old anyway,' she says, grey and proud now, and still cool.

As I write it all down, I'm cheered by how alike we are and how much, even if it's just dyeing our hair, we have in common. But I wish I was like my mother in so many more important ways. I wish I was more thoughtful, more organised, more generous, more caring, more naturally happy, less of a grump, and wiser. Maybe I will be one day. For some of us, Becoming Our Mothers would be a very good thing indeed.

GRACE: THE GRIEVING-HER-AS-SHE-LIVES DAUGHTER

Sitting around the table at the first Daughterhood meeting, feeling a bit shy, I begin talking by telling them about the car. That is where I spend a lot of time with my mother these days. We go for long drives, me taking the wheel and my mother in the passenger seat complimenting me, her only daughter, for being such a good driver.

'You must know all the roads in Kildare,' she'll say and I will smile and reply, 'Thanks very much, I do.' And a few minutes later Mum will comment on my driving again, 'You must know all the roads; you are such a good driver.' And I will smile and thank her. And this exchange might happen ten or fifty more times during the course of the outing.

Afterwards I will drive her back home, bring her safely into the house and get back in the car to drive home to Dublin. I will sit in the car. And I will cry. Heaving sobs. Fat exasperated tears. Cars are great for crying. They are little grief portals. There are windows so you can see and be seen, and yet it feels like being in your own little world. I cry a lot in the car.

It was my friend Ruby who told me about the message in *The Irish Times*. I was at a low ebb when I responded.

Dear Róisín

I am grieving for my mother but she is not yet dead. We never had the difficult relationship you mentioned so there is no way to improve it. But what we had, the wonderful mother–daughter friendship, is gone. It is never coming back. But I am finding a way to cope with the loss and trying to be there for my father. I'm not sure my story will fit in but I'd like to be part of your friend's project.

Grace

Growing up, I could tell my mother anything. She was one of those mothers. She got it from her own mother, Granny Nolan, who was the person on the street who used to counsel all the girls in their village in Co. Kildare. All those girls who said their mothers didn't understand them could go and be understood by Granny Nolan. That was back in the days when girls 'got into trouble' and disappeared off the street for ever, sent to England or sometimes worse. So growing up, my mother always said, probably because she'd heard her own mother saying it so often, 'You know, you can tell me anything.' And I did. Sometimes more than my mother wanted to know. And I always knew I was lucky in this. I had friends who couldn't tell their mothers anything and kept their lives private. My mother wanted the same relationship with me that she'd had with her own mother. She made a conscious effort to create that intimacy, that sense of trust. I know how lucky I was.

Now, of course, there were things I didn't tell her in my teenage years, things she found out about and was annoyed about but, as I got older, if I had problems, it didn't matter what they were, I'd head home and I knew she'd listen and that she would never judge.

I'm in my early twenties and it's off again with my on-again, off-again boyfriend. This time the off is permanent. I am heartbroken. It feels as though the world might end.

I remember getting the bus all the way back to the house

where I grew up, where my mother kept the bedroom exactly as I left it. I know however rotten I'm feeling – and emotionally I feel battered, as though my heart has gone ten rounds with Katie Taylor – I will feel better around my mother. I am more like my father, pragmatic and logical and a bit tough. My mother is soft and romantic and warm. I am drawn to the house and to her warmth like a little lost moth to a flame.

I get to the house and she makes me tea. We sit at the kitchen table. I take out a packet of Silk Cut Purple, even though I know that, in spite of all my openness, the one thing I have hidden from my mother is my twenty-a-day habit. I can't be bothered to hide it now, though, and she doesn't say anything as I fish a saucer from the cupboard to use as an ashtray.

I light up the first of several and I tell her all the latest gory details. Some are a bit shocking but I know, here in this space, where the black-and-white lino sparkles and the peonies on the windowsill are freshly cut, I am safe. I tell her everything and my mother arranges her face to appear as though she's heard it all before when I know for a fact she has not heard anything like this. Her life has been comparatively sheltered.

She lets me talk it out. She listens. Makes the right noises. Squeezes my hand. At one point she says, 'Here, have another cigarette, love,' and I know it might sound strange but that moment sums up my love for my mother, her love for me. 'Here, have another cigarette, love,' she says and I emerge from my emotional gloom long enough to celebrate the fact that my mother is encouraging me to smoke. That she can see it's soothing me through this nightmare break-up. This is love, I remember thinking, this is unconditional love.

I enjoy convalescing in my mother's house. I am minded, cared for, soothed back to emotional health. My mother takes me shopping. Cooks my favourite comfort foods. She offers the classic Mammy support. And she has always been like this. All my life. Always understanding, never judgemental. When I made mistakes she never asked questions like, 'What are you doing with your life?' My friends are asked those questions by their mothers. I was never told what I should do. I was allowed to be myself with all my flaws. Both of my parents are very loving, supportive people. My mother was born to be a mother. She just knew how it should be done. She made it her life's work. I'm lucky, I know. Lucky.

I started to notice something was wrong around six years ago. I remember talking to a close friend at work, at the time I worked in a bank, and confiding to her that, 'I think there's something wrong with my mother.' It was difficult to explain. She was saying silly things, telling stories that had no context. Always kind and caring, these attributes became exaggerated and, for the first time in my life, irritating.

When I'd call over she'd want me to sit down but it wasn't enough that I would be sitting on the kitchen chair, she wanted me to be lying on the sofa, she wanted this exaggerated version of comfort. Or she'd make sandwiches and tea, even when I said I didn't want them. But my brother and I really started to worry when my mother started telling the same stories about her childhood again and again.

At work the colleague I confided in said, 'You know all those things you think you'll do with your mother one day? Well, do them now.' So I took her to New York. We stayed in the Plaza, went ice skating in Central Park, ate watery hot dogs on street corners and trawled the galleries and museums. We talked a lot.

One day, strolling along the High Line, the long, narrow park in Manhattan which used to be a stretch of disused railroad, I suggested to her that maybe she needed a hobby, more activities in her life, that maybe that would curb the strange behaviour. It was a wonderful trip. And my colleague was right. Our relationship is unrecognisable now but we'll always have New York.

Back home I signed us up for art classes in a gallery in the local town hall but, while my mum loved drawing, she found it difficult to follow the instructions of the teacher. And I became protective of her, afraid that the curious glances and comments of the other students would upset her. We stopped the classes after a few weeks.

It was difficult to get her to the doctor but eventually we did, admittedly by stealth. After days of tests we had a diagnosis. It was Alzheimer's. That is when we found out it had been my mother's biggest fear since childhood. After the diagnosis I went into the blackest pit of depression. I was convinced I had Alzheimer's myself. I thought I was losing my mind. I went through a list of every terrible thing that could have happened to my mother and always, always, Alzheimer's came out on top. At the time I had a friend whose mother was dying of cancer, who had gone through such a prolonged and terrible leave-taking, and I remember thinking maybe that would be preferable. I was numb most of this time. I completely shut down.

I don't tell my mother much any more. When I do her responses are stilted and rehearsed, as though dragged from somewhere years ago when she knew how to make conversation. They are a hopeful stab at the to and fro of regular Alzheimer's-free mother–daughter chat. I go from wanting to be a good daughter and to be there for my dad, who is still a devoted husband

and is now also my mother's full-time carer, to being resentful that this is happening to me at a time in my life when I should be so happy. I am planning a wedding. I'm at such a hopeful, joyful time of my life, a time that my mother, before she got ill, would have been so enthusiastic about. The irony is I've never been that interested in wedding dresses or any of that. There is no bridezilla in me. But my mother has been talking to me about these things since I was a little girl. She would have loved to be properly involved. She would have been so thrilled to be organising dress fittings and flower arrangements. This was her dream for me.

I feel guilty. I try to see her every week but there are weeks when I just can't face it, and then what I call the double guilt spiral takes over. I want to be a good daughter but it's difficult. There are times, if I'm really honest, when I can't face going to see her. But then I know my mother is degenerating and I should be a better person when I am with her and that I will regret it when she goes.

I am ambushed constantly by sadness. I'll be sitting in a café and somebody will sit down with an older woman, someone who is obviously her mother, and they'll laugh together, talk over each other, dying to get the news out, to catch up. Sitting with my own coffee, observing the scene, I will suddenly be stunned, as though hit over the head, by the reality that I will never have that with my mother again. I'll never have that closeness, that friendship, that beautiful intimacy with her again.

I swallow the guilt down when I'm with her. I try to find ways to distract her from the endlessly repeated stories and the conversations that come from nowhere and have no context and no full stops. One day in town, frustrated and feeling like I wanted to escape, I brought my mother into the art and hobby shop. I spent a small fortune on paper and charcoals and took her to St Stephen's Green to draw the ducks. It was exactly what we needed. There we were, mother and daughter sketching away furiously in the park, laughing together, enjoying each other. We probably looked like two unhinged crackpots but it's one of my most treasured recent memories. I don't know how much more of that memory-making is left.

I always come back to the car. It is the perfect place to cry. To express the sorrow at what we've lost and the constant guilt that I'm not being nice enough or kind enough or patient enough. Never enough. I want to work on acceptance. Acceptance of what's happened. Of how I'm doing my best. Of the cards life has dealt my mother.

I am grieving my mother even though she is not yet dead. I look at Mum and I feel the same love I felt for her as a child and as a bolshie teenager and a heartbroken adult. My mother is different, unrecognisably so. But the love is the same.

Reflections on the Grieving-Her-As-She-Lives Daughter

When I – Natasha – sat on that bench outside the hospital, I was confronted with the unthinkable realisation that my mother will die. Having a sick mother forces all of us to face up to the fact that our mothers will be gone one day. (Not just yet, though. Please, not yet.)

My mother's prognosis was bleak and time was not on her side. The complications that both lupus and pulmonary hypertension were causing meant that the doctors had to do a very fine balancing act between the right course of treatment and the medicine they were prescribing for her. Of course I knew that she'd go some day, but her death wasn't imminent. She was in great health, really, in mind and spirit. So until I sat on that bench I hadn't given it a great deal of thought.

After the initial paralysing fear set in, the day-to-day realities and practicalities of having a sick mother took over. The in and out of hospital, the up and down spirals of her condition, the adjustments to her life and ours as a family, with regard to how much she can manage on her own. Planning her time in Dublin at my sister Sorcha's and her visits to my house.

The heroine in all of this is my mother. We call her Miracle Mary. Despite the initial very pessimistic prognosis and an onslaught of medical setbacks, she remains strong willed and stoic throughout it all. I have watched her as she struggles to accept her condition. 'I keep forgetting that I'm sick,' she says. 'Then when I have to take my pile of tablets I'm reminded of the fact.' Her pile of tablets and the excellent care she's getting from her doctors is both slowing down the effect of the lupus on her organs and managing her pulmonary hypertension.

As the years have passed, she has slowly accepted and adapted. My mother is a very reflective and spiritual woman and she has worked hard on accepting that this is the way it is and will be. This is her lot and that lot could be a lot worse! She gets deeply frustrated at times by her lack of energy. The way one task or small outing a day results in having to go back to bed for the rest of the day. She had such an active life before she got sick and coming to terms with her new limitations has been hard.

Even though my mother has accepted her lot I can't honestly say that I have. She is going to die on me some day. That initial fear of her not being here has never left me. It's a constant undercurrent that gently flows beneath the surface all the time. Sometimes

I allow it to rise up; I force myself to feel what it will be like when she is actually gone. It's the Life Without My Mother Test. I sit with that thought and see where it takes me.

In the early days tears welled up within seconds but now an image of a wide open space appears and I'm filled with dread. It's as though I'm preparing myself for when that time comes. I'm testing myself out to see if I've made any progress. And, at the same time, I'm so conscious of how lucky I am and so grateful for the borrowed time that has passed since she got sick.

I'm not alone in conducting what I call the Life Without My Mother Test. My great friend Veronica told me recently that she did something similar. She was driving to Galway a few months ago to see her mother in hospital after she had been diagnosed with a brain tumour. 'I was speeding along the motorway and I forced myself to imagine what it would be like if she died. What would my world look like?'

Veronica had to pull in on the side of the road, put on her hazard lights and have a good sob because she was worried that she might have an accident. (Anyone attempting this test should not do it while driving or while using heavy machinery.) Luckily her mother is now in remission and doing well. 'What annoys me', she said, 'is that just because my mother is eighty-one, I'll be expected to get over it pretty quickly when she does go. But losing her will have a profound effect on me; she is still my mother. I know it will take me a long time to get over it.'

For the daughters of women with Alzheimer's and other forms of dementia, this grieving takes place while their mothers are still alive. They don't have to do the Life Without My Mother Test. It's happening every day. The mother they knew is fading or is already gone because of this progressive neurodegenerative disorder. Her personality, her quirks, her outlook on life, all changed utterly and for ever. The disease robs daughters of their mothers in the cruellest way. Their mothers are there but not there. Still alive but different. Nothing near the mothers they used to be.

Ireland's – and indeed Western Europe's – ageing population means that the number of people living with dementia is expected to treble in a generation. There are currently almost 48,000 people living with dementia in the Republic, over half of whom have Alzheimer's. That number is expected to rise to over 153,000 during the next few decades. On a global scale, Alzheimer's Disease International figures show that nearly 36 million people are suffering with Alzheimer's or a related dementia, and two out of three people with Alzheimer's in the world are women. That is an awful lot of mothers and daughters dealing with the tragic loss of a relationship they can never regain. And feeling, like Grace, as though they are grieving their mothers before they die.

RÓISÍN: THE DEPENDENT DAUGHTER

My mother is in the top four people on this planet I like to spend time with. The others are my daughters and their father Jonny. Life feels better with my mother around. I make a point of including her in everything we do, not because I am a dutiful daughter but because I want her there with me. My mother improves every social occasion. A bit like crisps and cheese.

As part of my work, I get invited to lots of interesting shindigs. I quite often bring my mother. When I had to do a public interview with the Irish literary giant and all-round legend Edna O'Brien in Belfast, I asked my mother if she would come with me. Knowing she was in the audience gave me a confidence boost, while she adored bathing in the wisdom and intellect of O'Brien for what was a magical hour. I brought my mother with me to Ballyfin, probably the most luxurious hotel in Ireland, where we wallowed in the beauty of the place. I may not be able to drive a car but I can drive a golf cart, which was the main thing I learnt on that trip. I drove that golf cart around the grounds for hours, delighted with myself.

I bring her with me whenever I can because she loves me. Excuse me while I channel Sally Fields delivering her much-slagged-off Oscar acceptance speech when I tell you, tearfully and truthfully: 'She loves me, she really loves me.' And at a very basic level it is uplifting to be around that kind of love, so I drag her with me everywhere as much as possible.

It's the unconditional nature of her love that I'm grateful for. That, coupled with her intimate knowledge of me as a human being. She loves me. She understands me. She accepts me. Those three things together are a very potent cocktail, a cocktail I may or may not have become addicted to over the years. Perhaps it's a healthy addiction. Like the one I've been developing lately for tabbouleh. (Breaking news: bulgar wheat mixed with spring onion, coriander, mint and chopped tomatoes is tasty. The health freaks are not lying this time.) But I know that when I think of what I need to do with our relationship it's about not being so dependent on her for so much in my life.

When I sat with the other daughters at the first meeting I told them all of this. I also mentioned my tendency, when my mother and I go out to lunch, to talk about myself the whole time. It's not that I don't ask her questions, I do. But the joy of having my mother all to myself means I want to let her know every little happening and problem and triumph I have had. Sometimes she just doesn't get a look in.

I also came clean about our family gatherings. How when we've got together lately, a few of them were spoilt by me being argumentative with some of my seven siblings. When my brother came home from India a couple of Christmases ago, he organised a replica Christmas dinner, like the ones my mother used to do in Inglenook, where we grew up. (Yes we were stony broke but our house had a name. I like to think of it as beautifully aspirational on my mother's part.) There was only one sibling missing, Eddie in America, but when we sat down around the table heaving with beautiful Christmas food (albeit in November), a small grievance I'd been having with my younger sister exploded into full-on war. Cutlery was thrown, a glass was smashed and, as though no years had passed since I was a paisley-pyjama-wearing teenager, I stomped back to my own house around the corner in the rain. I know plenty of us regress when we are back in the bosom of our families, but I was taking things a bit too far. My mother was upset and the day was ruined, until it was salvaged by less volatile siblings.

In addition to my tendency to throw grenades into otherwise peaceful family gatherings, the appalling details of my dependency should be laid out here: I am dependent on my mother materially. If I lose my ATM card, which happens too frequently, or too many bills come in at the wrong time and I need a dig out, my mother is there. I pay her back, eventually, but I know that I shouldn't be relying on her in this way. A few years ago, I got myself into some serious financial trouble and she bailed me out to a significant degree. I know she was happy to do it but I also know that the funds she loaned me represent money she could have now been enjoying herself or using to splurge on her, wait for it, seventeen grandchildren, or using to help my other siblings out. I lean on her financially way too much. I need to stop.

I am dependent on her emotionally, too. Take the other night. I was feeling a bit fragile after a long day at work. I took a call from a well-meaning friend who started to suggest gently that I might need to take time for some exercise. He wasn't wrong. I DO need to take some time for exercise. But at the moment I haven't got the time or I find it difficult to make the time. So this well-meaning person's comments riled me. After I put the phone down, all my struggles with being fitter and healthier, mostly so I can run around after my children and not pretend I don't have a swimming costume just so I can get out of going to the pool, came bubbling up.

I talked to Jonny about it. And he was good and kind, as he always is, but I knew the only person I really wanted to talk to about it, the only person who would really understand why I felt so bad was my mother. So, instead of dealing with my hurt and confusion and frustration on my own, like a grown up, I rang my mother and spewed it all out down the phone.

I howled out my pain, I wailed, I talked for twenty minutes, hardly drew breath, and all the time my mother was there saying, 'I know, I know.' And she did know. Otherwise her 'I knows' would have irritated me. I *knew* she knew. And that knowing was like a balm across my heart, a salve for my soul. Eventually, I calmed down. I had been heard. I had been understood. I had been loved back to some kind of equilibrium by the only person in the world who could have done it: my mother. But is she the only person? No. I know my work with my mother is about learning how to depend on the other person who has the power to love me back to sanity: myself.

I'm six or I am seven and my mother is the centre of my world. I don't really know my father. Although he is there in the armchair, shouting at the horses on the television: 'Go on, ye daisy. Go on, my son.' Or he is holding my hand crossing the road past Ryan's pub on the corner where the smell of hops tickles my nose. Or he is at the door, a stranger with a beard, a brown paper bag full of sweets in his hand. I haven't seen him in a while and, with the new facial hair like Captain Birdseye from the fish finger ad, I don't recognise him as my father. I reach back through the years and I try to remember his touch or his smell but there's nothing. I can see a twinkle in his blue eyes, though. And I can hear him singing 'Tura lura lura' in his beautiful, warm, rich voice. I have a memory of that.

Daddy is sick, you see. He has schizophrenia, but I don't know what that means at six or seven. I just know he is not with us the way my friends' dads are. He is there but he's not there. He is a ghost in the house. With eight children, my mother is keeping the show on the road. We have no money because Daddy, a taxi driver, can't work. There are butter vouchers in the drawer, though; they are given out to poor people in 1970s Dublin and Miss Roddy, who owns the local shop, lets us buy other things with them. Bread and milk, whatever we might need. And the nuns down the road, the sisters of charity, bring us black bags of clothes, which we have great fun sorting through. At Christmas the bags are full of toys. It's where Santa gets his stuff.

Sister Agnes is the nun who helps us. She sits in the kitchen talking to my mother for ages while we run in and out and around her to the back garden where we make mud pies and construct elaborate obstacle courses. Before she goes back to the convent or on to the next struggling family, she hands an envelope to my mother and there will be cash – one note, sometimes two – folded neatly inside. I know all this. I know about the butter vouchers and the black bags and the charity but I never feel poor. I feel lucky. I am snuggled up with my mother on the sofa, beside the fireplace my father built, and there's a smoky smell from the briquettes and *Blake's 7* is on the telly, and I feel I am the luckiest girl in the world. That is my mother's gift to me.

One day, when I'm eight, my father, who has been promising to do this for quite a while now, kills himself. He takes a blue rope and he goes outside to our back garden and he puts it around his neck and he ties it to the tree and he hangs himself. We don't have a phone, so when my mother finds him in the morning she runs next door to Mrs Smith's house and she bangs on the door until they wake up.

The Smiths have a phone. It's in a specially built cubicle just beside their front door. The phone was such an important and glamorous item then that it had its own little house. My mother picks up the heavy black handset and dials 999 and the ambulance comes as quick as it can but it's already too late. When we wake up that morning my eldest sister says, 'Don't look outside', so I don't. I am grateful to my sister. I hope nobody else looked.

The thick blue rope is on a counter near the back door. The house fills with people. Daddy's dead. I'm floating above the scene. I'm not really there. I float out of the house because I'm going to school. I know what's what there. The house is confusing to me now. I float around for days. I float into Miss Roddy's, where she doesn't charge me for my usual brown paper bag of Fruit Salads. I float into the funeral home, where Daddy is in the coffin and my mother says he has donated his eyes to science and I think that means another man will be walking around with Daddy's eyes and I wonder will they still have his twinkle. I found out how he died from my brother Michael. A boy on a bike had shouted across the road to him: 'Your dad hung himself from a tree.' I got annoyed with Michael when he told me what he'd heard, convinced he must be lying. When I told my mother what he'd said, she confirmed it was true.

We younger children don't go to the funeral. We sit in the back room of the Borza's chip shop, which is three doors from our house. I love Borza's. We can have anything we like because we are children with a Dead Daddy. When I think of my father dying I taste hot, fat chips and a burger smothered in crispy batter. I see the goodbye note he wrote on my Peter and Jane reading book. All our names listed there in his bockedy handwriting. I have dreams that my father comes to visit me. But they are nightmares. He really is a ghost now.

My mother is my superhero. Her youngest child was one and her eldest sixteen when my father died. She is English and came over to Ireland in the 1960s after marrying and meeting my father there. She had no other family in Ireland except us. I will never stop being grateful for the fact that she raised me to care about the things she cared about – books and culture and being curious about people. That she didn't fall apart. That she managed the widow's pension and the social welfare payments and was able to give us the building blocks for a good life. Before Daddy died she had bought the entire set of the *Encyclopaedia Britannica* – the Google of the day – which we consulted on everything from quiz questions to school projects. She purchased it on the never-never from a door-to-door salesman, even though there was no money for luxuries. When Daddy died one thing that happened was the encyclopaedias were paid off because of some kind of insurance clause. I doubt he knew it would happen but I always think of it as his gift to us.

You try to join the dots in life but sometimes you can't. My father killed himself. Is that why I began to use food to comfort myself and still do? Is that why I was such a pain-in-the-neck teenager? Is that why I'm so dependent on my mother as an adult? I don't know. I just know that it would make my mother happy to know that I am finally sorting myself out and standing on my own two feet. I know that mothers like to be needed. But in my case I know my mother would like to be needed less by me. I will try.

I've been thinking a lot about why I'm so dependent. And the conclusion I've come to does not paint me in a good light. Somewhere along the way, when we grow up and away from our mothers, the mother–daughter dynamic is supposed to change. Where once it was a child and adult scenario, the daughter should emerge as an adult in the world and their relationship should, as a natural consequence, achieve a more equal footing.

This hasn't happened for me yet. When I close my eyes and think of my mother, I don't see her just as a woman, with needs and hopes and dreams. This is what I think when I think about my mother: she is there to mind me, to look after me, to keep me safe. She is there to keep the wolves from the door and the monsters from under my bed. She is there to rescue me from dragons and ride in on a white horse to save me from myself. Until I started really looking at our relationship, I hadn't realised this to be the truth. I think everybody else in my family probably sees it, which is why she sometimes gets called an enabler when it comes to me. I know it causes a certain amount of resentment. But perhaps that resentment is justified, which is something I never considered before now. I thought my work here was going to be about not taking my mother for granted. Now I see my work is bigger than that. I need to grow up. What a surprise.

I am the Dependent Daughter but I think I'm a Dependable Daughter, too – with some qualifications. I am one of the most squeamish people I know when it comes to hospitals, for example. I hate the smells. The unexpected sights. A surgeon's blood-splattered, slip-on shoes. Nappies piled neatly on a table beside an older person's bed. It's as though I resent being reminded of what actually goes on there and I find this resentment hard to hide. If I needed to go to hospital and wanted a friendly face to gaze on, I would be the last person I'd call. So take pity on my mother. Over the past few years, every time she ended up in hospital, it's been her hospital-phobic, decidedly non-nursey daughter who, for some reason, has been the one to accompany her. I was with her when she went to the doctors for a routine check-up and it was decided that she needed a heart scan. I sat petrified and resentful in St Vincent's for an afternoon trying to think of soothing things to say. Mostly 'You'll be grand', if I'm honest, although I didn't know if she would be. She was, as it turned out. I, on the other hand, needed a couple of days to recover.

Not long afterwards she went to Belfast to visit me. I had moved there for work and was always finding schemes to make her come and spend time up there with me. I once brought her up because the world record for most people kissing in one space at a time was being attempted. It was only when we walked into the space that I realised it wasn't exactly the most appropriate mother-daughter outing.

We went to the cinema to see *A Beautiful Mind* instead. We were walking up the steps into the cinema and when I turned around in the dark to ask her which row she fancied sitting in, she was gone. I followed a muffled groan to discover her lying on the plush cinema carpet mumbling something about her left arm. I can see us both now, whispering in case we disturbed the other patrons' enjoyment of the trailers. 'Are you OK?' I whispered. 'No, I think it's broken,' she whispered back.

Embarrassed, I managed to get her up from the floor and lead her out of the cinema whispering about whether we should get an ambulance to the Royal Victoria Hospital. We took a taxi instead. The first thing I did when we got there was ring my sister.

'Rach,' I said. 'I'm in the hospital with Mother. I think you better come down here.' The fact that my mother had said she didn't want to bother anyone else was immaterial. I was not about to start playing nurse when there was someone much more qualified a phone call away. I don't think I relaxed until my mother was so full of morphine she was in no position to judge my skills as a Florence Nightingale. We got *A Beautiful Mind* out on video a few months later. She cried.

The phone rang at around 9am one morning a few months later. 'Róisín,' she said. 'I fell down the stairs at work and . . .' She had broken her other arm.

Four months later, the right arm had not healed. An operation was called for. In an operating theatre in St Vincent's, a portion of bone was taken from her hip and grafted on to her broken arm. Everyone else was at work and, though I had deadlines looming, I was moved to action by the thought of her waking up from the anaesthetic all disoriented and afraid.

So, against my will, against every unbroken hospital-hating bone in my body, I was there, stomach squirming, as she emerged, an oxygen mask on her face and a drip coming from her arm, looking as confused as a child who has just awoken from a bad dream.

'Am I OK?' she asks and I tell her that she is. And she asks me to kiss her, so I do, on the forehead. I stroke her hair like I remember her doing to me when I was young. I listen to the nurses in the ward sympathising with this lady about her frail hips and that young girl about her accident. Smiling and joking and cajoling, even as they empty out bedpans and listen to pain and wipe away blood. I think they are some of the most incredible people I've ever seen. And I think I am one of the most cowardly.

But, I tell myself, I am here. And, though I don't believe her, my mother smiles over from her hospital bed and she tells me that is enough.

I've caused her so much grief over the years. And yet, she asks hardly anything in return. Like most mothers, I think. Ordinary mothers. Although, really, there are no ordinary mothers. And she is certainly not ordinary. I am writing this a few days before Mother's Day. But she doesn't do Mother's Day. Doesn't need cards. Doesn't want chocolates. There are no rushed, guilty trips to the newsagent. No buying overpriced bunches of carnations that still bear the sticker from the convenience store. No fussing over which restaurant to take her to. Happy Mother's Day? No way.

The Dependent Daughter wants to give her something anyway. A mother and daughter story: once upon a time there was a daughter who was not always kind to her mother. She stole coins from the drawer in the kitchen. She stole notes from the purse with the sticky clasp. She once lied so brazenly about where she has been until this hour of the night that the mother had to go searching the neighbourhood in a frenzy until she found her and dragged her out of the pub. The daughter hated the mother that night. But she appreciated the gesture when she realised what, and more precisely who, the mother had saved her from.

One day the daughter decided to run away. She had been given too much maths homework and, anyway, there was this boy she liked with white make-up on his face who looked identical, if you squinted, to Robert Smith from The Cure. He lived in Co. Wicklow, so she took a train to the end of the line and then a bus and then somehow she arrived at the right house on the dark country lane.

The boy had seemed full of encouragement on the phone but now just looked embarrassed. And she thought he didn't look that cool after all, in his posh school uniform, with no white face and no blood-red lipstick. Reluctantly, he agreed that the girl could live for a while in his garden shed. They ran across the lawn, which was sort of difficult when you were bent double so that his parents wouldn't spot you from the living room window, and down to the shed at the side of the house. It was a posh shed. With windows. Inside there was a mound of chopped logs. Her new home smelled like a Christmas tree. What a pleasing development, she thought as she settled down on a wood pile where she hoped some snogging might happen later.

After a while she got bored and the boy got worried, so he pretended to go and get them both a snack but instead he told his parents who told her mother who had to get a friend to drive her the 20 miles to the house late on that rainy school night.

On many levels the daughter was difficult to live with. She was full of anger, lashing out at everyone, making life a misery for the rest of the people in the house. She was a nursery rhyme – when she was good she was very, very good but when she was bad? Oh, horrid. The mother tried counselling but that didn't help. The horrid daughter just sat there looking sullen while the rest of the children told the woman with the understanding expression how their sister made their lives a misery. She slammed doors until they fell off their hinges and she pretended to be a witch to scare her younger brother.

All this time the daughter knew she didn't deserve the mother who would make beautiful meals: meatloaf and mashed potatoes, chicken pie and beans, a fry-up on Saturday morning, bubble and squeak with the leftovers of her perfect Sunday dinners, which sometimes featured big fluffy Yorkshire puddings. Nobody else the daughter knew had Yorkshire puddings. Sometimes the daughter would turn her nose up at all of this and buy chips instead. Knowing she didn't deserve this mother sometimes made things worse. She wanted to be good but more often than not it didn't work out like that.

This daughter was always saying, 'Sorry.' Sorry for bunking off school. Sorry for letting boys into the house when you were away. Sorry they then wrecked the house and stole the special bottle of Martini and broke her eldest sister's Spanish guitar. Sorry she got sacked from her Saturday job for liberating a packet of mouth fresheners from the shelf. She meant to pay for them. She forgot. Sorry for throwing a plate of spaghetti Bolognese at the wall. 'Sorry,' she said.

The mother was always saying, 'I forgive you.' I forgive you for worrying me to death. I forgive you for running away. I forgive you for being selfish. I forgive you this. I forgive you that. It seemed to both of them as though the cycle would never end.

But if mothers and daughters are lucky, the cycle does end. Eventually the daughter counts the mother among the people she can talk to most honestly and laugh with the hardest. The small encounters of their lives, the ones other people might be bored by, are discussed in detail. The daughter loves to listen to the mother's stories from her work. The tiny triumphs. The dramas and the politics. A perfect afternoon will be spent drinking coffee and eating cream cakes while the rain pours down outside. There will be no slamming doors. There will be no crying over spilt spaghetti sauce.

Because this mother is not ordinary. This one has superhuman strength. A heart that is always prepared and willing to give. Eyes that see through you, right into the beauty and the beast of you.

And still this mother manages to love you, no matter what demons are discovered inside.

The daughter still says sorry and she is still forgiven. So no flowers, only friendship and a Happy Unmother's Day every day. From the Dependent Daughter to the mother I need to start depending on a little less. The mother I need to start seeing as a person in her own right, and not just the most highly evolved support system I've ever had the pleasure to lean on.

I don't know how to make the transition from Dependent Daughter to whatever lies on the other side. I don't know if I have it in me. But that is the work I've signed up to do.

Reflections on a Dependent Daughter

I remember when Róisín walked into my office for the first time and I told her about my 'Ten Things to Do with Your Mother Before She Dies' idea. There was a split second when her eyes seemed to pop. I wasn't sure if this was a good or a bad thing. It turned out that, not only did she think it was a good idea for a book, it really struck a chord with her and she was clearly excited.

I had read Róisín's pieces about her mother in her column and it was obvious that she loved her. I was also struck by Róisín's incredible honesty when it came to confessing her shortcomings as a daughter. She was upfront about the fact that she relied on her mother a bit too much. But, in our early months working together, this wasn't that obvious to me. At times I wondered whether she was hiding her dependency. Sure enough, though, soon the curtains came down. One night we were in my house working on the book and my printer broke. Róisín, almost immediately, as if in default mode, called her mother and asked her to print out the thirty pages that we needed. Before I knew it, she was halfway across Dublin picking up the pages from her mother's house. It all happened so quickly that it was only when I stood at my front door, watching the taxi take off down the road that I thought, 'How did I let this happen?' How could we, two grown-up forty-somethings, end up asking a 75-year-old woman to go through the hassle of printing reams of paper at 9.30 at night? Clearly, I'm blaming Róisín entirely for this. The Dependent Daughter was doing what comes most naturally to her. She was doing what she had always done since childhood – leaning on her mother at the drop of a hat.

When I finally met Róisín and her mother together I saw how well they got on and how compatible they were. And I could see how easy their relationship is. So why wouldn't Róisín depend on her mother? Her mother totally got her. Over time, Róisín and I talked a lot about her wish to move away from being a Dependent Daughter and to start to see her mother more as a woman in her own right. Our 'mother' conversations were making her become much more conscious of the need to think twice before dialling 'M' for Mother.

It was clear that she was willing to participate and not just be an observer in The Daughterhood. In fact, from very early on, she was drafting all sorts of plans and lists of things she was going to do with her mother. But in making such a dedicated daughterly start, I was concerned that she would run out of steam halfway through. However, I realised The Daughterhood was having an impact on her when I got a call from her one day.

'Guess what? I went for lunch with my mother today,' she said.

'Brilliant,' I said. 'Did you go anywhere nice?'

'Never mind where we went, I didn't talk about myself once

through the whole lunch,' she replied with a sense of achievement in her voice.

Róisín was clearly determined to come out of this process a better daughter. If I were a betting woman, I'd have put money on her achieving the Gold Star of Daughterhood. Whatever way it was going to turn out, The Daughterhood would be with her every step of the way.

NATASHA: THE DEDICATED DAUGHTER

I have digital scales in my bathroom that talk to me in an American accent when I stand on them. Sometimes I don't like what I hear. I have the talking scales because I'm legally blind. In restaurants, friends are used to me pulling out my state-of-the-art magnifying glass. I always book seats in the front row when I go to the theatre. I don't drive and every document on my computer is presented in size 28-point font on my ginormous screen.

When my mother was pregnant with my older brother she contracted toxoplasmosis, a condition which can affect the sight and in many cases the brain of the carrier's unborn children. My brother wasn't affected but two years later I was born with the condition. My mother instinctively knew something was wrong. After a few weeks she brought me back to the hospital where I was officially diagnosed.

At the time, doctors told her I would almost certainly be blind and possibly – although they couldn't be fully certain – brain damaged. My mother refused to accept their findings and it turned out she was right. There was nothing wrong with my brain and I could see.

Still, they told her I would lose my sight and possibly suffer brain damage at some point during adolescence. It was only a matter of time. I did temporarily lose my sight as a teenager, but regained 30 per cent of it, which is what I still have today. Luckily my brain was never affected. What the condition did affect, though, was my relationship with my mother.

Looking back, it's as though my difficult start and her championing of me created an unusually strong bond between us.

Perhaps this is why I grew into the Dedicated Daughter. I was aware of her dedication as a mother from a very early age.

Having me as a daughter was a crash course in something all those baby manuals had yet to put a name on: attachment parenting. Family legend has it that I screamed the place down if anyone apart from my mother so much as looked as though they wanted to pick me up. I wouldn't even countenance my father being near me for those first couple of years. I wanted her and I wanted only her.

At my insistence, for the first few years of my life we were joined at the hip everywhere we went from a deserted beach to a crowded supermarket. She couldn't put me down to dry herself or even butter a slice of toast. As mother–daughter relationships go, we were deeply connected. We still are.

As it became evident that toxoplasmosis wasn't curable and that my sight would be severely limited, she was determined never to let the condition limit me. Instead of overprotecting me, she encouraged me in everything. She never made me believe that I was anything less and I never ever heard her say I couldn't do something because of my vision. Despite my condition, my mother always let me figure out my own capacity and levels, as did my brothers and sisters. Nobody was precious about my lack of sight. Quite the opposite, in fact. No one was ever found when I was 'on' during Hide and Seek. And, much to their joy, I always ended up with the least amount of eggs during the Easter Egg hunts. My lack of vision was never allowed to define me. My mother taught me to concentrate on the 30 per cent that I do have, as opposed to the 70 per cent I don't.

I joined every school activity, from hurling to cycling to drama, music and debating. I was sent to France on two student exchanges long before any of my siblings got to go. I was a ferocious reader, preferring a good book to climbing trees outside with my sisters. I have no doubt that my level of confidence in myself has come from these early foundations.

I love being a daughter. I actively take on the role of being a daughter. Now it clearly helps that I love my mother and want to do daughterly things with her and for her. I have the advantage in that I have more time than most as I don't have children. But I'm also driven by the belief that there are inherent duties that come with being a daughter, particularly as our mothers age. It's part of the daughter deal, it comes with the territory.

To a large extent our roles are now reversed. It's my turn to give back to her, to consider her needs, to show her that she matters, that she's important to me. I include her in lots of ways. We take regular trips together. I invite her to my house parties. Weekends at home with her and with me in Dublin are scheduled ahead so that there is never too long a gap between seeing each other. When I'm in town buying those outrageously expensive coffee capsules that you can only buy in one particular store, I buy them for her, too. When I see a bargain in the sales that I think she would like, I call her. I keep toiletries and nightclothes in my house for her.

It helps that my whole family are a part of this. It's not like I'm the only one that makes conscious decisions to include her in our lives. We are far from the Waltons in other regards, but at all times our mother is an automatic part of our decision making.

When my sister Sorcha and her husband Ron moved back with their three children from Mozambique a year ago, they and my brother Oisín built a bedroom and bathroom downstairs in their house so that she could go and stay with them for long periods of time. I donated the curtains and Cilian, my other brother, bought her a TV.

Being in Dublin for longer periods meant we saw more of her and she was included in our day-to-day lives, thus saving the two-and-a-half-hour journey to her house in Galway at the weekends. As the weather gets better in spring and summer, she moves back home to her beautiful garden beside the sea. This is where she is happiest. Many of our summer weekends are then spent over long meals sitting in the garden and swimming in the sea.

Despite her illness, my mother makes it easy for me to be a Dedicated Daughter. She's very aware that her illness has put further responsibilities on us and that she's more dependent as a result. She is forever telling me that she doesn't want to be a burden to us and it helps that she appreciates whatever we do for her. Above all, I know that she feels loved and secure.

Mary Troy grew up right in the centre of Frank McCourt's home city of Limerick in the 1940s and '50s. Both her parents were doctors and she was the youngest of five. Her father died when she was only ten, which left her mother to run their GP practice on her own.

After school she followed her parents' career path into medicine but only lasted six months in pre-med. She told me she couldn't think of anything else as a career choice but she soon realised she didn't want to lead the life of her mother. Her mother was on call all the time and it was really demanding.

She always had a sense of adventure and a huge appetite for life, which remains with her today. At nineteen she packed her bags and set off volunteering in Jerusalem and Palestine. At the time, it was unheard of for an Irish person to be travelling to an Arab country, and even more unheard of for a woman to do so. Her experience in the Middle East confirmed for her that she wanted to study Arabic and Hebrew. She came home after nine months and enrolled in Trinity College to do just that. Not only was she one of only two women taking this degree, but she was also one of the first Catholics to do so. 'It was 1962 and women had to be off the campus by ten o'clock at night. But that didn't stop us – we regularly climbed over the wall. We had great fun doing so.'

Knowing that having the degree in languages wouldn't be enough to get a job back in Bethlehem, she signed up for a social science degree by night at University College Dublin, or UCD as it is known. I'm still amazed that she even considered doing two degrees at the same time. Trinity by day and UCD by night. For a woman who tells me that she lacked confidence in her early years, I can't help but be inspired by her relentless focus and determination.

It was during those years at Trinity that she first met my father, Desmond Fennell. He was eleven years her senior, a very handsome intellectual from Dublin who had studied in UCD and then gone on to study at Bonn University. When she met him he had travelled extensively to far-flung countries, such as Japan, Hong Kong and South East Asia, and had already published his first travel book *Mainly in Wonder* in London. They made a very handsome couple. My mother was very beautiful – long hair, high cheekbones, beautiful full lips and a great sense of style. My favourite photo of them together is at their wedding breakfast.

My brother Oisín was born as my mother finished her second year in college. She was twenty-three. They went on to have four more children, Cilian, myself and then my two younger sisters, Sorcha and Kate.

My mother didn't go back to the Middle East for another thirty-four years. In the intervening years we moved to the west of Ireland to a tiny island called Maoinis that is connected to the mainland by a rickety bridge. It was 1969, the year after I was born, and my mother fell in love with Maoinis the first day she crossed that yellow bridge on to the island. The 1960s in Ireland saw a lot of people leave the urban lifestyle behind and head west to a simpler, less frantic place. My father also wanted somewhere remote where he could write, having become a full-time writer. Maoinis was and still is one of the most beautiful places I have ever known. When we lived there, it had a population of about 300 and most people earned a living by fishing, turf cutting and raising cattle.

We depended on rain for our drinking water. There were no phones on the island and very few people owned a car. It is also an Irish-speaking part of Ireland where the first language is Irish and at school all subjects are taught through Irish. It was a two-teacher, two-classroom school down the road that had forty pupils altogether. Irish was our native language – we all called our mother 'a Mhamaí' – and the first English words I learned were 'red handbag', taught to me by my grandmother. The move to Maoinis was a major cultural and environmental shift for both of my parents but one they immersed themselves in for the next eleven years.

My mother was only twenty-nine and she had three children when she moved there. Away from her family and friends in Dublin, she was learning to speak Irish like a native, as opposed to the Irish she had learned at school. She got a teaching job in the local secondary school three miles away and, along with my father, she got totally involved in local issues, the most significant of which was campaigning for self-governance for the Irish speakers in the province, which resulted in the founding of a national Irish language radio station that still exists today. She was also central to bringing running water to Maoinis in 1979, ironically the year we left.

Those summers in the 1970s were hot and our days were spent on one of the beaches two minutes from our house, jumping off the big rock on to the sand. My mother was a great swimmer and she taught many of the local children how to swim. She wore maxi dresses, made a lot of her own clothes and made us a picnic every day that kept us on the beach until evening.

At age eleven, we moved to Galway city, only an hour but a world away by very pot-holed roads. A few years later, my parents decided to separate and my mother got a job teaching in a Jesuit school in Galway. Through all those years since her early visit to Jerusalem, the wish to go back never left her.

At fifty-six, she finally returned. I was in college in Dublin when she rang to tell me. 'I've decided to go back to Trinity. I'm going to study Hebrew and Judaism for a year and then I'm going to go back to Jerusalem for my second year. I'm finally going back,' she said. It was one of the first times that I can remember seeing Mary Troy as a woman in her own right, and not just as my mother. She had reclaimed her identity.

It was the beginning of a new chapter in our relationship. I was now in my twenties and starting to carve out my own path, whilst my mother was doing the same thing in her fifties. Somehow it put us on a more equal footing and we moved away from just being mother and daughter, to being two women trying to fulfil their own personal ambitions.

*

As much as I might be a Dedicated Daughter, like most people I need deadlines. The Daughterhood meetings provided a structure and a time frame for me to do the things that I wanted to do with my mother. I saw these meetings as a kind of monthly 'mother check-up' where I would set aside some time to review how I was getting on. More than anything it encouraged me to have conversations with my mother that I had been intending to have but had been putting off. Some of you might find it unthinkable, but one of the conversations I committed to having with Mary Troy was to discuss her wishes with regard to her funeral.

But apart from anything, these monthly meetings had a profound effect on me. I was constantly moved by the willingness of these women to do what they could to work at their relationships with their mothers. Both Lily's and Sophie's relationships were so clearly fractured and yet, here these two women were in my kitchen trying to make sense of it all. I really hoped they would get something out of all of this. They needed The Daughterhood more than any of us.

Reflections on the Dedicated Daughter

As I got to know Natasha, I – Róisín – realised that I was the slow learner of this blossoming friendship with regards to my mother. I remember one day, not long after I'd met her, ringing Natasha to tell her about the developments in my mother's recently diagnosed Age-related Macular Degeneration, or AMD.

There is a wet version of AMD which is treatable and a dry version which is not. My mother, like Dame Judi Dench, has developed the wet version. I like that my mother has something in common with Dame Judi. Not that she didn't already – they are both beautiful, talented, strong women. My mother once dabbled in amateur dramatics and has cropped grey hair. That's an awful lot of common ground before you even get to the disease that causes gradual loss of central vision. Judi Dench can't read her scripts any more. My mother needs the print on her Kindle to be in a much larger font. If she ever meets Dame Judi, she won't have to worry about a conversation opener.

One morning, a few months after her diagnosis, my mother woke up and experienced a sort of swimming sensation when she opened her eyes. The doctor told her the AMD had progressed and she was going to have to go in for eye injections. Go to a hospital. Where they were going to stick actual needles in her eyeballs. Meanwhile, I stuck my fingers in my ears. I didn't want to know. La, la, la, la. My mother was not a patient. My mother was not weak. My mother was not someone who needed needles stuck in her eyes or anywhere else. My mother was not going to succumb to old age and the gradual decline that visits other mere mortal mothers with the inevitability of the tax man. Or – and I didn't want to go there – was she?

To be very honest (and cowardly), I didn't much feel like hearing about this mother who doctors said needed eye injections. I like the mother I already have, thank you very much. The one who, when I ask what she's done of a Monday, tells me she's been to see two movies (one of which had subtitles) on her own and that she treated herself to dinner afterwards in that new sushi place I still haven't managed to get to. I like the mother who goes to a creative writing class on Friday mornings and a memoir writing class on Wednesdays, and helps her wheelchair-user friend with his latest campaign to sort out reproductive health in Africa on Tuesdays. The mother I want is the social-media-savvy woman

who became active on Twitter (@anningle – she needs more fol-
lowers), Facebook and Instagram before I did.

The mother I want to hang out with and boast about and
cadge dinners from is the one who went on four holidays last year,
to beautiful Co. Mayo with me, to North Carolina to see my
brother Eddie, to Portugal with my sister Rachael and to London
to visit to my brother Peter.

The mother I've come to know, love and rely on is the
chairperson of the board of a local, not-for-profit community
newspaper. She energises the meetings, takes the minutes and
ploughs through the agenda, while I (she roped me in, too) struggle with my energy levels and eat too many sandwiches to get me
through the boring bits.

'So how is she?' Natasha asks me, snapping me from my mother
thoughts.

'She's fine,' I say, trying to close down the conversation. 'She's
grand. She'll just get the injections and it will be, you know, fine.
Her eyes will just go back to normal. She's fine.' I stop then,
trying to think of ways to change the subject and come up with
other words that also mean fine to get Natasha off my back.

This is what I mean by slow learner. But I was learning from a
woman who could give masterclasses in Daughterhood. Natasha
listens. And then patiently, warily, because she can hear the shrill-
ness and low-level panic in my voice, suggests that I might want
to ask my mother how she's feeling about the injections. Perhaps
I might enquire whether I could be of any assistance. Maybe even
make a plan to be with her in the waiting room or collect her
when she's finished. I do none of that, as it happens. My strategy
was to zone out when Natasha started talking about the injections
and just hope she'd stop talking about it soon. We were just at the

beginning of this thing, this non-journey, and the fact that I needed to really think about how I approach my relationship with my mother hadn't really sunk in yet. Or maybe I knew, but it took a while for me to do anything concrete about it.

It turns out the needle in the eyeballs episode was my own mini Bench Moment. I was starting to see my mother as someone who was failing, or at least growing more vulnerable. But I wasn't yet facing up to it in the way Natasha had. She accepted her mother's new vulnerability and made plans accordingly, but she still saw her as an independent woman in her own right. Natasha recognised the confusion in me regarding my mother – it was a bewilderment and resistance that I was trying to hide. I knew then that Natasha's call had come at exactly the right time for me, in terms of where I was at with my mother. I had that virtuous feeling I always get when I embark on something pure and healthy. The one I had at my first anti-gravity yoga class/WeightWatchers meeting/meditation course. But for once it wasn't a selfish mission. As the meetings continued and I got more clarity about what was lacking in me as a daughter, I felt I was about to start giving something meaningful back to the woman who had given everything to me. The plan was to become a little less dependent and a little more dedicated.

6: TWO MORE DAUGHTERS

In the beginning I – Róisín – wondered whether our fellow members of The Daughterhood would ever tell their friends about what they were doing. Membership of The Daughterhood wasn't exactly something they wanted to shout about from the rooftops. Meanwhile, Natasha and I couldn't stop telling people about our new club. It was talking about The Daughterhood to a complete stranger in a hotel lobby that led to Natasha recruiting Anna from England after two Daughterhood meetings had already taken place. Debbie, our final daughter, came to us at about the same time. We'll let them tell you the story themselves ...

ANNA: THE RELUCTANT DAUGHTER

I'm fifty-four years old and I never expected that in the autumn of my life I would be dealing with a mother whose winter is going on indefinitely. It's the responsibility no one warned our generation about.

One of the many reasons I didn't have children is because I do not have a disposition well suited to looking after dependents. I do not have a maternal bone in my body and, similarly, I feel awkward in the caring role. I could never be a nurse or a primary school teacher, yet put me in a war zone or at sea in a storm and I'd take charge and steer everyone to safety. I'm good on the high seas, not in a crèche or a care home.

My greatest fear is not that my mother will die; it's that she will outlive me and I'll never know a life free from her. There. I've said it now. I know that's a seemingly callous thing to admit but it's the truth; it's how I feel. She's eighty-eight now. Apart from horrible leg ulcers, she is as healthy as a moderately fit sixty-year-old. Her mind may be on the wane with the first hints of Alzheimer's but she's not about to keel over any time soon.

I don't, as a rule, tell anyone what I just told you. In the past six months I've started to take time off work to look after my mother. But I'm full of anxiety about it. I'm doing it through a sense of duty rather than love. I don't feel like a 'bad daughter' but I do feel something of a fraud, as I don't have that deep bond with her that daughters are supposed to have their mothers. I'm ambivalent about daughterhood. I am, in effect, waiting for her to die.

When I first met Natasha I was dubious about the project. She was presenting at a conference in a hotel on the outskirts of Dublin.

I had been flown over by my company – I work in travel, sending people away on singles' holidays. I am single myself and love travelling, although packaged excursions to the Med are not really my bag. I am more a backpacking in the wilderness kind of girl.

I was sitting in the lobby minding my own business when we started talking. And she asked me what I now know she was asking everyone: 'Do you have a mother? How do you feel about her dying?' I think she was taken aback by my answer. It's not something I would normally blurt out to a stranger. But it was one of those anonymous conversations, where you know there will be no repercussions. She told me about the book she was writing and about how surprised she had been to find that so many daughters were struggling when it came to their mothers. It didn't surprise me. The struggle has defined my life. But I've not let it hold me back. Natasha and I exchanged numbers. I didn't expect to hear from her again.

In fact, Natasha rang the next day. I was barely off the plane in London. She wanted me to think about being involved with her project. My first instinct was to say no and change my number so that I wouldn't have to think about it again. But another part of me was curious. Was there really anything that could be done when it came to my mother? Or was it just a trial to be endured?

I have only attended one Daughterhood meeting, when I was over in Dublin for business, but I like to think that I have done the correspondence course. The emails have flown back and forth. I've done my Motherwork, as well as I could in the circumstances. I'm a participant in the Open University Daughterhood Degree. By the time I met the others in Natasha's house it seemed the other daughters had clicked. Maeve wasn't there that night; she was on holiday with her mum. But Lily, Róisín, Cathy, Sophie, Grace and Natasha were ensconced on sofas, a tight little club; you could see there was a bond. They seemed happy to have fresh meat: me. They said I was to start at the beginning. So I did.

According to my mother I rejected her from the day I was born. I wouldn't take her milk. Apparently I howled whenever she came near me. This record played over and over from as early as I can remember. My mother told me so many times growing up that she did not want to get married, did not want to be pregnant and she did not want to have a child. She made very sure not to have another one after me. I grew up knowing that this life of domestic drudgery and motherhood and wifery was not what she had planned for herself; that in a parallel world she was living quite another existence. An opera singer, maybe. Or a model. In her twenties and thirties she looked like a Mediterranean beauty. Jet black curly hair, dark complexion, tall and slim. A complete catch. Like Sophia Loren with a 22-inch waist. But, in fact, she was from a dirt-poor London family with very limited experience of the world outside of Hackney. She had no sense of herself. No ability to fulfil her potential. Just a gnawing sense that things could have turned out very differently if life hadn't been so unfair as to land her with a husband and a daughter.

My dad was, like my mother, from a working-class East End background. He was from gypsy stock. He didn't even have a birth certificate.

He was forty-six when I came along; my mother was more than ten years younger. But, even so, she was marrying and having her first child very late for those times. To have your first baby at thirty-five was really unusual then. She'd left it as long as possible before getting married. Years later I read something from author Annabelle Charbit that struck a chord. She wrote that her mother belonged to that group of low IQ individuals who find everything alarming and who believe that raising your voice is the most effective form of communication. That is and always has been my mother – maybe not the low IQ, but she certainly has an under-developed curiosity about the world and other people.

I don't have any memory of being put in hospital at the age of three. They say I fell off a pony ride. Apparently, I came off the horse in a very unusual way and broke my arm in several places. All I know is that while I was in the hospital, in this children's ward where the windows had bars on them, I was physically abused. And while my memories of my time there are hazy, apart from being given dead legs and Chinese burns by one nurse, I remember connecting the sense of abandonment to my mother. I'd heard her enough times complaining about having had me. It seemed to me that I was being punished for being born. I don't want to overstate this incident but only mention it to show that from an early age I was aware of being a troublesome burden.

At home, I knew the set-up was different to that of my friends' families. Their parents had friends round for dinner and drinks. My friends had record players, put music on, had their mates round. That wasn't my life. My mother constantly moaned. She was never happy. She made mountains out of molehills and she never relaxed. I never got the sense that my mum and dad loved each other either. There was no intimacy between them. I firmly believe they had sex once, when I was conceived. They didn't kiss. They didn't hug. There was no tenderness. They'd slept in single beds since I was an infant. I expect it was because my mother was terrified of getting pregnant again.

We lived with my grandmother, whom my mother idolised. I would describe their relationship as uncomfortably close. Granny was the light of her world. Mum was an only child herself and went everywhere with Granny – a dynamic, feisty woman with whom I had a wonderful relationship. She liked a laugh and took an interest in me without moaning endlessly.

It struck me as odd that my mother and my grandmother constantly nagged my father, though. It was relentless. Granny even went on my mother and father's honeymoon with them. That's what I mean by uncomfortably close.

I felt sorry for my dad. And while I preferred his company to my mother's, he was remote and distant; lost in thought mostly. I could never get close to him. Before he married my mother he had a wild sort of peripatetic life; wherever he laid his hat was his home. He was a traveller in every sense of the word. He didn't seem suited to the settled, domestic life. He was a wanderer pinned down to a mundane routine. My mum would slag him off constantly until it would get too much for him and he'd go down the pub. When she got in a rage she would boil with frustration at her lot in life. And yet they stayed together – her cooking and cleaning and complaining; him just asking for peace and, when it didn't come, escaping to a place where he found more comfort. 'Don't ever get married,' she'd scream at me when the slam of the door signalled my dad was off down the White Horse. 'Don't get trapped. Don't have a baby.' And I never did. Funny, that.

I knew from about the age of seven that I would leave home as early as I could. The first time I went abroad was on a school trip to Belgium and Holland and I remember sitting in a dining hall with the nuns – it was a convent school – and seeing bottled water for the first time. And we were given horsemeat. I remember thinking, 'This is amazing', while most of my classmates were miming being sick. It was 1968. On that school trip I went wandering off. I found a free festival. Everyone was tripping their nuts off (although, of course, I didn't know that at the age of seven) and I was befriended by some hippies.

They gave me some coins to put in a machine that dispensed extremely bouncy Superballs. All the hippies were tripping, bouncing these balls around and laughing and I was happy with them. Then the nuns came. It was over. But I knew then that I was going to leave home as soon as I could and travel for the rest of my life. There was a whole other world out there, and it looked as if adults could have as much fun as children.

In the early-1970s, if you were a white working-class teenage girl in London you went one of two ways. You either became a teeny bopper, who worshipped the Bay City Rollers, read *Jackie* magazine from cover to cover every week and dreamt of getting married. Or, well, you explored the 'alternative' culture. For me, that meant reading Karl Marx, *The Little Red Schoolbook*, going on the children's school strike, getting into French existentialism and radical film culture and punk. I wasn't a *Jackie* kind of teenager.

I'd been having a close friendship with a teacher who was only a few years older than me. He was in the Worker's Revolutionary Party. We would go to parties with other teachers of a left-wing persuasion and sit around, smoke dope and talk about existentialism. If this sounds like the worst kind of 1970s radical chic cliché, it was. I used to wear a beret and smoke a pipe. My teacher opened my eyes, opened me up to learning, to revolutionary thinking, to Marxism – although our friendship would certainly be viewed very suspiciously by today's standards.

He was the first person to suggest I might go and do a degree. He encouraged me to take A levels and then study Art History. I never got any sort of guidance about school or study from my parents. They never had high expectations of me. My world at home was so narrow. I felt as though I lived with this really old couple. I had nothing in common with them.

They seemed impossibly out of touch. They read rubbish newspapers and watched crap game shows. They didn't know about Albert Camus or the Left Bank or any of the French intellectuals! I couldn't talk to them about surrealism and modernism and radical lifestyles. So, in my impetuous teenage way, I wrote them off.

And outside of the house I soaked up all this stuff wherever I could find it. I was becoming the person I felt I was meant to be. If my mother had taught me one thing by default, it was that you had to create your own life. Grasp it. She hadn't done that for herself and she was unfulfilled and miserable. She never went on foreign holidays. She'd never learnt to swim or ride a bike or drive. She never became proficient at anything that would have given her freedom or adventure. She had shied away from life and this was like a warning flag to me. I wasn't going to repeat her mistakes. I was off. And I wasn't going to look back.

But I've tried so hard, all my life, to make things better for her, to steer her gently towards making good decisions. The only time she ever left the country was when I arranged a holiday and took her and Dad to Turkey for two weeks in 1984. The only photo I have of her looking truly happy is from that holiday. There's something so melancholy about this person who never really adjusted to modern life, or even adulthood.

Something unknowable lurks in her history and I've never got to the bottom of it. Instead I have these faint memories of flaming, violent rows. A terrifying anger directed at Dad and at me. At Dad for going down the pub and being free, as working-class men were in the 1960s. At me for being helpless and noisy and messy. Working-class sulking. Dinners thrown at walls. Awful atmospheres and slamming doors. Was there post-natal depression? Undoubtedly. But no one even had a word for it then. It was one of the many things you just didn't talk about. Her parents were living with them, and my mother's close, cloying relationship with her own mother, plus a new baby, was a recipe for tension.

It was resentment built on poverty. A literal financial poverty, but also an emotional poverty – of not talking about feelings. Each person scurrying off into their corner and brooding or storming out and going down the pub. What did my mother do in those first couple of years after my birth when my dad was ostracised and badgered and driven to drink? There was no TV at home in 1961. There were no books in the house. There was just the kitchen, the wireless and the radiogram to break the silence. A person could go crazy with a small baby . . . That milieu, reflected so accurately in British films like *Billy Liar* or *Saturday Night, Sunday Morning*, and even sitcoms like *Till Death Us Do Part* – horrible suffocating décor, dark, heavy, wooden furniture, doilies and linen, and the older generation's foreboding that everything they had fought for fifteen years earlier in the Second World War was going to be dismantled by a force more alien than Hitler's war machine: make way for the youthquake of the 1960s and '70s.

Since I was old enough to write my name, I felt part of a very different tribe to that of my parents. Singing along to the piano was never going to hold any interest for a child whose ears were alerted to psychedelia, the Kinks, the Crazy World of Arthur Brown, Andy Warhol, and the explosion of the 'permissive society'.

I was aware I'd been born into an era of great change. By the age of seven I was glued to *Top of the Pops* and thrilled by Hammer horror movies. My mother hated it all. To think she was only in her early forties, yet to her even The Beatles were a sign that everything was going to pot. That reactionary thread of Fear of the New ran from right to left, top to bottom. Never has a generation of parents been as appalled as those of the late 1950s/early 1960s. Didn't matter if you were going down the pit for your living or looking after clients at a private bank – the youth were hairy, scary and had a radical agenda; they talked about revolution and got naked in Hyde Park. They had all the opportunities their parents had never been afforded because of the war. Resentments brewed but the old guard couldn't stop the tide.

They couldn't stop me. At the age of fourteen I had become a cuckoo in the nest, a swaggering arty-farty anomaly in this traditional East End home. I wasn't interested in going to catering school like my mum had expected. I was reading Kafka, studying photography and European cinema. There was absolutely no common ground between us. The gap increased until one day, age fifteen, I just left home. That's when I consider my real life started. I gave up school – I only had one O level at that point but I couldn't be bothered staying there. The revolution was coming and I was going to be prepared.

My dad sat there with a face like a lemon. He wasn't happy but he couldn't stop me. My mother wanted to know how I was going to look after myself and was full of dire warnings about how I would come 'crawling back', but I knew I was going to be OK and that I'd never live in her house again. There were no hugs at the door, but not really any rows either. I think they kind of expected it and they made no real attempts to stop me. I packed a rucksack and hitch-hiked to Devon with my best friend and her older brother. They had older siblings in the West Country who lived in a kind of commune – a tumbledown rural hippie haven where I could have conversations about metaphysics and creativity and God and art and feminism. I had visited them the previous summer and they'd taught me a lot. They were my kind of people. Vegetarian. Practising yoga. Living off the grid. And if that all sounds very worthy, it was tempered by dressing-up days, song writing and playing guitar and laughter and love and sharing and joy. Oh, to be surrounded by joy!

I lived between Devon and various squats in London, enjoying the punk rock explosion. I kept in touch with my parents but only the bare minimum. When I'd visit her, my mum would say, 'When are you going to get a proper job? When are you going to knuckle down?' My dear dad would give me money on the sly, but I was supporting myself by then – working in cafes and shops, getting an education. By the time I travelled around Europe in my late teens with a gang of travelling minstrels, I would write airmail letters home and Mum and Dad could see I was going to be OK. They knew I wasn't going to become a heroin addict or get pregnant or wind up in a gutter somewhere. They knew the path I was following was one of art and learning and adventure. And so their minds were put at rest.

I lived in a cave in Greece for a while and had all sorts of jobs. I was even a shepherdess at one point. I was in love with 'outsider poets' and musicians such as Leonard Cohen and Syd Barrett. I was a young, wild, romantic in a beret, smoking Gauloises. Mum and Dad would send packages of tea and tobacco out to me. When I'd phone home my mother told me they loved the letters I'd sent. They'd read them again and again. There was, finally, some acceptance of my unconventional life.

When I moved back to London in the 1980s, I got a degree

and a job in the public sector, and I began to have what might be seen as a more regulated relationship with my parents. I would go round there once a month, on a Sunday, especially when my dad was still alive. And it was totally amicable. We'd have Sunday dinner. I'd talk about what I'd been doing; and, as a young firebrand revolutionary, there would still be political arguments. I would carry on my diatribe about the fact they read the bloody *Daily Mail*. I would rant and rave about Thatcherism. I would talk about the riots, about how society was all going to come tumbling down. I was a bit of a political bore, really. I mean, in my 20s, when I should have been going to discos and having a wild time, I was going to Socialist Workers Party meetings and building barricades.

I have a friend, Jenny, who has worked hard on her relationship with her mother. She's been a big influence on me in trying to become more compassionate with mine. Now that my mother needs more help, I've started to work a four-day week. I spend my Fridays with her – making her meals for the week, sorting out her medication and hospital visits. Five years ago I started talking to her about moving to sheltered housing. Where she is now, the only bathroom is upstairs. It's not suitable. But she won't have it; she wouldn't even entertain a conversation. 'You are not going to put me in a 'ome,' she'll shout at me and anyone else who tries to bring up the prospect of her moving. She would only consider leaving when things have become an absolute emergency.

I am trying to do the right thing. But it's out of a sense of duty rather than anything else. I care about her. I do. I want her to be comfortable. I want her to be happy. But just as when I was growing up, no matter what anyone does or says, she will never be happy. She doesn't know how.

In April I bought her a special padded wheelchair, as she hadn't left the house since December because she can't walk unaided any more. I pushed her two miles down to the High Street. I took her to the pub for her favourite whisky and ginger, and I showed her the sunlight on the water of the local pond. There was no thanks. No 'What a lovely day; this is great.' No, instead, it was just, 'It ain't half cold.' Do you know what she reminds me of? *Steptoe and Son*. Steptoe and Daughter. That's us.

'It ain't half cold.' She repeated that twenty times over the next half an hour.

If she dies tomorrow, of course I will feel bad. Mostly because I couldn't ever get her to enjoy herself. It's as though she's spent her whole life with a cloud of negativity hanging over her. A yoke of gloom. I sensed it as a child. And I wanted to get as far away from that cloud as possible and try and be as positive and pioneering as I could. I did that. I got away. It's pointless wasting emotional energy on hypothetical regret. I realised a while back that I've just got to write it off.

It's the mystery of my mother that drives me nuts. I want to know what her problem is. I want to know why she never tried to live. Really live. If there is one question I have for my mother it is: 'why have you never taken a leap of faith? Why have you never once just thought 'fortune favours the brave'? She never cut her own apron strings from her mother; she never made that journey as a child away from the parent. She never rebelled.

I believe something very healthy happened at the end of the 1950s, when people started rebelling against their parents. They became a powerful generation, and made real changes for good in the world. But she never individuated, to use Jung's terminology. I don't understand why not. I'd like to understand.

I think it's too late, though. If I have work to do with my mother it's getting her to accept her own mortality. She's in denial about her mobility, her age, her oncoming dementia. I'd like to give her a good send-off, though. We're of a similar mind when it comes to green issues. She thinks the same way I do, that we are ruining the planet. I know she wants a biodegradable coffin and she showed me a brochure with a bamboo casket being carried into a bluebell grove. 'Isn't that lovely,' she said. So I suppose I could talk to her about that. I suppose that is one thing I could do.

My main preoccupation now is that I don't want to witness the cruelty of her at 100, or 103 or 106, dribbling and incontinent. I cannot be the one looking after her while the rest of my life stops happening.

Although it sounds awful and mercenary, the truth is she's sitting on a house worth a fair bit of money, simply because it's in London. I'd be lying if I said I haven't thought about the options open to me if I were to inherit it. I don't want to send people on singles' holidays. I want to see more of the world myself! I have a whole other part of my life to live. Reluctant Daughter? Reluctant is one word for how I feel. Frustrated is more accurate.

Reflections on the Reluctant Daughter

The only time that I – Natasha – can remember being a full-on Reluctant Daughter was during my teens. Our house was a very busy one. We were a very active family. The front hallway was clogged up with gear bags, dirty runners, rugby boots and hurling sticks. A busy house doesn't run itself. We all had house jobs. I had to keep the bathrooms clean during the week, and Sorcha was the best cook so she made dinner twice a week. My youngest sister Kate hoovered and Oisín cut the grass, fixed whatever needed fixing and decluttered the bulging garden shed full of bicycles, tins of old paint, rejected furniture and stuff with no name that found its home there from our already over-stuffed house. Cilian had to clear out the ashes from the fire and make sure that both the turf basket and coal scuttle were full. He was the biggest skiver. He regularly tried to pay one of us off to do his jobs.

Like millions of mothers, my mother was exasperated and exhausted with all this responsibility. As the eldest daughter, a lot of this was lumped on me. I knew that as the eldest daughter I should have pulled my weight and given her the support that she needed, but for those two reluctant years, I wanted out. Instead of going straight home after school to help with the chores, I spent hours in my friend Jennifer Cunningham's house drinking coffee, listening to CDs, analysing our lives and the lives of others. I escaped to my boyfriend's house as often as possible, too, which seemed like a sanctuary compared to the noise and chaos of the Fennell household. I also had a part-time job in the now world-famous Druid Theatre as a member of their front-of-house team. I immersed myself night after night in the world of Tom Murphy's *Conversations on a Homecoming* or Brian Friel's *Translations*. I didn't want to be my mother's daughter and I certainly did not want to be the eldest daughter.

During that time, my mother hardly got a look in. But somehow wisdom prevailed and I snapped out of my Reluctant Daughter phase. And that's just what it was. A phase. It never occurred to me that that reluctance might be with you your whole life.

In Anna's case she is a reluctant only child with no siblings to share the burden of looking after an ageing mother. What's worse? To abandon an ageing mother for the sake of your own sanity or to be in a situation where you feel you've no choice but to do the 'right thing' and look after her? They both sound like hell. Either you're plagued by the guilt that comes with not taking care of her or you endure the miserable existence of looking after a woman you can't stand.

In her brilliant memoir *Mother Daughter Me*, *New York Times* journalist Katie Hafner asks a central, crucial question: what is our obligation to our parents as they age, particularly if those parents gave us a childhood that was far less than ideal? Reluctant Daughters are the daughters who, like Anna, struggle to answer that difficult question, often for much of their adult lives.

DEBBIE: THE DISAPPOINTING DAUGHTER

I've come quite late to the Daughterhood party. Until very recently I worked in a basement office in Dublin city centre. I called it The Bunker. A couple of the strip lights in The Bunker didn't work, so every day from 7am to 4pm I sat in a pool of pale yellow, flickering light with my headphones in listening to people.

Lately, I've been listening to a focus group on catfood. 'Well, my Tabitha, Tabby for short, my husband calls her T, is not impressed with the salmon flavour. And I don't mind telling you I tasted a bit just to see, and she's right it IS too salty. Now she loves the duck one. Can't get enough of it. In fact, I tasted that, too, and it had a flavour a bit like foie gras to me. I had it once in Nice ...'

I didn't like The Bunker but I liked my job. If you are curious about everything, and I am (in Fifth Year I got the nickname Debbie the Nose because I was always asking questions), it's the perfect job. One day I'm listening to cat owners and the next biochemists discussing cures for cancer. What I do is type up conversations so the clients have a record of what's been said. I don't know what they do with it then – my job ends when I send off the transcripts – but what I do for the clients is get it all down. Every word. Well, not the 'ahs' and 'ums' and the 'likes' and 'yeahs'; people do a lot more of that than you might think. I get rid of them. I make people sound better on the page than they do in real life. I'm good at it because I type exceptionally quickly. My boss calls me 'the Mo Farah of the keyboard'. Mo for short.

But you're not here to read about The Bunker or my job or my boss's 'hilarious' line in unimaginative nicknames. You are here to

read about daughters and about mothers and how they get along.
Or don't in my case.

Sometimes I feel like an alien who has landed on planet
Mother-Daughter-Love. I look around and I see daughters out
shopping for special outfits with their mothers. Sharing intimate
dinners in restaurants. Laughing together in the changing rooms
of clothes shops. Friends tell me about what they are doing for
Mother's Day. They think carefully about the spa they've chosen
or the restaurant they are going to afterwards. I notice they seem
to be looking forward to these opportunities to be close to their
mothers. I have no reference points to share with them, no
common ground. But I don't tell them that. I nod and smile. I
make the noises I think might be appropriate. 'Oh, I'm sure she'll
love that,' I say. And I think about my mother and when they're
gone and I'm on my own I might cry.

My own personal survival technique is to cover it all up. That's
what I've always done. Not getting on with your mother is a
lonely place to be but I've been here for years and I'm used to it.
You try to assimilate. You find a way to fit in. You don't let anybody know. You keep it all in. I mean, you tell me, what kind of
dysfunctional freak doesn't get on with their own mother? Who
wants to hear about that? Who wants to talk about it?

At last, it seems as though somebody does. And I am here to
transcribe their discussions.

Smokers, I have a question. (Non-smokers, you might also find
this interesting.) Did you know that the amount of nicotine you
have in your toenails could predict your risk of developing lung
cancer? Until yesterday neither did I. I've been transcribing the
keynote speeches from an international chiropodist's conference.

Fascinating stuff. Researchers took toenail clippings of male smokers who developed lung cancer over a twelve-year period and compared them to clippings from non-smokers. The ones with the highest nicotine levels were 3.57 times more likely to develop lung cancer. So there you go. I love my job.

My boss smokes. His fingernails are a mustardy yellow and he stinks of Benson & Hedges. There's a courtyard at the back of the office, about the size of a napkin, where he goes to suck cigarettes and think up nicknames for the staff. My mother doesn't smoke. My dad did. I was always trying to get him to give up but in the end it wasn't the cigarettes that got him, it was this thing in his head that had been growing, the consultant reckoned, for around twenty years.

It couldn't have been stopped. There was nothing we could have done. But you never believe that, do you? When you are left behind you wonder what if, and you think you should have noticed something, and you remember something that might have been a sign, like the time he left the keys in the door, which really wasn't like him, and every so often you notice a bitter taste in your mouth and that is the guilt.

All those emails dripping with guilt from daughters Natasha spoke about? I don't mind admitting I gave a little inner cheer when I heard about them. I think what they are doing is great but Natasha and Róisín seem to have the kind of chocolate-box relationships with their mothers that I've always dreamed of. But these other women who wrote in – I felt they were in my head. The relief. What is it that woman sang years ago? They were 'strumming my pain' with their words.

I related to Maeve and I understood her craving for intimacy with her mother. And the story of hiding from her made me laugh. In one way I felt sorry for her mother, you know, being turned away. But part of me admired Maeve for being able to stand up for herself. Your mum wouldn't just turn up at your office in town and say, 'Stop working, here's your lunch.' And I was chilled by Lily's account of her adoption and her mother's narcissism and rejection of her. It's always secretly a relief to know that no matter how bad you have it, somebody else is going through far worse. I started to work on The Daughterhood file, even though I was running late on other more urgent files. I couldn't wait to hear what happened next. I listened and I just kept thinking, 'It's not just me; I'm not the only one.'

Maggie, who sits two cubicles to my left, has been assigned a mediation case involving a couple who are fighting with the couple next door to them over a tree that is blocking their light. She's been listening to them for weeks now. 'If I hear one more effing word about that effing tree I'll climb the nearest one and, so help me God, I won't come down from it until Basil has assigned this to someone else,' she said the other day while we shared a bag of Skittles in the kitchenette. Maggie talks with a slight lisp and so my boss calls her Toyah, after Toyah Willcox. He is tall and annoying and a bit mad so we call him Basil after Basil Fawlty. Behind his back, obviously.

Maggie is very jealous that I have The Daughterhood files and not the Mad Cow files, as she calls them, because one half of Couple Number Two is having a bit of a nervous breakdown about the trees. Maggie's always looking to know what's going on. 'You mean to tell me that this is a group of women meeting to bitch about their mothers?' she asked me when I first told her, not really believing. I had become enthralled by their monthly gatherings. It was like a soap opera. I was dying for the next instalment.

'They're not bitching,' I said.

'Well, I bet they are bitchy,' Maggie said.

'I wouldn't say they bitch about their mothers. It's more a reflective chat,' I answered defensively – I became very invested early on with the project and felt a kind of affinity with the women. 'They share their stories and offer each other support, and just a listening ear. They talk about their mothers but they also talk about themselves as daughters. They say they find it cathartic.'

'Cathartic, my arse,' said Maggie, but it's just because she's driven mad listening to the dimensions of that pine tree and the shadow it casts across Couple Number One's decking and all the rest. 'If my mother knew I was meeting to bitch about her with a group of women sitting around eating – what did you say they had the first time?'

'Chilli with brown rice, and I think some sort of vegetable roulade and home-made garlic bread.'

'Eating chilli with brown rice and roulade, or whatever you call it, she'd be appalled. Do they tell their mothers what they are doing?'

'No, that's not the point. The point is they are figuring out how to be better daughters and how to—'

'Well, I personally think it's disloyal,' said Maggie. 'Where would they be without their mothers? Nowhere, that's where. And how do this bunch of ingrates repay their mothers? By sitting around a table telling each other how terrible their mothers are? It's not right!'

'How is your mother?' I said then, to shut her up more than anything else. And it worked. She spent the whole rest of our lunch hour, and there's no other word for it, bitching about her mother, without seeing the irony of it at all. I love Maggie.

*

Sometimes I can't hear myself think over the hum of the air conditioning system in The Bunker. I'm sitting here, trying to ignore the buzzing, wondering what I'd have said if I met Natasha on a bus or on a train or a plane and she asked me about my mother. If she asked me, 'How is your mother?' I wouldn't know what to say. Because, right now, I don't know. She has run away to my sister in Australia. She won't answer my calls. She is grieving for my father who died last year but it's a private, personal, secret grief and she doesn't want to share it with anyone, least of all me.

My father – clever, intuitive man that he was – predicted as much.

It was cancer. There was nothing the doctors could do. We found out and then three months later he was gone. You read about it in the papers, these kinds of things happening, but it's always to other people. Now we are the other people. I miss him.

A few weeks before he died, before he sort of went into himself, into his head and you knew he wasn't coming out again, he said to me, 'Look out for your mother when I'm gone.' He knew what would happen. He said she'd run away, as far as she could get, he even mentioned Australia, instead of facing up to the grief and to the loss and all the rest of it. Everything he said has come true. She has been to Australia twice since he died. She says she is going for a month and she ends up staying for two.

My sister works in a legal firm. She's out at 7am in the morning and she often won't be back until 7pm. Her husband is out at work, too; he works in financial services. So my mother is at home with the nanny and my sister's two small children all day. She is bored, I think, that's what she says when she does decide to call on Skype. My sister's been reporting back that all she does all day is sit there on her iPad. I wouldn't mind if she was reading.

But she's not reading. She's playing games. Angry Birds and solitaire. (She is seventy-four.)

My sister's place is quite isolated. One of those posh, gated estates, a cul-de-sac of eight identical detached houses. My mother doesn't drive so she can't go anywhere. Behind the houses there is a huge forest 'full of snakes' my mother says but I think she's exaggerating. So she's trapped in a way, or that's how she sees it, and she won't come home. Well, she will at some point but then she'll be off again. Running away from the grief.

So, Natasha, in answer to your question that you haven't asked me but you might had we met somehow on a plane or a train: I don't know what to tell you about my mother. Since Dad died I feel as though I've lost her. Or she's deliberately losing herself. I can't talk to her about anything. How does she feel? Does she miss Dad? When is she coming home? When I try to go there she clams up or something mysterious happens to the Skype connection. She is escaping into herself. Into her games. Bloody, jaysus, pigging Angry Birds.

I went to some grief counselling after Dad died which helped and I tried to get Mum to go. But she was having none of it. 'You don't need to talk about all that, it just makes it worse,' she said.

How is my mother? Good question. Missing in action. I think she has been all my life. That's what I'd say.

I'm five years old. I'm sitting on my Granduncle's big red couch. Uncle Tom is sitting beside me eating his sweets out of a bag. They smell like cloves, the ones Mam stuck in the oranges over Christmas and hung over the door with a red ribbon. The sweets are red and white but I don't like them. I like my sweets. The ones in my bag. They're called satin cushions. They're all different colours and some of them have stripes across them. They look like presents. Inside the presents once you've sucked them a good bit there is a surprise and the surprise is chocolate. It sort of melts all out of the cushions, like the stuffing coming out of a real cushion that's been stuffed too much, and it tastes gorgeous. When Uncle Tom eats his sweets he makes this sucky, clacky sound. Sucky, clack he goes. And then I go crunch, suck. And I don't say anything but I think we sound like an orchestra I saw on *Blue Peter* except, instead of instruments, we have our mouths and our sweets. Sucky, clack. Crunch, suck. It's a sort of music.

My parents have left me here while they've gone shopping. It's the first time Uncle Tom has minded me all by himself. He's lived alone since Aunt Margaret passed away before I was born. They asked him loads of questions before they went. 'Will you be all right with her?' 'You won't let her have any sweets, will you?' 'Will you make sure you ask her if she needs to use the loo?'

I don't know why they asked him so many questions. I love Uncle Tom. He's kind. As soon as they were gone he got a bag of my favourite sweets from behind the Bible on a high-up shelf and gave them to me with a big wink. 'Our little secret, eh, Debs?' he said. 'Our secret, Uncle Tom,' I say back and I try to wink but I just scrunch up my whole face and that makes him laugh.

My favourite programme is on the telly. It's called *Wanderly Wagon*. It makes us laugh loads. Uncle Tom's laugh is a kind of wheezy one. Haahahazzzzzz. Like that. Sometimes I'll hear a little rattle and it sounds like it's coming from his chest but I don't say anything because I'm so happy. Uncle Tom says, 'We'll have a little fire, will we, Debs?' and he reaches down to strike the match off the mantelpiece and then he throws it into the fire and I love the crackle it makes and the way the newspaper curls up and dances in the grate.

I'm five years old and I am sitting beside my Uncle Tom eating sweets and listening to his rattling chest and I think I can trace it all back to what happens when Uncle Tom leans over to me and says, 'I'll just throw another log on the fire, shall I, eh, Debs?'

They have started talking to me now at their monthly meetings. Addressing me, which almost never happens in this line of work. 'Transcriber,' they say, 'don't transcribe things like "pass the wine", you'll make us sound like alcoholics.' 'Transcriber, sorry about the clinking of knives and forks.' I feel as though I know them now. I listen to their stories and I think about my story. About my mother and the distance between us. The other day someone from Natasha's office rang up to ask whether they could have the latest transcript a bit quicker. She asked whether it was the same person transcribing all the sessions and I told her, yes, and that the person was me.

And then she asked me what I thought about it all. What did I think? I think it's essential listening. I think it's making me feel less alone and odd. I think I want to read this book and get my children to read it when they're older. 'I don't really get on with my mother,' I told her. And she said, 'You're not on your own there.' And I remember laughing and I found myself telling her how much I was enjoying listening to The Daughterhood. It just sort of happened. Then she asked if I'd like to join. My first instinct was to say that my story wasn't interesting enough. But then I got a bit indignant with myself. My story is as important and as interesting as anybody else's. Plus, I spend so much time thinking about my mother it might do me good to let it all out. So I said yes. Yes, thank you for asking, yes I want to talk about my mother to people who will understand and who won't judge. Yes. I put the phone down and I realised that I'd been waiting to be asked all along.

I'm not going to pretend it didn't feel weird heading out to my first Daughterhood meeting. It did. I was a bag of nerves. Maggie from work couldn't believe what I was about to do. 'But that's ...' she said, struggling to find the right word, 'it's ... unprofessional.' I knew what she meant but there had been a certain development in my business affairs which made me not worry too much about professional decorum.

I had escaped from The Bunker. I had got a loan from the bank. I was setting up on my own, transcribing from my house when the kids were asleep or when they were in school and whenever I could get a chance basically. I had some clients who were willing to come with me. Including The Daughterhood. Maggie was stuck in The Bunker so I could understand her frustration. But I didn't care. I was going to address something in my life that I had spent years running away from. I was going to face the problem of my mother.

But I'm a wuss at the best of times. This meeting was in Róisín's house, which as it happened wasn't too far from where I lived. I sat in the car outside her purple door for half an hour before I went in. I was worried. I thought I was being disloyal to my mother. I was fretting about what my father would have thought. I felt shy. What would the others think of me? In the car on the way over I was just chatting to myself, like a little train from *Thomas the Tank Engine* – can-I-do-this, can-I-do-this, can-I-do-this. Stupid really. I always imagine before I go anywhere that everyone is going to be like Marilyn Monroe, perfect, and I'm going to feel inadequate. But nobody was Marilyn. (They never are.) They were all just normal and welcoming and nice. I was early. Róisín was there and Natasha. And it all felt much more natural than it should have done. I nibbled at a bowl of crisps and had a laugh about recognising people from their voices. They all arrived. Lily. Maeve. Cathy. Grace. Sophie. Anna was in London but had sent a welcoming message. It was like meeting characters from a book in real life. I recognised their voices. I knew them but I didn't know them at all.

I broke the ice by telling them to go easy on the cutlery clanging, explained how it distorted the sound on the Dictaphone. We laughed about the fact that, later, I would go home and have to transcribe this meeting, clanging cutlery and all. Like most people I hate the sound of my own voice. I wasn't looking forward to it. I'm like my mother. We are both quite self-conscious, nervous people. I learnt it from her. She panics if the phone rings.

But this was my first meeting and I was the main event. I started talking and it was such a liberating feeling to talk about my mother without censoring myself that I thought I might never stop.

First, I told them about what had gripped me listening to their conversations. I'd remembered at the first meeting Natasha being surprised that people could not get on with their mothers. 'How could they not?' she had asked. And what was amazing, I told them, was that some of you didn't and that you were all able to sit around a table talking about it. I told them how much I related to Maeve hiding from her mother. Because I do that with my mum. I'll be working and she'll need to talk but I need to get my work done and so I have to shut her out. I remember thinking, 'I'm not alone. I'm not the only person in the world who does this.'

When I listened through my earphones, it was like eavesdropping on a group of friends who I had so much in common with, even though I had never met any of them. I thought of my mother-in-law and my sister-in-law, a mother and daughter, who are thick as thieves and go everywhere together, and even live beside each other. It made me wonder what was wrong with me. Am I abnormal? Am I the only one in the world who doesn't want to be beside their mum?

When I said that, Róisín laughed and said, 'Well, you are in the right place to say that out loud.' And it did feel like the right place.

I told them about my dad dying. And how since he died everybody has been saying to me, 'How's your mum? How's your mum?' And how I just kept telling them, 'I don't know. I don't know.' This week I don't know because she's gone off again to Australia, even though it was the first anniversary of my father's death. I was upset. Everybody coming up and remembering the anniversary and asking what we were doing and saying, 'How is your mother?'

I haven't even spoken to her in two weeks. She refuses to use an ordinary phone. She will only Skype and I hate Skype. I don't like seeing myself. And I like to be doing something else while I'm talking – filling out an invoice, say, or peeling the potatoes – and I'd prefer her not to see that. Also, my kids come in and start trying to use the computer and putting things up on the screen and . . . I know I'm behind the times but I just feel like it's not a proper conversation. She won't use the ordinary phone because it costs money and she's obsessive about saving money.

Then I told them about the struggle of the past year with Daddy dying. And how he said to me before he died, 'Look out for your mother.' And how he told me exactly what was going to happen and how every single thing has come true. And then the group wanted me to go back to the beginning and by now I felt comfortable and at home in the strangest way. It sounds cringey but it was a safe space. I didn't have to pretend. I've spent such a long time pretending.

I told them about my little brother Billy. He was born with Down's Syndrome and associated heart problems. He had to have lots of operations when he was a baby and I suppose what happened was that I took on a lot of the responsibility for my sister, Edwina, Billy's twin. My mum was always so worried about Billy. She would run here and run there, taking him for this operation and that operation, and I think it was back then that I started to distance myself from her.

And then I went back a bit further. I told them about the day thirty-eight years ago when I was five years old and my parents went shopping and left me with my Granduncle Tom.

I described the room, how the carpet was red, and so were the sofas, covered with some sort of bumpy material like a circular corduroy. I used to sit on the sofa rubbing it, feeling the bumps in the material.

And I sat on that sofa for what felt like a lifetime, rubbing the bumps to comfort myself while Uncle Tom lay unconscious on the floor. He was blocking the door so I couldn't open it to tell anyone. I just rubbed the sofa and looked at the telly. And then the dog, Uncle Tom had a Border Collie named Shep, just started to howl and I couldn't get the dog to stop.

I said, 'Uncle Tom, wake up, wake up.' And I kept saying it. But eventually I thought, Uncle Tom is not going to wake up so I will just sit here watching *Wanderly Wagon* until my mum and dad get back. And it seemed to take them ages. And Uncle Tom never did wake up.

When they did get back from the shops all hell broke loose. An ambulance arrived. I heard a man say 'massive heart attack' and I was shoved into a bedroom upstairs. My mum took me to the doctor a few weeks later because apparently I had become a bit withdrawn. The doctor said, 'She's five years old; she's not going to remember this.' But I do remember. I remember everything. I remember the red and gold swirly pattern on the wallpaper, the ticking of the huge mantle clock, the fire crackling and then glowing and then dying and Uncle Tom's dog howling, howling, howling, and the crunch of sweets in my mouth.

The funny thing is I never thought about it much. I didn't spend years trying to figure out how that incident had affected me but I know it did. About thirty years later, I'd been suffering with depression and I went to a counsellor. That's when it all came flooding out. A dam burst. That first day the counsellor told me to go home and talk to my mother about it. So I did. And she wouldn't talk. Just refused. She said, 'I don't want to talk about that, it's in the past.' And then she said, 'You don't need to talk about it. That's nonsense. Leave it be.' And, 'You're fine, you're fine. You are just over-analysing.'

Our relationship deteriorated from that point. But I think the start of the deterioration was when I was five. She thought she was doing the right thing, taking the doctor's advice, not talking to me about it. But it was the wrong thing and from there we started to grow apart. And then Billy was born and I had to take care of Edwina and gradually, over the years, a coldness descended between us. When debs time came around, it was my dad who took me to choose the dress. Imagine, my dad doing the thing that everyone else did with their mum. It's sad, when I think about it now.

I felt I'd been going on for ages but the group never made me feel like that. I told them that my mother's relationship with my father was rocky. They were always close, they did everything together, but were never friends that you would have noticed. As he was dying, you got a tiny glimpse that they loved each other but when I look at it now I think that my mum and dad just weren't meant to be together.

It wasn't right. My dad was deeply antisocial, didn't like going out, didn't see the point. But my mum wanted to meet people, to chat, have a glass of wine. My dad would say, 'Why waste good money?' And so she stayed at home, too. Dad's perfect Sunday was a roast with his nine grandchildren around him. So they were different people but they stuck together because there would have been no other option in their minds.

I can forgive my mother. I can leave her lack of compassion for five-year-old and 43-year-old me behind. I don't know, though, if she can forgive me. I feel I disappointed her. The usual teenage shenanigans that people get up to, well, I got up to them. But my mother could never get over it. I'd let her down. And this has carried on. I constantly feel like I don't live up to her expectations.

I came home one day to find her sorting my husband Stephen's underwear drawer. I know it sounds funny, but she was doing it in an exasperated way. In a way that suggested I was useless and couldn't even manage my own home. And the other week she was going to have my eldest son, Ryan, who is fifteen, to stay in the sunny south east with her. He's a great boy. I told him to pack his blue bag with enough clothes for a couple of days. And he did. I picked up the bag and threw it in the car. Ryan got into the car with no shoes on – he was too busy with his iPod.

I only noticed his shoeless state when we were halfway down the N11. I thought it was funny. When we got to my mum's, he walked down the drive to the house in no shoes and then I realised I'd brought the wrong bag. He had no shoes and no clothes, other than what he was standing up in. He and I were laughing at our silliness. I gave my mum some money and asked her to pick up some cheap stuff for him in Penney's. She went mad with me. Really hysterical.

'You should have checked. You are his mother. Are you stupid? You are stupid!' This was all in front of Ryan. I get this all the time from her. My house is a mess. I don't do enough for my children. I work too hard. The truth is, I don't feel good around her. I feel like a failure. If I decorate the kitchen she'll say, 'That paint is a little bit dark in that room.' It's the negativity that is the hardest thing to bear.

But then lately I've been asking myself, what do I do to make her feel good? Does she feel good around me?

Maybe it's just not the right time for this Daughterhood business. She is still grieving Dad. He's only dead a year. I'm self-employed and working ridiculous hours. But she's been brilliant with the children, minding them down at hers during the summer holidays so I can get work done. I arrived to bring them back up to Dublin on Sunday night. I could have sat and had a cup of tea with her before we went to bed, or we could have watched a television programme we'd both enjoy. Instead, she sat playing Angry Birds on her tablet and I got the laptop out and started to do some typing in bed. We have bad mother–daughter habits. I

lon't know what to do to change that. I don't want to disappoint
her any more. And I want her to stop disappointing me.

Reflections on the Disappointing Daughter

No book on mothers and daughters would be complete without
the Disappointing Daughter. Perhaps you recognise her already?
I – Róisín – do. I don't think I am disappointing to my mother
and yet I still feel a bit of a disappointment. Let me count the
ways:

1. I haven't sorted my finances out. I am forty-two. I still treat
her like she's a branch of my local credit union. The other day I
lost my bank card and so I went around the corner to borrow
hers. 'This is the last time,' she said. I laughed. I'd heard that before.
I always wonder if it really will be the last time until she bails me
out again.

2. I still haven't got my issues around food (too much) and
exercise (too little) under control. She is very understanding of
this, more than anybody else because she knows all the reasons
behind it. But I would like to get this sorted so that she doesn't
have to worry about me as she gets older.

3. I rely on her too much. She doesn't mind my constant need
to run things past her, to ask her for favours, to spill out my innermost grievances, but I know she's concerned that I'll be lost
without her when she's gone.

And I will. I will be lost when she's gone. That's me saying that
as a grown-up adult woman. It was worse when I was younger, in
terms of the grief I caused her. Although I do think teenagers are
supposed to be a bit disappointing. It's almost part of their job
description.

You give life to these children, you feed and nurture them, you do your best for them, you fall in love with them, and then adolescence comes along and replaces your child with a raging (I was an angry teenager), white-haired (I had a thing about Billy Idol for a while), pyjama-as-daywear-advocating (blame Morrissey) monster.

In a family of eight children, I was the bane of her life. I spent a lot of my teenage years trying to get out of going to school. I had a repertoire of 'tummy aches' and 'splitting headaches' worthy of an Oscar winner. I wasn't a morning person. A lot of things 'weren't fair'.

School wasn't fair, for example. I always felt it should have started at a reasonable hour, like noon. This ludicrous 8.45am kick off was all too like we were heading out to put in a day's work in an accountancy firm.

But nobody agreed with me and so I faked illness as often as possible. Sometimes it worked but most of the time my mother could not be fooled. So when I think of my teenage years I remember countless duvets being reefed off me in the cruel, cold morning light. I taste neat vodka and hear the 'Wham Rap!' which I still know off by heart. But as I grow older the specifics, the details, get further out of reach. Which is not necessarily a bad thing.

All I know is, like a lot of teenagers, I was a Contrary Mary. One day bunking off school to get Gay Byrne (the Irish equivalent of Michael Parkinson; I told you I was contrary) to sign my copy of his autobiography, the next stalking silver-voiced buskers on Grafton Street. One minute wishing I could be as cool as the people who hung around with a Dublin band called The Garden Hasn't Changed Much and the next cuddling up with my mother on the sofa to watch Barry Manilow television specials.

'What was I like as a teenager?' I asked my mother recently so my memory could be jogged. 'I don't keep those things in my head,' she said. She's blanked them out, more likely. I wouldn't leave it, though. 'What was I like? What are your memories of teenage me?'

She thought for a minute and then recalled, 'The time you ran away from home to that boy's house and I didn't know you were gone until the boy's mother rang to say you were there.' She was on a roll now. 'Even when I made nice dinners you very often wouldn't eat the vegetables and filled up from Borza's instead,' she continued, making me yearn for fish and chips from my childhood haunt. I suppose they were nice dinners. But I always craved something else. I spent years wondering what that was. I'm still figuring it out. 'You did wear some strange clothes, which upset your sister when we visited her in Glasgow.'

Oh, excuse me. That was the brilliant paisley pyjama top which I wore as a shirt every day that summer. I was too cool for my entire family. They just didn't get it. They didn't get me. I slammed a lot of doors. 'You know I can't think of anything too terrible but there must have been some bad things because why did I ring whatever organisation it was that mothers who can't cope turn to?' I do remember a family counselling session where all my family sat around in a circle and I seemed to be the problem. But it's all water under the teenage bridge now.

'You did bring some strange people into the house, but then I was used to that,' my mother added. She brought a few strange people into the house herself, if she didn't mind me saying, especially during her Internet-dating phase.

There was silence then. Each of us trying to remember.

I do have a memory of one night when I spray-painted my

wardrobe with black flowers. In the morning my mother tried to get me up for school as usual. I couldn't talk, couldn't move my legs or arms. Overnight, the fumes from the spray had rendered me incapacitated. Of course, my mother thought it was another one of my classic put-ons. Later, when I could move again, I celebrated my bona fide day off school in front of the telly with a waffle and vinegar sandwich. In *How to Build a Girl*, Caitlin Moran refers to the teenage years as a time 'when you veer wildly between thinking you are a nuclear accident and thinking you might actually be here to save the world'. Sometimes I still feel like that. The teenager hasn't changed much. Some of us don't. And that's not necessarily a bad thing.

I feel I disappointed my mother then, but she doesn't see it like that, which gives me a sort of absolution. I don't feel I disappoint her now. But I do disappoint myself; that's another story. Absolution. A clean sheet. The chance to start over. We need that from our mothers. They are supposed to be the people who can wipe the slate clean without it costing them a thought. If we don't get that, if the disapproval never ends, it can be devastating.

7: THE MOTHERWORK

I – Róisín – was never great at getting my homework done at school and I knew I would struggle with this most important part of The Daughterhood. From the very first meeting we decided the most appropriate name for the work we had to do with our mothers was Motherwork. It was like homework except it was all about our mothers. Naming the work made us more conscious of what we had to do. Without the concept of Motherwork, we were just women meeting up for motherchats. We needed something concrete and the idea that we had work to do gave us much-needed focus.

In the beginning we had ticked off the 'things' we could do with our mothers. The trips, the exercises in patience, the lunch dates – but in a lot of cases as soon as we ticked the boxes we promptly forgot about our Motherwork. As our mothers know well, us daughters lead busy lives. But over the course of a few months, Natasha and I would gently remind the daughters and ourselves of all the things we had signed up to do at that first meeting. We met every month over dinner in Natasha's house or mine and gave each other updates about how we were getting on. Emails and texts were sent between meetings, gently encouraging and cajoling each other and reminding ourselves of what we were trying to do.

In truth, after the first meeting we didn't know what to expect. To go back to that rookie orchestra analogy, we were playing it by ear. We had started a club and, from our experiences of other clubs, we knew it was likely that at least one person would bail from the proceedings at some point. Perhaps the whole thing would collapse after a few meetings under the weight of promises none of us could keep. There was also the risk factor. Some of our daughters were dealing with extreme situations in their mother relationships and we were hardly equipped to advise them if something went horribly wrong.

Our hope was that The Daughterhood would operate, with apologies to Simon & Garfunkel, as a bridge over troubled daughters, but it was also a potentially explosive social experiment. Anything could have happened. Here's what actually did.

THE BUSY DAUGHTER'S MOTHERWORK

Maeve had written to us because she kept hiding when her mother turned up unannounced for lunch bearing a variety of home-made pickles. She wanted to deepen the connection with her mother and let her in more. Here's how Maeve got on . . .

There's a reason I never go away with my mother and I suddenly remember it as I'm standing in line waiting to check in. She has already vetoed the check-in machines. 'I don't trust them. I want to check in with a human being not a computer screen,' she says. I'm about to lecture her on the time-saving benefits of the machines when I catch myself. I've been doing a lot of that with her lately. If there is one thing I think has happened since this whole Daughterhood business began, it's been me biting my tongue in the presence of my mother. It was hard at first. Sometimes half a critical, chastising sentence would come out, 'Ah, Mam, please don't give me any more gherkins, I'm coming down with—' before I'd stop and change the sentiment to a more positive one. Then gradually it got better. 'Ah, Mam,' I'd say, and then stop myself before going any further at all.

All I can tell you is that I've become more conscious of how I am with my mother since that night a few months ago when I first sat down with all the other daughters. Although nothing much happens at the meetings, exactly – we just catch up on what's been happening in our daughterly worlds – somehow talking about your mother on a regular basis, in a conscious way, seems to have the effect of altering your behaviour. It has in my case anyway. I'm blaming hormones, too, though. You see, I'm six months pregnant.

I knew this at the beginning of the process, which is why I wasn't knocking back the wine. I'm normally a big wine person. And then the night I told the others I was pregnant they were madly curious as to how it would impact on my relationship with my mother.

I played it down. I mean, I didn't know. Maybe she'd only ever want to talk about the baby and start telling me how to rear it and what foods to give it to eat. As it turned out, it's been exactly how the other women said it would be. We've grown closer. But I think the closeness is definitely due to me learning how to bite my very loose and sometimes cruel tongue.

But here I am at the check-in desk. She's asked me if we are going to be late for the flight around seven times now. She has worried about whether her extra baggage would be too big and whether her 50ml cosmetic bottles in her hand luggage were actually 100ml or 200ml. I stood there thinking, 'Three days and three nights of this … I don't actually know if I can handle it.' But before I left I made a little contract with myself. I was going to make this trip with my mother as good as it could be. And, of course, I knew I'd have to report everything to the others so that kept me straight. If I wasn't censoring myself, I'd have told her to chill out a thousand times by now. 'Chill out, Mam. Would you just relax, everything is fine.' And I'd have got myself irritated and she'd be worried that she couldn't open her mouth. So, even though all her worries were hard to bear, not voicing my annoyance was already making this trip better than it might once have been.

I had decided to bring her away last Mother's Day when we were having dinner together. I'd had a voucher for a new French restaurant and I wanted to make a special effort, partly because I always make a fuss of her and partly to have something to report to the other women. Since I became pregnant I could sense this need in her for more intimacy. But we were also easier together. I think my mother had worried that I would get so wrapped up in my job and in searching for work that I would forget to have a baby. When she tried to bring it up before, I'd shut the conversations down. Now my mother could relax and I could almost feel her exhaling and our relationship had grown calmer as a result.

We just sat and talked for a couple of hours in the restaurant. We had steak and chips with peppercorn sauce. The crowd was buzzy, just the kind of atmosphere she likes. My brother Peter and his wife, Ann, had just moved in with her while they waited for their home to be renovated. We talked about that for a while and how Mam hadn't realised how much she enjoyed her own space until she had to share it with her son and his wife. She made jokes about the fact that Peter's habits hadn't changed much. She said she found herself picking up after him and scolding him to finish everything on his plate. Her daughter-in-law wasn't impressed. Peter and Ann had said they might join us for dinner and I was relieved when they didn't show. I was realising that I operated better with my mother one on one. In crowds, at family gatherings, I often become irritated just by my mother's ways. Her manner, her quirks. She was selfless and well meaning, but it was too much to take sometimes.

My mother is obsessed with this baby. Sometimes I think she's even more interested in it than I am. And I let my guard down with her. I let her rattle on about the clothes she was going to knit and the cot she was going to buy. I was moved by how much she cared. I realised how lucky I was.

Over that Mother's Day dinner both of us seemed to relax. I had bought her a face cream for a present, and she was so delighted it touched me deeply (although it might have been because I was a bit weepier than usual on account of all the pregnancy hormones). That night she texted me thanking me for the present and for the treat of dinner. I texted back asking whether she wanted to come to Portugal with me for a few days. 'Travel with her' – I hadn't forgotten that it was top of my Motherwork list.

We got to Portugal without any arguments. An achievement in itself. The place we'd booked was perfect. That first night we went to a restaurant by the sea and had beautiful seafood and she had her glass of wine. I knew that she needed this time away. She had told me about a friend who had let her down very badly. And it was a good way to open a conversation that I'd really wanted to have with her. I've always felt she was too giving. That she didn't concentrate enough on making herself happy. I really wanted to know if she was happy. In her own life, I mean. And if she was happy, what was the cause of the happiness? I suppose I feel a lot of the time that there are self-improving things she could be doing – reading the newspaper, going on courses, up-skilling – that might make her happy. I wanted to find out if that was just an assumption on my part.

I was surprised by the conversation and by her answers. As the water lapped on the shore and a loud Portuguese family celebrated the birthday of a little girl and the wine waiter kept saying, 'Irish, eh? Roy Keane!' she told me that she *was* happy. Really happy. And that what made her most happy was her children being happy. That her whole focus in life was the pursuit of our happiness and she didn't want to change that.

She knows I'm the kind of person who is always striving. I need to change focus constantly; I need new projects and new challenges. But talking to her that night, I discovered something that was really quite comforting and surprising. She is happier with a smaller lot. And my expectations of what should make her happy are very different to the truth. I told her I worry about her sometimes that she is anxious and highly strung and that she can often focus on the negative. I told her that I think we are very alike in that way, in our insecurities and tendency towards thinking the worst. 'I wouldn't view myself that way at all,' she said, looking out at the ocean, really thinking about what I was saying. 'I feel confident in myself, confident in where I am and what I am and I'm happy, too. I'm happy.'

We talked about my dad. It's always awkward bringing him up in conversation. But, because this felt like a more relaxed and open conversation, I even steered the chat around to the age gap between him and her and whether he was the right choice, given she was left quite early on as a single mother. Then she surprised me again. 'I have no regrets about your father,' she said. 'I want to be really clear about that; I want you to understand that.' She told me some of the things about my father she first fell in love with, how he made her laugh and how he always remembered the little things about her that nobody else noticed. She said she wished he hadn't died when I was so young because I would have loved certain aspects of him. And that I was like him in certain ways. She had never told me that before.

It was a beautiful few days. There were slightly tense moments. She kept offering me money to help for when the baby comes, but I don't want to take her money. So I tried to be diplomatic while turning her down. As we sat eating lunch she must have asked me twelve times whether I thought the way I was lying on my lounger when sunbathing was going to hurt the baby. But we laughed about it. I was able to say to her, 'Mam, you have to stop saying that now.' And she didn't get offended. I looked at her on that holiday full of wonder; especially since somebody is going to be calling me Mam in a few months. I saw traits in her that maybe I recognised in myself – that slight anxiousness, a perfectionist streak. I was looking at my future self, I thought. And it didn't seem so bad.

The Busy Daughter writes to her mother:

Dear Mam

It feels very strange to be writing you a letter because I don't think we've ever communicated in this way, apart from the odd holiday, pre-technology, when I was away for the summer. Or maybe I'm thinking of those unpunctuated emails you sent during the years I was abroad.

I'm really glad that I've taken this time recently to focus consciously on my relationship with you. Some of that was making more of an effort to spend time together and get to know you, but also what was important for me was thinking and focusing on our relationship. What it means to me. How I can cherish it that bit more.

We've always had a close relationship. We see each other and chat regularly. Maybe in many ways I took that for granted, the fact that we have that closeness and that you'd always be there. I know you won't, though. To think about that is very difficult.

I love being in your company, your philosophy on life, your vivacious personality. I enjoy making you laugh. I do realise that a lot of my criticisms of you, when they arise, come from my own impatient and intolerant personality traits.

I manage to censor that with most people. But it's the ones you love the most that sometimes bear the brunt of our weaker moments. We are so very alike in many ways. We know each other well on many levels. But, then again, I feel I have held back from telling you everything that was going through my head or in my life. You have probably done that, too, in terms of your past history. I think perhaps it's good for us that there are some elements left unknown.

You are an amazing mother. Totally unselfish, all-giving and full of unconditional love. Sometimes I think that can both overwhelm me and make me protective of you. I always want to make sure you're getting everything in life that you want and have always wanted for me, in terms of happiness and fulfilment, achievement, respect and love.

I hope your life, despite some of the challenges and traumas, has been a happy one; that you've felt loved, fulfilled and rewarded for your self-sacrifices. I hope you are proud of who I am. And I hope I can be half the mother that you are when my time comes.

Love, your daughter,

Maeve

THE DAUGHTER OF MADNESS'S MOTHERWORK

Sophie wrote to us about her mother who had suffered with mental illness all her life. She wanted to cultivate more of those As Good As It Gets moments. Here's how Sophie got on . . .

There is a rocky path that winds down to a small swimming cove near where my mother lives. She loves to swim but only in sea-water. She's always had a thing for sea swimming. I have childhood memories of her getting up at 5am, when it was still dark, and waking me up in her swimming togs. She'd drag me half asleep into mine and down we'd go, with the waves higher than she was sometimes, in all weathers. I'd shiver on the shore, afraid to go in. Madness when I think about it. But I knew no better at the time.

'It wakes me up,' she used to say when I was small. 'The salt is good for the bones.' She had a thing about chlorine. The toxicity of it. So she never took me to the pool where my friends were with their parents, doing normal parent things. But I'm grateful to her because swimming in the sea is now a panacea for everything I've carried into adulthood. I'm not fond of swimming pools myself these days. Like mother, like daughter, in this if nothing else.

Since I joined The Daughterhood I've been trying to find more of those moments when I can manage my mother and be in her company without feeling hopeless and too full of rage about everything I never had. About all that she has never been able to give me. Telling the group about my desire to find more of these moments with my mother has spurred me on. It was at one of our meetings that I remembered how much she used to love swimming in salt water. I gave her a call one Friday afternoon.

She had been waiting for me to ring, which I found touching. 'I was hoping you might get me out of here,' she said. By here she meant her home, although she made it sound like she was incarcerated. Life with my father is tough. I sensed her need to escape so acutely, it seemed to spill out of her down the phone line. Her life is lived that way. Wanting to escape but incapable of doing anything about it; that's been her way for so long now. She's like a small animal in a cage. The cage door is swinging open but she just doesn't have the strength to crawl out to freedom. I have accepted that I cannot help her but it still makes me sad.

'What about a swim?' I said.

'A swim? Well, now . . . I don't . . . would I be able? A swim. The seawater. But I don't know . . . Do you know where my swimming hat is, the white one? I don't know . . .'

I was expecting this, the stream of consciousness uncertainty. I could see her standing in the hall, lips pursed in confusion, doubting herself, doubting me and my motives. I pushed my annoyance away. 'Of course, a swim. I've my bag packed here anyway,' I lied. 'The togs are wrapped in a towel; do you remember the way we used to roll it like a sausage? I can be over to you in twenty minutes. Where are your black togs? And that big flowery towel? Can you have everything ready?'

'I could, I suppose,' she said. I left it there before she could come up with an excuse. I grabbed my gear and headed over, wondering whether she'd actually come with me.

As I drew nearer to the house the anxiety came over me again; it happens when I'm with either of my parents. It's the unpredictability of their behaviour. I never know what to expect. I can't rely on either of them. I'm on the back foot the whole time. After the first Daughterhood meeting, I was overwhelmed by some of the other women's obvious love for their mothers. Natasha even said, and she may have been joking, that she was going to wear a vial with her mother's ashes after she died.

When I went home after the meetings sometimes I would get upset thinking of my mother. The guilt and shame was immense. I thought at first I was betraying her in front of all these women; that she would die at the thought of me speaking about her. But as the months passed this changed. I began to realise that by being forced to go through this period of reflection a new respect for my mother was blossoming. I could go to the meetings if I kept remembering this. I was starting to accept her as she is. And this acceptance was allowing me to break the cycle, to free myself from the past, so that there was even more space to invest in my relationship with my daughter.

I drove up the path to the house and sat there, just breathing in through my nose and out through my mouth, the way my yoga teacher taught me. I grew calmer. When I walked up to the door she was standing there waiting on the other side. I could see the shadow of her. She opened the door clutching a plastic supermarket bag, it had holes in, I noticed, and she had put on her old swimming hat. One of those padded ones with a strap under the chin. Seeing the way her skin was pinched there choked me up. With what? Love? I don't think we've ever had that between us. But, as I led her out of the house and into my car, I realised that I still, despite everything, had an urge to protect her. The fact that I cared enough to want to mind her seemed like something good I could hold on to.

Since she came out of the hospital after her last breakdown, my sister, who was home from America, had taken charge of her. They have an easier relationship. Stacey was away when I was left minding my mother in the house during the worst of her breakdowns. She doesn't have the same memories of her illness as I do. She wasn't burnt as badly by those experiences. She was glad to help and I was happy to let her. But she has gone back home now. Back to her husband and her family and a life where she is too far away to feel too much guilt about her mother back in Ireland.

We parked up on the grass verge, close to the path. My mother didn't want to get out of the car for a while. She just sat staring out to sea as the cruise liners crossed the bay. 'They want to knock the chimneys down,' she said after a few minutes of silence.

It was in the news that the electricity board were planning to raze the Poolbeg stacks, an old electricity power station, and there was a campaign to keep them. The chimney lovers were never off the radio spouting eulogies for Dublin's own twin towers. I followed her gaze over to the red and white chimneys by the sea, landmarks of my childhood. I remembered the sight of them coming home when I worked in London during the nineties. I used to see them from the aeroplane window and get that sick feeling in my stomach. They made me anxious. Reminded me of what I was coming home to. My mother loved them, though. 'They won't knock them, Mam,' I told her. 'There'd be war.'

My mother is not at peace. When I'm around her I feel the crackling tension of all that she cannot express swirling around inside of her. I realised sitting there looking at the Irish Sea that I am getting better at detaching myself from all the crossed signals and the noise. I know at the Daughterhood meetings I had talked about how you have to make a decision to forgive. A decision to accept the things about my mother I cannot change and will never be able to change; that serenity poem really does say it all.

Here is where I am now with my mother: she is an old woman who needs help. An old and vulnerable woman. But I can make a choice. I can decide to dump the baggage; I can jettison the rage about how useless she was at motherhood. I can leave that all behind. I've spent years trying to figure out the steps in this detachment dance and now I feel I can do them without even thinking. This might not seem like much to anyone else, but it's huge for me. It's progress. I'm detaching from her; detaching with love.

She got out of the car eventually. Being much frailer since her last episode, she couldn't really decline my offer to take her arm. So I took her elbow in my left hand, noticing how much thinner she has got, feeling the loose skin on her forearm and the birdlike bones underneath. I walked her down to the sea thinking how it wasn't so bad. I could do something like this now and again. We took off our clothes and got into the water, which was freezing with only a pale heat from the sun. I saw how her togs hung off her, and wondered how long it had been since she had worn them.

It was my other sister Deborah who said it to me, the last time she was over. 'The things we don't get from our family, or our parents, the things we feel we should have been given, we need to go out and find them somewhere else.'

There's a woman I'm seeing now, a counsellor I suppose, but she's become more than that. She's in her sixties, around twenty years older than me. She could be my mother, really. Money changes hands after our encounters, though. It is a professional service. And yet our interactions give me a sense of what I might have had if things had been different with my mother. I talk to her about my relationship, about my daughter or about challenges at work. This woman is full of good advice. My mother has never offered me advice about anything. She isn't able. This woman, Margaret, is maternal. I recognise it from films and books and from friends I have who are close to their mothers. I know that money alters a relationship – I am not reading more into the acquaintanceship than I should. But she is going away for five months and she said I can email her if I need to. I think I will. Deborah is right. You have to go out and find what you need somewhere else, if you never had it before.

Part of my Motherwork was to concentrate on the good times with my mother. Moments when we felt close. I don't have any, though. I've been trying but I don't. This makes me feel ungrateful. If she only gave birth to me, isn't that something amazing? Isn't that the ultimate thing anyone can do for you? I'm trying to remember. Once I mitched from school with a boy in primary class and we were found out. I remember the next day, when people were pointing at me and the teachers were giving out, I remember her saying, 'Don't worry about them and what they think.' She said I was to hold my head up high. I also know she would have done anything to bring us anywhere if we were invited to a party or got an opportunity to do something. She paid my rent for a few months when I had no money. She did what she could. I'm glad I remembered those things. They are important acts of kindness and I had pushed them out of my mind.

Since joining the Daughterhood I started to dig out old photos; it was a way to look for clues. Moments with my mother that I might have missed. One photo came as a total surprise. We are in Co. Mayo, in the west of Ireland, and I am holding her hand. She looks gorgeous in a denim mini dress. She always had cool clothes and was stylish in her own way. In the photo she is holding my hand. I must be about six. She is holding my hand and the sight of her hand in mine made me cry. I thought, 'My God, we must have had moments when I went to her for comfort. There must have been times when she tried her best to love me.'

I've put the photo in a frame. It's on the mantelpiece in my sitting room beside a photo of me and my daughter. These are the memories that I am going to try to keep at the front of my mind. I want to see about creating some new memories. I want to put in more time with her and support her, if I can, in her old age.

My mother swam out farther than I would have liked. For someone so frail, so jaded and so tormented, she has these strong, expert strokes, and her little white hat bobbed away from me. I stayed close to the shore treading water and did a bit of doggy paddle. I didn't want to join her. She seemed to be in her own world. When she came back I can't say she was smiling but she looked, what is the word, serene.

'The salt water wakes you up. Will we go back, now, Soph?' she said softly, rubbing herself with the towel. It gave me a jolt. She rarely used my name. She never said Soph. Only my close friends call me that. When we walked slowly back up to the car, she turned around to face me. 'I want to thank you,' she said. I stood there all casual, trying to act like she thanked me for things all the time. She rubbed her cheek with the towel. 'Thank you for being so very kind to me when I was sick. It was very good of you.'

And that really is As Good As It Gets. I don't think we're ever going to have any life-shattering, filmic moment when we declare that we really feel close or love each other. She is not that kind of mother. But who knows? Since I've been detaching with love I've noticed a protectiveness for her kicking in, a realisation that, my

God, I really do care about her. I am compassionate. I want her to be happy, even if she never really can be. For so long I felt like a bad daughter because we never had a mother–daughter relationship. I don't feel like a bad daughter any more. I want peace for both of us now.

I look to the future. To more gentle, simpler times, when we can just be together like we did that day down in the cove. And perhaps we can make peace with each other in that way. I am making more of these moments happen since I joined The Daughterhood. And I am increasingly grateful for them.

The Daughter of Madness writes to her mother:

Dear Mam

This is a difficult letter to write as I still struggle with how I feel or what our relationship means. I suppose the sad thing is, for a lot of reasons, we never had a mother–daughter relationship. We never shared very close moments and, to be honest, early on I realised that it was pointless to look for comfort or advice from you, as I was nearly always left disappointed.

You are a good, kind and caring person but the role of mother was never within reach – perhaps because of all the madness that surrounded you at home within your marriage and your bipolar condition. It's really only since I've had my own daughter that I realise what was lacking for me growing up, so it makes the loss all the more intense. But, at the same time, I also feel for you and what you were going through.

I still feel the loss and hurt and, in a sense, I grieve for what we never had.

At this stage of my life, after a certain amount of counselling and work that I've done on myself, the only way to cope is to 'detach with love' and try and ditch the anger and the sadness. I think you did your best at any given time but that was not enough and children need more security and emotional care.

Now that you are getting close to eighty and are sick, I want to help you and be there for you and I hope that you can accept this from me without being suspicious. I hope that you can finally accept that I do care about you and that I would love you to have some peace and happiness before you die.

Love,

Sophie

THE DAUGHTER OF NARCISSISM'S MOTHERWORK

Lily was rejected by the woman who adopted her, a woman she believes is a narcissist with no capacity for or understanding of motherhood. She was searching for acceptance and forgiveness. Here's how Lily got on . . .

I told them at the beginning there would be no happy ending with me. I felt I needed to manage expectations. And the ending is not happy but something has shifted in me just by telling my story to these daughters. I feel validated, I think, is what my counsellor would say. For so long I blamed myself for being rejected by my mother. All the time I was thinking, 'What's wrong with me?' and 'Why am I such a bad daughter?'

This will be short. It is hard to do Motherwork when you don't know where your mother is. I've narrowed it down recently to Co. Limerick. My mother's friend, the neighbour who has taken it upon himself to manage her affairs, let it slip to my aunt. So now at least I can picture her in sheltered housing in Co. Limerick somewhere. One of these days I will make a list of all the sheltered houses and narrow it down even further. Or maybe I won't.

She has taken calls from me on her mobile a few times. At an appointed time. I know well enough now to plan what I will say in my conversations. I keep it light. No matter what response I get, I stick to my script. It has worked well so far.

I don't actually think about her very often, which is another welcome development. I know she is receiving good care. I know she is safe. I go about my life as though she doesn't exist.

My Motherwork is work I have to do on myself to undo the damage she has done over the years. My Motherwork is to become more confident and change my way of thinking about myself. I want to be happier, more sure of myself. My mother and I were intertwined in my mind for so long, it took time to separate myself from her. My Motherwork is making that separation permanent. The counselling helps.

In the meantime, I've been trying to get back in touch with my birth mother. The only contact we had is around the time I got married when I first discovered I was adopted. I let it drop then. My life got busy and I was so happy with Rob and all our plans, I didn't make time for this new mother relationship in my life. When I contacted the agency they told me that she didn't want to rekindle the contact at this time. She 'has too much on in her personal life', they said. They didn't think she could deal with hearing from me again.

I understand. I appeared and then disappeared from her life just as quickly. If I were her, I'd probably be wary, too. I've asked the adoption agency whether she would be open to receiving a letter from me without any need for a response. I'd like to explain how my life has turned out. I don't want to make her feel guilty for putting me up for adoption, but I do want to tell her why I left it so long to get in contact. I hope she might be open to an explanation. But if she isn't, I will understand.

Natasha and Róisín asked me how I would feel if my mother died tomorrow. The word that comes to mind is relieved. I don't mean that in a bitter way. I'm not saying I'd dance on her grave. There would just be a sense of relief that this sadness, this painful part of my life that has hung over me and, in the last few years hung over Rob, for so long would be over. On a selfish level I'd feel my life was now my own. That I was no longer defined by her actions and words. The words said to me and whispered about me. The lies.

I know I will cry when she dies. There will be tears over the loss of so much life and love. But I've been mourning her loss as my mother for a long time. I spent a long time wondering how a woman could choose one baby from a room full of babies, the way she chose me all those years ago, and then reject that baby when she needed her most. As a child. As a teenager. As a young woman making my way in the world. I have compassion for my birth mother. I know the circumstances she must have faced were appalling when she had to give me up. But the rejection by my adopted mother, a woman who must at one point have desperately wanted a child, has caused me unspeakable pain.

When the time comes for her passing, I don't think it will be that hard to deal with it. For a long time I thought it was my fault. I don't believe that any more. I have compassion for her now. She is not well. The words were rattling around my head for ages. I do feel so sorry for her. Sorry for this woman sitting wherever she is sitting, in whatever sheltered house she is in, living beside strangers, all on her own.

Her death, when it comes, will signal the final closing of the door on my former life. I am part of my husband's family now. I am enveloped in their love and in their traditions. I am accepted by them for who I am. I am so grateful for that.

I've been thinking a lot recently about what I'd say to other daughters in my situation. All the other rejected daughters. The daughters of narcissistic mothers.

The first thing I would say is – don't feel guilty. It sucks the life blood out of you slowly but surely. If you've done everything to be a good daughter, then you have been a good daughter. You've just been unfortunate not to have the mother you deserve. If your mother cannot love you, if she cannot respect you and your life, your opinions, your choices, then she doesn't deserve you in her life. It is her loss.

My advice, the thing that has worked for me, is to seek out and nurture relationships where your contribution is valued and you are treated equally and loved unconditionally. By lovers or by friends. You deserve love and you are not unlovable, no matter how your mother made you feel.

Learn to love yourself. When your self-esteem has taken a battering from a mean mother it is hard to feel good about yourself but don't let that stop you trying. Accept people's love and kindness, it will help you heal.

Being rejected by your mother is horrible. But she is only one (admittedly one very important) person in your life. Don't let her define you. Don't let her ruin all that is good in your life. Write new chapters. Open a new book.

If you can, go and see a counsellor. If nothing else, it's a release to rant and rave with someone who is trained to listen. Someone who is not family. Someone who will not judge. And if counselling isn't for you, set up a Daughterhood. Seek out people who will listen without prejudice. It has helped me, it might help you.

The Daughter of Narcissism writes to her mother:

Mother, I'm sorry.

I'm sorry I've disappointed you as a daughter. I'm sorry that you can't trust anyone in your life ever. I'm sorry that life seems to have disappointed you. I'm sorry that you can't/won't know the true love of family and friends.

I'm sorry that you miss Dad so much. I'm sorry that we don't know one another better and I'm sorry we never will get to know one another better. I'm sorry you don't know what it is to be honest with yourself and others. I'm sorry I didn't do more or see what was going on with you sooner.

I'm sorry you only know how to lie and manipulate people. I'm sorry you don't know what unconditional love means. I'm sorry I don't love you as a daughter should. I'm sorry you've never seemed to be truly happy.

I'm sorry you could never just be you and not care what other people thought of you. I'm sorry that you can't even tell me or your sisters where you are. I'm sorry that you probably have dementia and don't even realise that the reality you see isn't real, right, correct.

I'm sorry that you were never the mother I deserved and I'm sorry we've ended up like this.

Your daughter,

Lily

THE BECOMING-MY-MOTHER DAUGHTER'S MOTHERWORK

Cathy wrote to us out of a fear that she was becoming her mother. She also wanted to be more patient with her mum and stop telling her what to do. Here's how Cathy got on . . .

If I were to tell you in one word how things have changed or improved since I began consciously focusing on my relationship with my mother I would use the word: communication. As a family, we never stop talking. But since joining The Daughterhood I have done a lot of thinking about the way I communicate with my mother. How I speak. The quality of my listening. The subtleties of our exchanges.

The phone is a case in point. In our house growing up, you never stayed on the phone too long. You might be blocking an important call, after all. Somebody might, at the exact moment when you are waffling on about your Spanish homework, be wanting to get through to report some Big News. A house burning down in the next village, say. The latest political scandal. In my house you answered the phone and got off it again as soon as you could.

Without really realising, I carried this on with my mother when I left home. Our phone conversations were hurried. Full of basic facts and rushed arrangements. But as part of my Motherwork I had committed to listening to my mother more. The results have surprised me.

One thing I discovered during these long conversations on the phone is that my mother's hearing is getting worse. Sometimes I felt I was shouting at her rather than speaking to her. We chatted about everything. She was feeling old. She didn't know what to do about her friend Mary who was worried her children were thinking of putting her into a home. My first instinct when I gave my mother the space to talk at length about these issues was to offer advice. To fall back into old family habits and meddle. But I held back. I was learning that my mother wasn't telling me all these things so that I could fix them. I realised she just wanted to say these things out loud. Just to be heard.

I started calling her on Fridays, putting an hour aside to listen to whatever she wanted to say. Before the call I'd remind myself of the purpose of the chat. I was to listen. I was not, unless specifically asked, to offer some kind of advice. After a few Fridays I hardly needed to remind myself at all. It began to feel natural. She talked. I listened. I could sense an unburdening I'd never allowed to happen before.

These conversations allowed me to get to know my mother better. Something I hadn't realised was so important to me. When we are close to people we can often think we have them sussed. We put them in a box marked x or y and we become attached to that version of them. We are reluctant to let them evolve. But my mother had evolved. Kathleen was seventy-nine. She was growing ever more uneasy about getting older. Having spent decades rearing children in a house as busy as Grand Central Station, she had to adjust to a lonelier, smaller kind of life since my father had died fifteen years ago. As I listened to my mother on the phone every Friday, I began to find out who she was now. Not my idea of who she was – the reality.

'I hate it; I hate being old,' she'd tell me. It was a phrase I had heard from my mother a million times before. And usually when she said this I would try to rationalise with her, talk her out of this negative thinking. Before, my response would have been preachy, hectoring, exasperated even. 'Sure aren't you almost eighty, Mam?' I might have said. 'Aren't you relatively healthy with your friends around you and your whist outings twice a week?' I dismissed her complaints. But that was before I had started really listening. Now I said nothing. I let her talk.

'I hate being old,' my mother repeated, in the gap where normally I'd have interjected in a bid to dampen down her flaming negativity. So my mother got to expand on her point instead of being stopped in her tracks. 'I hate it. People treat you like you're an eejit. I don't like the way my bones creak when I move. I hate the fact that I'm invisible to some people in the supermarket. Getting old is horrible. There's nothing good or nice about it and don't let anybody tell you any different.'

I listened to my mother. I heard this strong, witty, sharp-as-a-tack woman objecting to the physical realities of ageing. She also struggled with what she saw as the mundanity of life as she headed into her eighties. 'It's just completely dull, Cathy,' she barked down the phone, and I bit my tongue because I couldn't get my head around the concept of a 79-year-old woman experiencing the kind of boredom my teenage son often complained about. But I let her explain. She told me about how she used to love the spontaneity of life. She had never been a planner. She lived in the moment. 'Now,' she said, 'I have to plan everything. Will I go to the shops in a minute or later? Will I have enough time to get all the things I need to get?' Everything, daily rituals she took for granted, were more of an ordeal now. Old age had taken the freshness out of things.

My mother talked a lot about her friends during these Friday phone chats. Her friends had always been a very important part of her life. A wide and varied network of people my mother had cultivated over the years. Now they were few and far between but her regular whist outings had introduced her to a new group of friends. Every Friday she had another story to tell. They went on outings to stately homes, trips to food markets and car boot sales. It seemed these women genuinely enjoyed my mother's company and wanted to be around her. The knowledge of this new group of people outside of our family who were all mad about my mother gave me something to think about. Something new.

My older sister Lorraine is dying. We found out a few months ago. She has stage 3 breast cancer. She is not going to get better. We're totally devastated. Having children myself, I can't even begin to imagine what my mother is going through right now. I want to be there for her through what I know will be one of the most difficult times in her life.

If Mam was the mothership in our family, Lorraine was the anchor – keeping the family local, never wandering too far from all she knew or, more crucially, from my mother. She went to the nearest college and married her first boyfriend. She will leave behind two teenage children, which doesn't bear thinking about. Growing up and even into adulthood I'd always been jealous of the relationship Lorraine has with my mother. And now all I feel is sorrow that my mother has to come to terms with the fact that this relationship with her first born is coming to an end. 'I love when Lorraine comes over,' she'd say to me. Before she got ill, Lorraine would visit practically every day. She knew how to flatter and cajole my mother in a way I never could. One day I came downstairs as Lorraine was telling my mother some story about a neighbour, a woman who was younger than my mother. 'I saw her in the shoe shop buying insoles. She looks twenty years older than you, Mam,' Lorraine said and my mother loved it.

I'm useless at that kind of thing. It doesn't occur to me to flatter my mother but it comes naturally to my big sister. And I was never interested in spending as much time with my mother as Lorraine did either. My mother would say, 'Oh, I haven't seen Lorraine for two days.' And I'd give out to her, 'Do you need to see her every single day?'

Now I'm so glad Lorraine was that kind of daughter. That my mother knew that kind of closeness with her eldest child. I feel my mother's fragility more than ever as my sister begins to slip away.

'It's not natural; it's not the natural way of things,' my mother keeps saying. It breaks my heart.

At the last Daughterhood meeting Maeve talked about her holiday to Portugal with her mother and how she had really enjoyed spending some 'alone time' with her. My mother rarely left County Clare and I thought a small break from everything that was going on would do her the world of good. So I invited her for a weekend to Cork, which she reluctantly accepted. I decided for once this visit was going to be all about her. I talked it over with The Daughterhood and I had a clear plan in place. The monthly meetings had made me grow increasingly grateful for the fact that I had a mother to love. A mother who loves me. Flawed and irritating though she can sometimes be. Flawed and irritating as I am.

I prepped my children before she came. 'Granny's coming to visit and she's going to be the centre of attention while she's here.' They laughed. Making a fuss about my mother was not something they'd seen me do before. But I will from now on. And I'm not going to waste time feeling bad about the fact that I hadn't prioritised it before.

Graham and I picked her up from the train station. We drove through town, which I knew she would love. Even though her mobility is limited, she still likes to feel she's seen the sights. At home, when the observations about my house came, I bit my tongue. She talked about the new colour on the walls and a lamp I'd bought, whether it was suitable, and, as she spoke, I realised there was no malice intended. She was just doing her thing. To an extent she has stopped evolving. She comes out with the same lines. About the state of the country and the economy and she enjoys setting out her stall and so what if it's the same stall she's been standing at for decades? I had heard it all before. But so what? She still reads two newspapers a day and has opinions on how things are. Those opinions are predictable now but if I get to seventy-nine myself and I'm reading two newspapers a day and still have strident opinions, I'll be doing very well.

It's night time. Mam is sleeping in the spare bedroom opposite our room. It has been carefully de-cluttered for the occasion and there are fresh flowers on her bedside table. I leave the reading light on for her, so she can see her way to the bed. Books are left on the locker because she likes to read. In the morning I go in and I watch her sleeping – this small figure snoring softly, childlike in her slumber, her face so innocent. I love my mother, I think to myself, as I watch her.

I sneak back to bed. I know that's what she wants – that morning time alone with my children. If I had my way I would be out there with them, joining in. But this is my mother's time with her grandchildren and I let them be. Her best time is morning.

'Would you ever tell your mother to bring you to the barber's? I can't see your lovely face under all that hair' I hear her telling my son. And she uses the same tone she always used with me. It's the tone I use with my children, too. But they just think Granny is being funny and they don't take her seriously. There's a lightness in the air.

She stays in her dressing gown for hours. She is a dressing-gown person. When she comes I have a new dressing gown for her and she takes it back home with her. She's a woman who likes to go home with something new in her bag. When we left her back at the train station it felt different from other weekends. She had a good time. A good weekend. It felt unforced and I hadn't sniped at her about comments I didn't like. I loved her. I just loved her and minded her.

Two weeks later, Lorraine died. My big sister. Gone. And at the funeral my mother walked behind the coffin linking arms with Lorraine's husband. The strength etched in that woman's face, I can't describe it, except to say it was otherworldly. I can see her now, a few days after the funeral, sitting at the dining-room table, holding a cup of tea, looking out the window. She can tell you where the birds' nests are and which birds built them and what they are all up to. She sits there for hours. Very still. And when she's not doing that she bustles around, preparing meals or reading mass cards or talking to visitors who call to talk about Lorraine. There's a clear delineation. Sitting at the table, drinking tea and looking out of the window is her grieving time, her time for reflection and remembering.

And then life has to go on and she does all the things that need to be done.

She keeps telling me she doesn't need to be minded. She doesn't want to be told how she should feel.

'I don't need anybody to tell me what I should think or what I should do. I knew Lorraine longer than any of you. I know how I feel,' she says.

I'm full of admiration for her. She is showing the rest of us the way with this quiet, dignified grieving she is doing. I tell her that. I say 'Well done' and 'You are brilliant' and I remind her, gently, that she has grandchildren and that we are all there for her and that we need her.

And so, if I really am becoming my mother, as my eldest says I am, I will take the annoying parts, the sayings my children will tease me about, the autocratic hectoring of other people about what they should do with their lives. I will take those parts because of what else becoming her will mean. Becoming strong. Becoming dignified. Becoming my mother.

The Becoming-My-Mother Daughter writes to her mother:

Dear Mam,

Do you know what a brilliant mother you are?

Let me tell you.

You reared three children and, you know what, we're not too bad. We're nice people. We care for others, have good friends, strong values and take our responsibilities seriously.

You always reminded us growing up to love each other, to look out for each other, mind each other and never fall out. And we didn't and haven't.

You made our home a haven for all of us and for our friends. It became a Mecca of good company, where everyone could have their say and be listened to. With you in the centre enjoying the banter.

Our friends saw you as their friend, ally, and second mother, and, to this day, ask how you are and call to see you, long after we've all left home.

I can't conceive of how you feel right now. Lorraine is gone. Your little star. I can't imagine, as a mother myself, what it must feel like to lose a child. It's not the natural way that it's supposed to happen. In the last few months of Lorraine's life you were stoic and incredibly brave and set an example for all of us. I was so proud of you. Only occasionally did the curtain fall.

Lorraine absolutely adored you and you her. You realised and understood that she needed to know that you would be OK and you maintained this stoic appearance throughout her illness, all the time fading inside.

And now you sit, looking out the window, expecting her to arrive at any minute for a chat or for her favourite lunch, tea or dinner.

But it will never be the same again. The spell is broken. The circle of three kids is broken. And you don't care any more. You minded us for all those years only to lose the star on the last bend.

I'm so sorry, Mam, and I know that you would happily have gone in her place. I remind you that you need to stick around for the grandchildren. They adore you and have their stories of you that they love to tell others. They need you to stick around and I need you to stick around. We're still here. A smaller, tighter circle. And at the centre is you. Stay strong.

Your daughter,

Cathy

THE GRIEVING-HER-AS-SHE-LIVES DAUGHTER'S MOTHERWORK

Alzheimer's had robbed newly engaged Grace of the mother she used to know. She came to the group struggling with the guilt of not doing enough for her mother and coping with the loss. Here's how Grace got on . . .

Mum came to my wedding but she wasn't there, not really. I remember standing at the altar and looking over my shoulder to where she sat. She had insisted on wearing a flimsy pink slip she found at the back of her wardrobe and it gave her the appearance of a lost little child who had turned up at the wrong birthday party. It was very cold for April and the church was freezing. My dad put his tuxedo jacket around her and tried to keep her from wriggling in her seat and wandering around.

She was singing to herself as I said, 'I do', belting out some rambling tuneless dirge. Outside the church she kept gathering up the cherry blossoms from the ground, throwing them up in the air and laughing. She couldn't sit still for the meal. My father took her for a drive instead and missed the speeches. Later that afternoon, when one of her sisters took her home, I felt relieved. And then guilty for my relief. What kind of daughter was I?

When I had told Dad I was getting married, I could see how relieved he was. It was at least one thing in life he didn't have to worry about any more. I was settling down. I had someone to look after me, is what he was thinking, in his old-fashioned way.

In a way, my biggest guilt and grief is around my father. What I had with my mother has been gone for five years now. I've had all this time to get used to the loss. I worry that I don't do enough to help Dad. That my one afternoon a week is only a fraction of what I could be doing. He is Mum's full-time carer. He gets no help and I know he needs respite. My husband is helping me organise this but my father feels it is his duty and it is difficult getting him to see that he needs help with Mum.

One of the clearest memories of my childhood is being in the bath and my mother soaping my back while singing our favourite Abba songs. When the bath was finished, I'd stand up and wiggle my bottom like Agnetha. My mother would laugh and pretend to be cross. 'Don't you wiggle that bum at me, my girl,' and then she'd bundle me into a huge towel ('Oh I do, I do, I do, I do, I do, I doooo') and carry me down to the sofa in the front room ('Waterloo! Couldn't escape if I wanted to . . .'). It was Sunday night and she'd stick on some children's choir programme or the *Antiques Roadshow*. We'd snuggle up together, my mother and I, in front of the telly. My dad would sit in his armchair, reading the paper. My two older brothers would be outside still playing on the green. In my memory there's a crackling fire in the grate and I can hear the clock on the mantelpiece ticking loudly. There's the smell of tea-time fried eggs. And the blue shampoo that stings my eyes.

I thought of that bath when I went to my mum's house on Monday as usual. I know what to expect now. Her make-up was applied the way I used to put it on my dolls. Electric blue eyeshadow smudged as high as her eyebrows, an ill-advised red slash of lipstick somewhere near her mouth. She had been at the powder puff again, clearly. There were talcy, white smudges on her cheeks and neck. Her hair was matted, stuck to the side of her head and sticking out in comical scarecrow angles on top. 'Come on, Mum, let's make you gorgeous,' I said, and she giggled like a six-year-old at a birthday party. She was going out with her sisters that night.

I washed her hair as I always do now when I go to visit her. Then I blow-dried it into the bouffant style she likes. As I wiped her doll's make-up off and applied a more subtle look, I noticed a bit of a smell. It was a hot day. I wondered whether I had applied my deodorant that morning. But the smell was coming from my mother. A sour odour that suggested she might not have showered in a while. The thought of her going out to see her sisters while smelling that way made me sad. 'Mum,' I said in the gentle, coaxing tone I use with her all the time now. I have to choose my words very carefully. She can get very defensive. 'Why don't you just hop in the shower there? It's a boiling day outside. You want to be all fresh and lovely for your sisters. All you gorgeous girls together. Your hair is lovely, your make-up is great and if you had a little wash you'd be all set. Wouldn't a shower be nice?'

I expected a protest. Sometimes she throws little strops, stamping her feet, like my friend's toddler daughter. But I must have phrased the question the right way this time because she threw off her clothes and hopped into the shower. I took the shower handset and helped her wash. She poured too much of the orange soap wash into her hand and started singing 'Dancing Queen'. I got a sponge and began soaping her back, there were bubbles everywhere. ('Young and sweet only seventeen.')

I didn't bother to try and stop the tears. I was laughing through them anyway. 'Stop wiggling your bottom at me, Mum,' I said, but I knew she wasn't having a flashback to the mid-1970s and tasting the cup of cocoa she always used to give me when she sat on the sofa later, brushing the tangles out of my hair. We will never share a memory again. We will never be on the same page. I've lost her. And I am living with that. Every day.

My Motherwork is different to any of the other women in The Daughterhood. I don't plan holidays. Or dinners. I can't even have a cup of tea with my mother, believe me I've tried. A cup of tea with my mother is not easy. She sits there wiping the table, standing up, sitting down again, banging the table with a tea-spoon, standing up again, dancing around with the full cup in her hand. It's easier for me if we go out. I try to do it as often as I can. I take her for drives around picturesque places. Walks around the shops looking at clothes she'll never wear except in her imagination.

Natasha asked me once about my motivation when I'm with my mother. It was an interesting question. I am motivated by love, I think, most of the time. But the guilt never leaves me. The odd thing is I feel more guilty about my father. When my mother dies I don't think I will have too many regrets about not doing more with her. Our time together as mother and daughter is over. We clung fast to our relationship when she started to get sick. We made memories that will stay with me for ever. Like in New York, when we stood in Grand Central Station and mar-velled at how our voices magically travelled through the whispering gallery we'd spotted in the guide book. 'Love you, Mum,' I whispered into the arch diagonally across from where she stood. 'Love you, too, Grace,' her voice came back to me as clear as if she were standing beside me, speaking her love into my ear. She loved me. Nobody in my life will ever love me better than she did. Part of my Motherwork is the acceptance of this fact.

So I don't think I will regret not spending time with her. We've had our time. I don't think we are missing special moments now. I won't regret not taking her out. But I worry that I will regret not helping my father more. He is very good about it. 'You have your own life,' he tells me. 'We've had our life, now you have to live yours.' His attitude is that he and my mother had a good life and I should not worry about them. But of course I do.

I think every day about how lucky I am to have had such a lovely relationship with my mother. I am so grateful for that, especially now. I never had all the passive-aggressive interactions that seem to be the norm for a lot of daughters with their mothers. She was unusual in that way. She never said to me, 'You're getting a bit fat there, stop eating bread,' which is something a friend's mother said to her last year. Most of my friends have fractious relationships with their mothers. 'You should try being a size eight for once,' is another thing a friend of mine gets told by her mother. There is a lot of this really crazy talk, a lot of jealousy and tension. In my whole life I never experienced one single moment of that with my mother. She was exceptional in the way she was always there for me. We used to laugh about it. She was always trying to look after me. It was her mission in life.

I am very aware of what I've lost.

I don't think I'm dealing particularly well with what's happened. Or I'm dealing with it in my own way. Which is to say, I compartmentalise my mother. I don't bring her with me to work. Or take her out with me in my head when I socialise with friends. I do think I'm still in running-away mode. I do my duties and then I try to shut it off, shut all thoughts of her off, for another week. It's my way of coping. This is the only way I seem able to cope. When I think back to when my mother was first diagnosed with Alzheimer's, I was in such a huge state of shock. Everything had fallen apart. I was free falling in the horror of it. I was bleak. I don't know if you recover from that. I don't think I have and maybe I never will.

I'm dealing with it the only way I can. My older brothers have been trying to get us all to have family gatherings, which we never really did before. We were all independent types and didn't do get-togethers. I don't want to start now. It wasn't going to work for me and it wasn't something my mother was able to appreciate any more. So I put the kibosh on that.

I have faced her illness more fully now, though. I know she's getting worse. I can see it in her every week. There's no denying what's happening and coping with it continues to be difficult. It never gets easier. You never accept it. You never get to a calm, easy, spiritual, peaceful point where you are sanguine about the situation.

Sometimes I sit in my flat and daydream that a call has come through on my phone and a voice is telling me that my mother has died. She's gone peacefully in her sleep with Dad beside her. It would be a relief. It would be terrible. A terrible relief. Because there is no hope for my mother. All that's ahead of her now is misery and suffering and pain. And all of that's ahead of my father, too; my beautiful, funny, caring, devoted father. You can't say her death would be a terrible thing.

Her sisters look after her during the week, so my dad can go to work. They take her to lunch and go for walks with her. It's funny, they say, that my mother had, from a very young age, a fear of being put into a home. 'Please never put me in a home,' she said when she was first diagnosed. My father probably feels like he has that added issue to deal with. He's been listening to that for years.

I look at my dad and I wish he could get some comfort somewhere. If he turned around to me and said he was having an affair, that he was in a relationship with another woman, I would say, 'Hallelujah!' I wouldn't think he was cheating on my mother. I want my dad to have a whole other life. He deserves that.

If he tells me he can't put her into a home, I will tell him he must. She's not going to know what's happened, not in the painful way she might once have known. He must not feel guilty. He has cared for her for five years and he has a life to live, too.

My mother is not the woman she was. In some ways my father needs me more than she does. My Motherwork is really Fatherwork. I have figured that out now.

The Grieving-Her-As-She-Lives Daughter writes to her mother:

Dear Mum

Thank you for looking after me all through my life. Thank you for being a mother I could tell anything to – I've learned how rare that is and I feel so lucky to have had that experience with you, even though it has been cut far too short. I love you so much and not having your support and kindness surrounding me is almost unbearable.

I know this is a letter that you will never and could never read and understand now, but I hope that all of what I've said so far, I've expressed to you before and that somewhere inside your mind you know how much I love you and how much you mean to me.

Seeing your beautiful personality fade away every day is killing me. I just hope that you're living in your own, blissfully oblivious world and that you're not suffering.

I feel so sad to be losing you bit by bit, but so grateful for all of the wonderful memories I have of our time together, from my childhood right up to the extremely precious time just before things started to change.

I hope that you can forgive me for the times that I lose my patience or can't face going to see you – I really am trying and I will love you for ever.

I will mind Dad for you, Mum. I will love him for you.

Grace

THE RELUCTANT DAUGHTER'S MOTHERWORK

Anna told us that her biggest fear was not that her mother would die, but that she would continue into her nineties or beyond, which would mean that the entire value of her property (Anna's inheritance) would be whittled away by care fees at the same time as her mother's quality of life diminishes. She wanted to be more mindful of her daughterly duties. Here's how Anna got on . . .

My mother has gone downhill mentally so fast since I joined The Daughterhood that the only way I can deal with it is by treating her as a 'case study' – my default coping mechanism in times of extreme crisis. I know it sounds as if I lack compassion, but this history is complex. I left home young to get away from her, in case her misery was infectious. I grew up listening to her moaning and blaming circumstances or other people for why her life has been so disappointing. It seems she has never had an iota of self-awareness or an inkling of how she's coming across to others. And I thought I'd long escaped the reach of her negativity, keeping my distance whilst being polite and kind and suggesting options to improve her life. But now, with my dad gone and her mental health failing, she is dragging me back into her orbit like a black hole, or a melancholy planet with a fearsome gravitational pull. She is the death star.

The other women in the group were a bit shocked when I told them my greatest fear is that she will outlive me; that she will be the world's longest-lived woman, seeing off little old Japanese ladies who have eaten nothing but seaweed for 120 years; making a laughing stock of Central Asian women from the

Hunza Valley who have stayed young on a diet of grain and apricots and know the secret of the jojoba nut. One only needs to glance at her to see the genes of longevity: that dark olive skin without wrinkles or blemishes; the mitochondria that replenishes itself, impervious to free radicals; that strong shrill voice that has never shown regard for its audience's ears as it recites its litany of all those who have done her a mighty wrong; a belligerence that would wear down the determination of the most ardent interrogators. It's all there: unceasing, unsleeping, vitriolic, incorrigible.

And yet, and yet, there is evidence still of her physical beauty – even as she approaches the age of ninety. Physically she had been truly blessed, but her inability to see life as an opportunity blighted her soul. Instead, the miracle of existence was for her a drudgery that was doing its level best to make her life a curse to be endured. Her mouth has always been downturned and glum, her eyes burning with grievances: Hitler, the war, her background, the lack of money, my father . . . me. 'Of course, there were no opportunities left for me because I had to look after *you*.'

Yet I do care about her. I don't want her to be uncomfortable and I certainly don't want her to suffer. But we have never bonded and there is seemingly no underlying, unifying, flesh-and-blood factor that would have me rushing unquestioningly to her defence like 'family' are supposed to. And for that, of course, I feel guilty. We are like matter and anti-matter – I am strangely repelled by her, always have been, and this is not done out of bloody-mindedness but out of self-preservation, in order not to be tainted by her mindset of doom.

Certain pre-industrial, shamanic societies would describe her as a 'bad-luck soul'. She knows it, and knows I know it too. She is the mother who always spoke in negatives; who labelled herself a 'Jonah'; who would jinx any initiative by involuntarily sucking the positive energy out of it. If there is something in the primitive belief that 'like begets like', then my mother has proven the theory time and again. One hundred women could buy the same article of clothing but my mother's would be flawed in some way and a replacement unavailable. One hundred travellers could set off on the same journey but my mother's path would be visited by tornados and blocked by landslides. One hundred houses would receive a free gift through the post but her envelope would be empty.

Do we make our own luck? Do we bring back upon ourselves that which we project? In her case, the prudence of expecting the worst never meant she was pleasantly surprised. Was it predestined that my mother would never have anything go right for her, or has a lifetime of moaning and blaming painted her into a corner of her own self-fulfilling prophecy? What happened to make her the way she is? Did something really bad occur when she made her first explorations of the world as a toddler? Was she hurt or harmed whenever she first tried to venture into the unknown? Never have I met a more narrow set of habits or tastes. Never have I met anyone, of any age, who is as reluctant to try new things as my mother, be it food stuffs, modes of travel, ways of thinking, hobbies or even TV channels.

I know people who are cautious of stepping outside of their comfort zone, but in my mother's case the zone in which she has been stuck has never made her happy in the first place – has never been a 'comfort'. It is as if there has been a force field around her, preventing her from seeing things from a different angle, from taking a chance on anything, from listening to others who were trying to advise her. She has never planned for the future and refuses to see the truth of the past. Her MO of 'worrying about it when it happens' has not been born of an easy-going nature but rather a refusal to accept the inevitability of change.

And there is always someone to blame. The hospital 'killed' my father with MRSA. The fact he'd had seven strokes and a heart attack and was eighty-six years old was nothing to do with his death. 'He'd still be alive if it wasn't for that bloody hospital.' (Even though he'd be 101.) The fact her legs are painfully swollen with cellulitis and oedema is not because she is too elderly to exercise and could help herself by keeping her legs raised, but because 'that foreign bus driver' didn't lower the bus for her to get on the platform and she fell, causing an injury that has led to complications.

And while her ailments are those common to elderly women – arthritis, aches and pains – she has by her own estimation been 'very hard done-by'. She knows ninety-year-olds who go jogging and have never had anything wrong with them, so why does she have to suffer such pain? She forgets that, apart from those common ailments, she has never had anything wrong with her. There has been no cancer, no hysterectomy, no heart disease, no diabetes, no stomach ailments – not so much as a cold.

But now there is something really wrong and she won't allow it to be discussed or acknowledged. She has Alzheimer's. And I'm sure she's really frightened but she is covering her fear with such aggression that I can only suppose she expects her unpleasantness will repel meddlers. Like a squid squirting ink, or a tarantula throwing spiny hairs, she expects her tactics will see off those who 'mean the best for her own good' and want to 'stick their noses in'. She has twice refused Social Services when they have come to make a care assessment.

I have begun taking videos of her on my phone and I'm building up a movie library of unreason. In one, she is telling me it's not just that I am on 'their' side but I am 'directing them all'. 'I loved you so much,' she wails in one short clip, and now I've 'turned around and betrayed' her by letting 'them' interfere. When a woman from the memory clinic came to tell her of the facilities available to her she told her to 'piss off', that she'd pack her bags and one day we'd come around to find her gone. She carried through with the packing of the bag, which I later found contained a soft toy, a plastic box of loose change, some tea towels, a large old-fashioned alarm clock and some press cuttings about crocuses. The pathos of this did not go unnoticed. It was like a little girl's attempt at copying mummy packing to go on holiday. I discreetly put everything back in its proper place and she forgot all about 'them' until a few days later when I was advised to move her bed downstairs to encourage her to go to bed at nights, instead of sitting in the armchair and not resting her legs properly. All hell broke loose and those vocal chords were exercised to a maximum impact of rage and accusation and conspiracy theories.

And so I go about shadowing her in her own home: picking things up; cleaning the burnt plastic from the oven where she has tried to cook food whose containers should never be heated; sifting through the endless old newspapers and magazine cuttings; secretly disposing of seventeen packets of beetroot – each in its own state of browning discoloration and decay – that she'd hidden in a cupboard; unravelling tightly rolled £20 notes totalling hundreds of pounds that she'd put into old soup cans and paying them into her bank account; cleaning and sweeping and gardening and mending things and cooking her lunch when I go round there once a week. The routine is always the same: get her pension, do her shopping, cut the grass in the front garden, put the rubbish in the right order, hoover the house, clean the bathroom, air the bedroom, and check she hasn't thrown out her jewellery.

Since I met everyone at The Daughterhood, I've been aware of needing to cultivate something positive with my mother. I certainly have been trying to help her since my dad died in 2000. I helped her to move house just after his death, and have subsequently tried to get her to move house more recently, as everyone can see the stairs are too much for her and the only bathroom is upstairs. She's refused to budge. And now we are veering towards a crisis of care management. I fear that it's too late for heartfelt chats. She doesn't remember the sentence I said 20 seconds ago. She can no longer follow the thread of what anyone is saying. One could never really hold a 'conversation' with my mother, in any case. She never seemed to understand the usual back and forth of adult discourse. She was locked in her own thoughts.

I think she's been able to understand that I care for her, although at no point have we discussed the gulf between us in terms of our world view and personality types. It really is like the meeting of people from different millennia, rather than a generation gap of thirty-five years. Still, I like to help with her domestic duties. She has a small front and back garden, and I enjoy the physical work which maintaining them entails. I know she loves ice cream, so I wheeled her to a delightful French brasserie and bought her an ice cream sundae and a beer, which she really enjoyed.

It's very hard work answering the same questions over and over, but it feels good to be able to bring some variety into her life by wheeling her around the area and just doing really basic things for her like bits of shopping.

Finally, as of August 2014, we have an official diagnosis of mixed dementia from the brain scan my mother had back in June. A psychiatrist from the local memory clinic came round to tell her the news gently. She used words like 'atrophy' and 'anosognosia' – the doubly cruel aspect of some dementias, which means a person cannot see they need help and that they are causing stress to others. She sat there, nonplussed, grumpily declaring, 'What do you expect? I am eighty-eight years old!' The doctor gently assessed her, asking questions as part of general conversation, but she couldn't remember my birthday, how long she'd been at her present home, or what I did for a living. She refused the chance to try medication which might help slow down the deterioration. Twenty minutes later, after the doctor had left, mother asked me belligerently who 'that woman' was and why she was there. And, yes, of course she'd take medication. Why didn't they bloody well write a prescription for her?

Our relationship is fractured by this disease of old age, but I am not emotionally wounded by the loss of 'the person she was' like other daughters I have read about whose mothers have succumbed to Alzheimer's. There wasn't much of a relationship to lose. We were always poles apart in attitude, interests and awareness. I am not grieving for my 'best friend' or the person who always looked after me. I am, however, deeply saddened by the mental decay of someone who, in nine decades, has never examined herself, and the opportunity to begin that process has now gone. The frustrating mystery is always in the back of my mind: I cannot fathom how someone so naturally bright, intelligent and well-informed, before the dementia seized her, could not once step outside of herself and exercise reason, practise mindfulness, or make a decision about her future. She went round and round in the same very small circle all of her life; unable to throw anything away; unable to let go of her own mother; unable to break free of her conditioning and background and *live*. She will die less than five miles from where she was born. A life lived so narrowly seems to me a life wasted.

I will struggle when I have to speak at her funeral, as the truths of other people's family histories are usually peppered with fond recollections of hobbies they loved or groups they joined, or things they made. There is none of that with my mother. She went shopping, watched television and cooked my father's meals. And moaned and moaned and moaned.

I have tried to bring some simple happiness into her life since joining The Daughterhood, taking her outdoors on sunny days, buying her Sunday lunches and the *Radio Times* (not that she can make any sense of it any more), and have made her comfortable, brought her soft blankets and cushions. I shop for her and buy her favourite foods and enjoy cooking for her. She doesn't remember any of it. In the same week as I spent a full eight-hour day with her, serving her meals and taking her out, she told the long-suffering neighbour that she hadn't seen me 'for weeks' and that I'm 'probably abroad somewhere', which reaffirms the neighbour's portrait of me as distant and uncaring. She is refusing Social Services help or any kind of care package. She insists that she is perfectly able to look after herself, although she is no longer capable of making herself a hot meal.

If she does live for another ten years, she will end up in a dreaded care home – a place she said she would rather die than enter. The news reports are so ghastly and depressing about such places, I empathise with her fear. I would do everything to ensure she was well cared for but she would have to be dragged there kicking and screaming, and I don't think I can face the trauma unaided. The charges are atrociously expensive: £3,500 per month, on average. More than three times the cost of the revenue I'd get from renting out her property to help pay for it. And when she does pass away, the house would be sold to pay the outstanding debt – unless, of course, she lives so long that the entire value of the place is drained to the last penny. It's the sorry story of what is happening to my generation across England (rules are different in Scotland, where care of the elderly is free). The side-effect of increased longevity is penury for the children.

I cannot lie: I could use the inheritance to admirable means. I would be able to realise my life's dream: to sail across the Pacific Ocean, volunteering on marine conservation projects and helping to raise awareness of what's happening to our seas. While I'm still relatively fit, I could work for environmental projects and contribute something really worthwhile to the planet without having to worry about working the nine to five.

But, instead, the value of the house will most likely be spent on maintaining the ancient life-form that is my mother as I, too, grow old and my scuba-diving, hill-walking years pass into history. It's possible I could be in my late sixties before she dies. The futility of that makes me feel very depressed. I have a lot to offer the coral reefs of the Pacific and the orphaned animals of Central America. I need to be keeping very fit, but as long as I stay in an office job in a city, that's unlikely to happen. In my bleakest moments I worry I'll drink myself to death instead. This crisis in mother management has driven me to the bottle. I am managing this completely alone as the only living relative. The healthy way out of my alcohol dependency will be travelling and plenty of outdoor life. The alternative is a liver transplant.

I've been trying to focus on the positive with my mother. She was always good with money and alert to world news and politics and aware of environmental destruction. She joined Greenpeace in the 1970s and I was proud of her for that. She was always kind to animals and loved pets. But she even denied herself the companionship of a pet after Dad died because something might 'go wrong'. Her life motto has surely been the opposite of 'Go For It'. What would that be: 'Don't Dare Risk It'?

I find it so sad that she never joined a club or went on day-trips and got to know people. She had so much to offer – she could talk the hind legs off a donkey and had a keen sense of aesthetics. She was always generous, a good cook, a fantastic gardener, and very aware of maintaining good health. She could be nicely turned out, with beautifully styled hair that she did herself in tiny pin-curls, which took hours. She cared about how she looked. She could even have met another man after Dad died. Why did she continue to always expect the worst?

I wish I could go back and meet her as a young girl and help her be more open-minded, show her the beautiful world that is out there. She always loved hot weather but never seemed motivated to try a foreign holiday. We were quite badly off when I was a kid, but we could have afforded a package trip to Spain. Going anywhere outside of the UK was as likely as a trip to the moon. I worry sometimes that something really awful happened to her when she was young, to make her so resentful and fearful. Different kinds of abuse cause personality disorders and anger. Was all her moaning about the war and Dad just a smokescreen masking something far more traumatic? I can't bear to think she might have suffered at the hands of an abuser; that all this self-denial was down to a simple lack of confidence. People of her generation and class didn't talk about 'those things' and it's far too late to raise the subject now. I will continue my Motherwork out of duty and, yes, out of a kind of love. But the mystery of my mother will never be solved and there is no one around to ask.

The Reluctant Daughter writes to her mother:

Dear Mum

I wish things could have been different. I wish you could have been happy. I wish I'd been able to get through to you, to penetrate the wall of resistance that repelled every suggestion made to you for how you might make your life easier and more enjoyable. I wish you could have understood something of my world and my interests. But those things never registered with you — you hated modern music and modern art and anything intellectual. It was obvious early on that I was not going to live a life you could relate to. I wasn't going to get a little catering job and get married to a traditional 'fella'. I studied surrealist art and psychoanalysis and was swept up in the counter-culture and alternative lifestyles. I never got married and I never had children. I know what a disappointment that has been for you. I guess we were both disappointments to each other. I've never seen you read a book and find that terribly sad, as books are one of the most important things in my life. We've never been able to have a conversation about the popular classics. Not even Chandler or Orwell. You never read them.

I know you were proud of me at particular points — when I got my degree; when I was published; when I taught myself various skills — and you were proud that I've always worked since I was a young teenager — but you could never seem to get past how my achievements were down to the opportunities my generation had, and which you didn't have because of the War. I know, I know, but I cannot help when I was born. It must have looked to you as if I had a charmed life, with my pop posters and fashion magazines, student parties, international travel and free, liberal arts education, whereas you suffered the Blitz, poverty, sexual discrimination and the narrow-mindedness of the times into which you were born. What would you have been like if you had been born just twenty years later? Would you have been freed from that appalling negativity? You never seemed able to let go of the War . . . you were always talking about it. Always. Every time I've come to visit you I've been told the same stories over and over about the War. I know it was epic and huge, and in the past I encouraged you to be interviewed for archives and reminiscence workshops, which you did. But it was a very, very long time ago and only lasted for six years of your extremely long life.

I have never known what to say to you or how to make conversation so that you don't turn it into a diatribe of how awful things are/were. As a child I was embarrassed by your dogged refusal to embrace the changes happening in society. Next to my schoolfriends' mothers, you were sullen, unsociable, almost wilfully dowdy, cramming your beautiful hair under a scarf — but you didn't have to be like that! You could have blossomed and embraced change and enjoyed the easy living of the New Britain. You chose instead to blame my father for everything we didn't have. You didn't want to have people round to our house, so I spent most of my evenings after school at other people's homes and I saw how different their lives were.

In the 1970s it seemed everyone was having fun, having dinner parties, trying out new foods, going for days out together, enjoying themselves. But not us. You always made the excuse that our house wasn't well-decorated enough to have visitors, but it really wasn't that bad. It's as if you denied yourself the pleasure and contact of friends. I even used to pretend I was part of someone else's family so I could feel something of that bonded love and warmth that was missing in my own home: dads who would chase the kids round the garden, drive them to camping adventures, have a barbecue, ride bikes etc. And parents who would show each other affection – what a shock that was! In later years, Dad's stroke was the reason people couldn't come round, as you didn't want them to see him like that. Always something. Always a reason not to socialise. And yet, when you found yourself in social situations in public, you were chatty, informed, charming. These situations had to occur spontaneously; they could never be planned, as you would refuse to attent such gatherings.

I tried so hard to get you to embrace an optimistic outlook, but you weren't having any of it. You would tell me again and again how Dad was unambitious and wasted his musical talent. How you could have made something of your life if it hadn't been for Dad or for having me. How your life was blighted and thwarted by bad luck. How it's 'too late now' (it was 'too late' in 1970, according to you, and in 1980 and 1990, and you're finally, definitely right, because now it is too late).

I see archive film of the 1920s and '30s and I'm looking at a lost world, a country that might as well have sunk into the sea. It has changed so radically as to be unrecognisable. The twentieth century saw more changes than any century that preceded it – being the most troubled yet most exciting time there's ever been. Even radio was a new invention when you were born. And those of your generation, creaking towards three-figure ages like soon-to-be-extinct beasts, must surely feel so alienated by the modern world. I'm sorry I am part of that which you reject. I'm sorry I couldn't be the daughter or friend you wanted. I apologise for being so unlike you. The gap was just too big.

    In love and sadness,
    Your daughter, Anna

THE DISAPPOINTING DAUGHTER'S MOTHERWORK

Debbie, our transcriber, felt as though nothing she ever did was good enough and she wanted to find a way to get her mother to put down her Angry Birds and talk to her. Here's how Debbie got on . . .

If this Daughterhood were a degree and if I were in university I'd be in serious trouble with my tutors. If I were being marked out of ten, I'd be lucky to scrape a two and a half. I am failing at my daughterly duties in quite a spectacular way. I just can't seem to make any of it work.

The plan was that I would bring my mum away with us on holiday. We hatched it at one of The Daughterhood meetings. I would find some quiet time with my mother. Nothing too dramatic. A quiet walk on the beach maybe. A cosy lunch on a shady veranda somewhere while Stephen took the kids off on an adventure. I'd tell her how I've been feeling. She'd nod and say she understood. She'd put the iPad away and say, 'That's enough Angry Birds for now. I want to spend some quality time with my daughter.' Reader, it didn't happen.

The camping holiday in France was a disaster. Mum was sick before we left with a terrible chest infection and for a while we thought she wasn't going to make it on holiday at all. I had a bad case of Undaughterly Thought-itis. I know she didn't get sick on purpose but the timing was terrible. It was going to be hard enough keeping her happy without the added pressure of her being sick away from home.

She rallied for the first couple of days. It was almost as though she was making an effort, although she was never far away from Angry Birds or her iPad. But her condition got worse, the kind of sickness that renders the most mild-mannered person cranky. My mother is not a mild-mannered person. I insisted she go to the doctor. That morning I planned to take her for coffee after the appointment, just the two of us. Maybe we would get to talk. But my two eldest boys had been pushing my youngest into the hotel swimming pool and they were banned from a planned beach trip for misbehaving. So they came with us, too. That slimmest of chances for some mother-daughter time was lost.

The rest of the time she was unbearable. If she wasn't criticising all of us, especially the children, who she said were too boisterous and loud, she was holed up in her 'room' in the tent communing with the Angry Birds. On the last day of the holiday she annoyed my husband so much with her bickering and negativity that he fecked off on his own for a few hours and left me to deal with it all.

And, of course, the car broke down on the trip home and we had to call out the AA. This led to another barrage of criticism from my mother, which led to another painful bout of me feeling like a disappointment to her. When we finally got home, she went straight to bed.

She was up the next morning and went off to meet some friends for coffee. She left immediately, without even saying goodbye to the children, who were all still in bed. Her parting shot was a story I've heard so many times before – this is the abridged version: she cannot cope with the chaos of my house and the lackadaisical way I parent my kids. And that I need to 'sort myself out'.

She hasn't spoken to me since. I've phoned a few times but she doesn't answer.

I'm a useless member of The Daughterhood. I can't seem to make any kind of progress at all. I feel like writing to Natasha to tell her I want to quit. But being a Daughter isn't like being in The Bunker. You can't just up and resign. Not from the role of daughter. It's a position that never ends. There is no way out of this gig and, anyway, there's nowhere to go even if you wanted to.

Despite everything, though, there are days when I still feel hopeful. I have a clear idea of what I need to do with my mother so that some measure of healing can happen. I would like to sit down with her and talk through her problems with me and mine with her. If I got the chance I would tell her that, yes, my house may be a mess, my life may be chaotic and noisy, but that doesn't mean it's wrong or bad or that I'm a failure. It just means my life is different and, perhaps, strange to her. It's a world away from her very ordered existence where everything is in its place and she can lie in her bed and play Angry Birds to her heart's content.

Now is not the right time for this Motherwork. Sometimes in life the timing is just off. I get the sense that my mother is still grieving so much for my father that she cannot deal with anything else. I worry that she is suffering from depression. When I'm not giving out about her childish addiction to computer games, I'm conscious those very games may be an important escape from all that she doesn't want to face. It's better than a whisky habit.

I've been thinking a lot about motherhood and daughterhood. It's only for a certain period of time that your mum is there for you and, after a while, the tables must turn. You have to be there for her. It may sound simple and obvious but this has been a huge realisation since I first started listening to The Daughterhood files.

I'm trying to hold on to the good parts. I never witnessed much love or intimacy between my mother and father but she showed her love during his illness in a profound and inspiring way. He couldn't walk and he could barely talk, because the cancer had advanced so far. She nursed him at home until the end. I was there every single weekend to give her a break, just to go to the shops or to get out of the house. Friends and neighbours also helped out but she didn't like to impose.

I was down there helping every chance I got. I knew what she was facing. And during the really difficult time when my father was first diagnosed, she would have phoned me up just for a chat. She said things during these conversations I could never have imagined her saying: 'I love you. Thanks for helping me. Thanks for listening. I really miss you.' We had a closeness then but it just seems to have melted away.

She is lonely, sad and angry. It hurts so much that I can't help her with that. There is still an unspoken bond between us, but no real closeness. I could, I suppose, drop everything to attend to her. Couldn't I? No, I could not. The demands of work and family are too great at the moment. Dropping everything is not an option. This does not make me a bad daughter. I just have to keep telling myself that.

The Disappointing Daughter writes to her mother:

Dear Mam

I am not quite sure where to begin, or where to end.

You have been with me and for me, in your own way, for all of my life. But there are still a few things that I want to explain and maybe to understand as well.

Becoming a mother myself has helped me make sense of a couple of things that puzzled me. One was that you cannot always fix

things with words. Sometimes silence and brushing things aside is
what is needed. A good night's sleep fixes a lot of things and
everything is back to normal and makes sense again the following
day.

Secondly, there is no such thing as a perfect parent. Everybody
basically muddles through. When I look back now at things that
annoyed me as a younger person I can see, completely and clearly,
that you were just doing your best, always.

I also see that you were taken for granted, not listened to, hurt,
disappointed and unappreciated by me.

While I feel I can talk to you about anything, I don't. Your
reaction to many things I discuss with you is not what I would expect
at times. And I must admit I wonder to myself about your own state
of mind, and your own issues. You are not my care-giver any more.
You are your own person again and I must look after myself.

I have been so hurt over the last couple of years with many of the
things that have been said and done. While I realise you have to keep
everybody happy in the family, there have been moments when I just
cannot understand your motivation.

That being said, I want to thank you for being the best mother
you were able to be. For all the selfless and thoughtful things you
have done. For being there for me in times of strife and picking up
the pieces and making me move on. For being a wonderful Gran and
giving my children the love and affection that I don't always have
time to give. They love you to pieces.

This letter started in my mind as a list of criticisms. A flurry of all
the times in the last several years that I have been hurt or
misunderstood or felt hard done-by. When Dad was dying, I did
spend many moments alone with him talking about the past, trying
to fix things that needed to be mended and saying sorry for all the

things that I hadn't done. We realised quite quickly that we didn't need to. It might sound trite but the unconditional love a parent has for their child and that a child has for their parent, even when there's been years of misunderstanding and arguments, really does conquer all.

But as the words fill the page it becomes even clearer to me that all my gripes are insignificant and can be put aside. I just want to say two things: thank you and I love you.

Debbie

THE DEPENDENT DAUGHTER'S MOTHERWORK

Róisín wanted to stop relying on her mother as much as she did and to stop being the cause of ructions at family gatherings. Here's how Róisín got on . . .

I got email spammed halfway through this Daughterhood non-journey. Spammed. I woke up one morning to observe that overnight I had apparently sent an email about a weight-loss product costing 128 euro to the several hundred people in my contacts list. Oh, let us rejoice on this happy day.

I have quite a few mental blocks around technology. I sat there blinking at my screen thinking about all the people I hadn't talked to in months, possibly years, suddenly getting an email from me suggesting they could do with shifting a few pounds. Just what you want to wake up to on a Monday morning.

Lots of people contacted me to suggest I send everyone on my contacts list a message informing them I'd been spammed, so they wouldn't accidentally buy a bottle of weight-loss pills for 128 euro. But I couldn't figure out how to do that. Also, I reckoned that most of my contacts were shrewd enough to realise that I wasn't actually sending them an email asking them to shell out 128 euro for a weight-loss product. Most of my contacts. But not my mother. So I emailed her within minutes of realising the scam to tell her not to press the button. To tell her I didn't really think a bottle of magic pills was going to do anything for me.

Ever since I was old enough to be slagged for being 'fat' (around the age of fourteen when, in fact, the pictures show I wasn't), my mother has listened to me about weight-loss woes. As I already mentioned, we both like our food a bit too much and, in my case, use it as a panacea for all kinds of ills that will not be cured by a bag of chips. Believe me I've spent a lifetime trying. Handy tip: chips will not cure what ails you. Fact.

Together over the decades we've spent hours discussing the Atkins Diet, WeightWatchers and Unislim, Motivation Weight Management Clinics and Cabbage Soup Diets. We've talked about the 5:2 Diet and the South Beach Diet and the 'fact' that *French Women Don't Get Fat*. In the last couple of years, my mother, using none of the above methods funnily enough, has managed to lose and keep off two stone. She did it by sheer willpower and not eating when she wasn't hungry. (She should write a book but it wouldn't sell because there's no gimmick. In the diet game, as in one of my favourite musicals *Gypsy*, you gotta have a gimmick.)

My mother inspired me with the slow, methodical way she achieved a weight loss that was motivated by her ambition to live until 100. She had looked around and seen that women of 100 years of age were generally skinnier than her. Ipso facto she wanted to be a bit skinnier. She wants to see her youngest grand-children grow up to be young men and young women. Her motivation was pure.

(As an aside – and this will be a long aside so bear with me – I want to make it clear that it is my daughters that are my main motivation for trying to become healthier, not any idea of what society says that I or any other woman should look like. I genuinely don't give two figs what society says I should look like. I wrote a column once inspired by Tara Erraught, an Irish opera singer, who was slated by critics in four broadsheet UK newspapers for her size. During that week in five separate reviews, five senior opera critics reviewed *Der Rosenkavalier* at the UK's Glyndebourne Festival and chose to focus on the body of this mezzo-soprano instead of her voice. The Dundalk woman was dismissed by them as 'a chubby bundle of puppy fat', 'dumpy', 'unbelievable, unsightly and unappealing' and 'stocky'. These men from *The Times*, the *Telegraph* and the *Guardian* thought this singer's body shape was more worthy of comment than her voice, the instrument that is her life's work. One of them said Erraught was not a 'plausible lover'. 'Look at her,' I imagine them thinking, 'how SHOCKING. She's supposed to be a love interest. How are we supposed to believe someone could love THAT?'

I wrote about the big fat lie. The idea that there is only one kind of lovable, sexy, seductive person. Look around. In real life people love all sorts. Men love women who are 'stocky'. Women love 'chubby' men. Fat men love 'dumpy' blokes. Skinny women love larger women. 'Fat' people succeed. 'Fat' people fail. We live out our lives the same way people who look good in skinny jeans do. We dream. We laugh. We feel sorry for ourselves. We snap ourselves out of it. And mostly when it hurts, it's because somebody has reduced us to the number on the label of our dress or our trousers.

I don't have any interest in being a size 10 or a size 12 or a size 14. If there has to be a label, I think a size 16 is what I naturally should be, as it happens. I have no truck with thighs that never rub off each other or thinspiration hashtags or seeing people's collar bones or ribs. I have no interest in size 0 skinny or congratulating women who 'get their figure back' quickly after pregnancy so that they hardly look as though a baby came out of them at all.

A broadcaster in Ireland, 2FM DJ Louise McSharry, who also wanted to be a healthier weight, told listeners to her radio show one day that she was going to make some lifestyle changes. Louise was engaged to be married at the time but had made no mention in her talk that these lifestyle changes had any connection with her wedding. A tabloid subsequently wrote a story with the head-line: '2FM's Louise McSharry is on a mission to fight the flab before her wedding.'

'No, I'm not,' Louise explained on Twitter that day. 'My wedding is not my motivation. As I said, health and fitness and a future where I can run around with my children are my motivation. I don't want to be connected to the idea that brides need to diet before their wedding. Every bride is beautiful, no matter their size.' I cheered and the tabloid amended the story, apologising for their 'mistake'. End of aside.)

I had a great year when it came to my own fitness challenge. I started running with one of those Couch-to-5k apps. There was a polite young Englishwoman in my ear saying 'well done' or 'slow down now' or 'you've done great'. I wasn't running really, I was slow jogging, slogging, if we're being factual. My sister Rachael stuck a big huge skyscraper-sized carrot in front of my nose – a trip to New York if I'd do the Dublin Marathon with her. I did the marathon but not with her. Always a bit of a whippet, she became a lean, mean running machine, while I trained to walk the marathon with a group of other women, led by Breda, a kind, older woman who got in touch with me through my column asking did I want to start walking at weekends.

I had been walking with Breda and co. for weeks. It was Breda who had the idea of starting the marathon at 6am in the morning instead of the 9am official start. It took us eight hours and we got lost at one point in the Phoenix Park due to the fact that the signage wasn't up yet. But I did it and that Christmas I felt better than I had in years. I had conquered something.

After Christmas the self-sabotage crept in and halfway through the Daughterhood 'journey' I was back where I started. I was in a worse place than when I'd started. I would sit at my mother's kitchen table in the blackest of black moods and she would sit there looking at me and trying to encourage me back to some kind of positivity. 'You can do this,' she'd say. 'I love you. I love you whatever size you are but I know you are not happy. I want you to be happy.'

'I can't do it,' I'd tell her, crying now. 'I can't. I'm an idiot. A self-sabotaging moron. I am a bad mother who can't even run around after her children.' And I know she has been worried about me lately. About my mental health, as much as my physical well-being. And when she got that spam email, she was so wrapped up in trying to help me, so worried about the state I'd got myself into that she clicked on the button.

She spent 128 euro, money she can't afford, on a bottle of weight-loss pills. She sat there looking at her screen, only recently returned from her American holiday and jetlagged. Seconds later I emailed to tell her that I'd been spammed. She was mortified. A week later the package came with the pills. She tried to get the delivery man to take them back but he said he couldn't. They are still in their packaging on the top of her wardrobe, never to be opened, making her feel stupid every time she thinks of them.

And worse. They reminded her that her love for me, her desire for me to be happy and sort out my long-standing problems, had seriously clouded her normally excellent judgement.

'This has made me see that I can't help you with this anymore,' she said to me in the kitchen after confessing to falling victim to the scam. I had at that exact moment come to the same conclusion. 'I don't want you to help me,' I said. 'I need to do it on my own.' My mother should not, at the age of seventy-five, have to take on my personal struggles. I know she will always support me.

I know that nobody else on the planet will be happier than she will when I finally get this one licked. But I am on my own in this. I don't feel as though I've lost something with that realisation. I've feel I've freed my mother from an unfair obligation and finally taken responsibility for something only I can fix. That's some serious Motherwork right there.

One of the other things I told the Daughterhood group that I wanted to change was how self-absorbed I am around my mother. I challenged myself to bring her out for lunch and consciously talk much less than I usually would. So I arranged a couple of lovely lunches in places we'd never been before. And during each meeting, I blabbed on about myself, as usual, perhaps even more than usual. It was only at the end of each lunch that I remembered what I had been trying to do. It seemed my habits were so ingrained around my mother than even when I consciously tried to do something different, I just carried on in the same vein.

That's when I came up with the idea of interviewing my mother – conducting an interview with her as though she was someone I'd have to interview for work. In that kind of interview scenario, I generally just ask questions and don't volunteer anything about myself, which is an essential part of the process. There are exceptions to this and they occur when I am also trying to be best friends with the person I'm interviewing. (Sorry Caitlin Moran/the Dalai Lama.)

I brought my mother to Cleaver East for the interview – that place where the dishes are so small you worry you'll be starving afterwards but you don't have to worry because you will be full up at the end. I promise. The timing was good because she had recently been getting treatment for her AMD. As I've previously mentioned, the treatment involved monthly injections right in the eyeball, so I knew there would be some fresh angles to explore.

When we sat down I put the Dictaphone on the table and, as if by magic, I managed a two-hour conversation with my mother where I mostly just asked questions and cooed over the food. ('You have to taste this salmon, mother; it's like they've turned fish into silk. I bet there's one of those sous vide yokes from *Masterchef* involved.') She just talked. And talked. And as with all the best interviews, I learnt a few things about my subject I didn't know before:

1. My mother would quite like some more 'alone time' with all of her children. One-on-one meetings. Without their partners or children. (No offence to either of these valued communities.)

2. She would quite like to go to Venice. It's been a dream since the 1980s when she first saw that 'just one Cornetto, give it to meeeee' ad.

3. Sometimes when she doesn't hear from me for a few days – probably the longest I ever go without getting in touch with her – she'll be delighted. This might not sound right but the reason she'll be delighted *not* to see me is because not seeing me means I'm OK. That I'm getting on fine without her. I found this very surprising and was a bit ashamed of myself at the worry I cause her. I thought about all those times I turned up at her house wearing the long face I generally try to hide from the world and just sat at her table luxuriating in my sadness. Hearing how worried she gets about me made me resolve not to burden her in this way any more.

4. She'd like to feel a bit more cared for. When she came back from getting her eye injections last week, she had to take to bed because the ordeal had taken so much out of her. She would have liked if someone, one of us children, would have noticed that it was the day of the injections and had rung to inquire how she had got on. Sometimes she thinks that because she's relatively healthy (apart from the sleep apnoea and the macular degeneration) she doesn't get minded as much. 'Everyone thinks I'm grand and fit and well and they don't need to worry about me. But I think I'd like people to worry about me a bit more. I think I'd like that,' she said, offering me a (stunningly executed) courgette chip.

5. She doesn't like being patronised or talked over. 'Mother wouldn't like that' or 'Mother isn't getting any younger' are things, which after interviewing my mother, I know not to say – at least not within her hearing anyway.

6. She would like to feel more appreciated. We were going into rhapsodies about this little lobster number or maybe it was the slow-cooked veal when she reminded me of all the energy and thought and love Jonny and I put into raising our girls. 'I did that for all of you,' she said. 'I did that; I put so much energy and time into it and I loved it. I wanted to do it. It was my job. But sometimes I don't know whether people are grateful to me for that. I'd like to have more of a sense that I was valued and appreciated.' Then almost in the next breath she blamed herself for the idea that, as a family, we don't show our appreciation to her more. She took a sip of water. Speared an asparagus tip. 'Maybe it's the way I

brought you up. I told you I didn't want any Mother's Day cards. I told you all to go off and do your own thing. When you left home I didn't want you to look back. But you'd wonder sometimes. Do they really love me?'

This was a bit of a bombshell. I wondered how the rest of my family would feel about this.

A couple of hours after we sat down, apart from having a sumptuous and surprisingly filling lunch with my mother, I felt I'd gleaned some valuable insider information. These were things I'd never have discovered had I not sat down and interviewed her. She told me afterwards that she enjoyed being the centre of the attention during our lunch and when I played back the recording I could hear how, by asking questions and taking myself out of the picture, I'd left room for topics of conversation that would not have been covered had I not been in professional interview mode.

Some of the fallout from the information I gleaned during this interview was that, as a family, we clubbed together and bought her a trip to Venice. My sister Rachael has made plans to take my mother out to lunch, just the two of them. And I've been trying to remember her medical appointments so that I can show her I do actually care.

So the message here is if you find yourself unsure what it is you could be doing for your mother, try interviewing her. You might be surprised by what you find out.

Apart from listening to my mother more and talking less, I also had some Motherwork to do around family gatherings. When my brother Brian came back to Ireland, this time from Ukraine (he gets around), we decided to try to have a sibling dinner again. No partners and no children, just us eight brothers and sisters as it used to be around the table in Inglenook.

Brian was staying with me at the time and was helping to get the roast chicken dinner ready. As we chopped and basted, I reminded him of the fact that he can sometimes antagonise some of our brothers and sisters and that he should bite his tongue at all times. He reminded me of the fact that it was my fault not his that the last sibling gathering had gone awry. He had a point. But this time I was determined that ructions would not happen.

I was on a mission – a mission to bring peace. I know, because she has said it to me a million times, that my mother gets no greater pleasure than just looking around a room where her adult children are gathered, seeing everyone getting on together, enjoying each other's company. What she hates is when that family harmony is disrupted by pointless, petty arguments. Today, for our roast chicken sibling dinner, I was on the case.

It was all going so well. The roast chicken (free range, organic) was beautiful, the vegetables (spiralised with a new kitchen gadget) were a triumph, and the roast potatoes (secret recipe, I'd have to kill you) were Michelin-star worthy.

Then my mother started talking about how much she enjoyed living with my younger sister. She wanted us all to know that she was happy there, that she wouldn't want to be anywhere else and that we should all appreciate the fact that my sister was very good to her. (That sister wasn't at the dinner – perhaps avoiding the inevitable ructions, I don't know.)

Now, on a normal, non-peace-seeking-mission occasion, I would have had a lot to say to my mother about this. Not necessarily all of it peaceable. I mean, I would like my mother to live with me. Katie gets a live-in babysitter along with my mother. She gets to live with the person who makes the best lasagne outside of Pisa. It's hardly a hardship. I would have said it all, probably until a row erupted.

But post-Daughterhood I kept my powder dry and, instead, found my Dictaphone, placing it strategically next to my mother. This conversation could be good material for the Daughterhood, I was thinking. An innocent enough thought. I'd been taping all my conversations with her since I started this project. But with this one movement I detonated a bomb.

Before you could say Big Brother another sister had spied the Dictaphone and decided my decision to tape the family conversation surreptitiously was bad form. Which, when I type it now, seems perfectly reasonable. But not at the time. No. At the time, with chicken congealing on plates, I freaked out and my sister freaked out and she flounced off and then I flounced off and another sister joined in and my mother was upset and in tears. My peace mission had been sabotaged. By me.

It took an hour for things to calm down. After a while, a box of childhood pictures were produced by the offended sister, and nostalgic comments about a certain appalling item of 1970s clothing were made by the offending sister. Peace came dropping slow. My mother looked happy. But I wasn't. I had done it again. I had done it, even when I was trying very hard not to do it. What was the point in trying?

The point, I realised afterwards, is that bad motherhabits don't just disappear because you want them to. The point is you have to keep trying and keep failing until you want the change so badly that one day it happens. Samuel Beckett once wrote in a completely different context: Ever tried. Ever failed. No Matter. Fail again. Fail better.

That's the best I can say. That I've been failing better when it comes to my mother. And it looks like this: one day you will walk into an Italian restaurant where all your family and your mother are gathered and you will wrap your resolve around you like a bullet-proof vest. You will choose your seat far down the table from people you sometimes spark off. You will be out of earshot of some conversations, instead of having your ears flapping waiting to be antagonised. You will ignore things you hear that for some ridiculous reason displease you and concentrate on the ones that bring you joy. You will keep your mother at the heart of the occasion and notice when there are moments that could bring disruption. Like a motorist keeping an eye out for potholes, you will swerve around those moments. You will be impervious and so serene that at one point your mother will try to get you to join in with her slagging of one of her daughters and you will nobly refuse. She will look at you funny, as though she doesn't recognise you. But it will be worth it because at the end of the meal there will be no broken glass, no bruised egos and a mother in the centre of everything smiling beatifically. And you, the Dependent Daughter, will be the reason for her smile.

This exact scenario happened to me near the end of the Daughterhood. And it tasted like success.

The Dependent Daughter writes to her mother:

Dear Mother

Remember that song? The one with the chorus that says 'Look, Mummy, no hands.' Fascinating Aïda wrote it but then Camille O'Sullivan did it in her fishnets and top hat and made it even better. (Fishnets and a top hat make everything better, in the right hands and on the right legs.)

We'd seen her in the Spiegeltent together. She was on a trapeze, as is her wont, and you could almost see and hear the old-fashioned merry-go-round that was spinning around in her head. She conjured up this whole world of childhood. And afterwards, going home, you sang it in your slightly off-key voice, your voice breaking with emotion, those tears that come so quickly for certain songs, like Don McLean's 'Vincent' because it reminds you of Daddy, threatening to spill from your blue eyes. And I laughed. With you, not at you. I understood. At least I thought I did.

Remember the fair, Ma,
The two of us there, Ma,
By the merry-go-round?

Remember that song? I didn't know really what it meant until this past five years as a mother. I didn't know how it made you feel at a cellular level inside. But now I sing it and think of Joya and Priya. They need me now in a way I've never been needed by anyone. It scares me. They need me in the way I needed you when I was small, to keep me safe and wipe my tears and tell me everything will be all right. You never seemed scared. You were my champion. Mammy the Champion of the World. In your arms the monsters came out from under the bed and everything was OK. I learnt the lyrics off once; I wanted to sing them to you. I sing them to you now.

Look, Mummy, no hands;
I'm riding the roundabout all by myself;
Look, Mummy, no hands;
I called as I passed her,

Faster and faster;
'Hold on tight, darling!'
She called out in fear;
But I laughed and pretended that I couldn't hear . . .

Do you remember the time I got my head stuck in the railings of Sandymount Green and the fire brigade had to pull me out? Remember that other time I bumped my head and a cartoon bump appeared? We went on the bus to the hospital. You held my hand. Remember that time you reefed me out of the pub when I was hanging around with a dodgy crowd? I screamed at you all the way home. Remember?

I do.

Remember the years.
Of the sulks and the tears?
Do you recall? I hated you when
You said 'Be back by ten,'
I knew it all;
Always asking to know what I'd done;
When as far as I knew, I was just having fun;

I was just having fun. But I know it's all ahead of me with the girls and:

Remember the daughter.
And all that you taught her?
She's grown up at last;
With a child of her own.
She struggles alone
As the years all rush past;

But now you're not there to answer her calls;
You're not there to catch her as she stumbles and falls;

*You'd be bawling by this point. You'd be in absolute bits. And I
know why now. The thing about me and that song, the difference is I
still have you here. We have years left, I hope. You aren't gone so I
don't have to miss you. Yet.*

Look, Mummy, no hands;
I'm having to do it all by myself;
Look, Mummy, no hands;
I used to dismiss you,
Now I just miss you;
    . . . How careless we are when we're young . . .

*How careless. For me, the biggest learning and the biggest
realisation from this Daughterhood business is that I need to be more
thoughtful and appreciative of you as you grow older. You are going to
be weaker. You are going to need all of us more. And, in the
meantime, just because you are seventy-five and hale and hearty,
doesn't mean you wouldn't like a bit of mollycoddling. I know there
is a time coming soon, hopefully not too soon, when I am going to
have to give back to you in a bigger way. I need to start adjusting to
that. Preparing for that time. And that's what the Daughterhood has
been for me – a wake-up call that things need to change.*

*I don't want to be careless when it comes to you any more,
Mother. My love for you is slowly coming of age. Thank you for being
the best mother in the whole wide world. And for all the laughs.*

Your daughter

Róisín x

THE DEDICATED DAUGHTER'S MOTHERWORK

When I started this book, I wanted to call it Ten Things to Do with Your Mother Before She Dies. *I wanted to get across a sense of urgency with this project. The reality is we may not have as much time to work at this relationship as we'd like. Before I started The Daughterhood, I had already begun my ten things and I've continued to do them since. They are like my Ten Commandments of Daughterhood. You can make up your own commandments but here's what I do or try to do with my mother.*

1. Get to Know Her

As we grow up, the story of our mother is handed down to us through scraps of conversation, photographs and funny incidents told on a loop over dinners and family get-togethers. At least a version of the story gets handed down. The story of our mothers then gets stuck in one place. We grow up and sometimes we decide we know our mother's story and that there is nothing else to learn about her. The story stops evolving. If there are gaps in the narrative, they don't get filled. But when my mother dies, I want to know her full story. I don't want there to be any gaps – well, as few as there can be. So as part of The Daughterhood I asked her to fill in some of the gaps that had been niggling at me.

I'm lucky because my mother is an open book and I can ask her anything. I was always interested in my mother's relationship with her mother. She lived with us in a granny flat beside the house and we all adored her. But, even as a young child, I sensed that there was tension between them. I had never really asked my mother about their relationship. It was something I was very curious about, though. She was such a wonderful mother, had she had a good role model herself?

As we sat in my kitchen having dinner one evening, baked sea trout and asparagus, one of our favourite meals, I gave her an update on The Daughterhood. It really is pot luck who ends up being your mother, one of the most important lotteries in life, and I brought up the subject of my grandmother. 'I found my mother very controlling,' she said, taking a sip of wine. 'You wouldn't have noticed, Natasha, but I often came out from the flat crying. She was so impossible at times. I felt like her maid.'

'Do you think she loved you?'

'I know she loved me, although she didn't tell me till very close to the end. I remember it so well. One night when I was in with her I gave her a glass of sherry. I had one, too, and we both relaxed into a conversation about the horse racing that day. The chat led on to other things and she asked for another sherry, which was unusual for her. I don't remember exactly the words she used but the sentiment of what she said stayed with me. She told me that she appreciated the care I was giving her.' My mother said it was a special moment. 'I held her hand and told her I loved her. I had never told her that before.'

On another occasion, I asked my mother about her love life; she had asked about mine. It was a spontaneous conversation that kept us at the kitchen table in her house for hours. 'Did you have any boyfriends before you met Daddy?' 'Did you ever have your heart broken?' I listened to her as she drifted off into a reverie of remembered romances and flirtations. I knew that I was connecting with Mary Troy the woman, rather than Mary Troy my mother. It reminded me that there are so many layers to her life and that I'm only one of them.

Your mother might not be an open book, though, and you might have to tread a bit more lightly in your investigations. But most people enjoy talking about themselves and telling their stories, so you might be surprised at how much your mother has to say when you start to ask the questions. But you need to ask.

2. Travel with Her

I used to do it all the time. On trains, buses, planes and boats all over the world. But since my mother got sick it has required a bit more planning. Here we are, my mother, my sister Sorcha and I on a plane to Oslo. My mother wanted to see the ice cliffs of the Antarctic. But her lupus meant we had to downgrade that one, so we are off to the Arctic instead to see the Northern Lights. We just dropped the Ant. We knew, because of her health, it would be our last chance to make this trip happen, so here we are, my sister Sorcha, my mother and I, arriving in Tromsø, Norway. It is snow covered and one degree Celsius. We are scheduled to board a ship to see the Northern Lights the next day so we have a night and a day to explore this picturesque town.

We have come well prepared for the cold. Layers and layers of thermals, jackets, ski gloves, woolly hats and socks. We tramp like Michelin women through the ice-slippery streets to the polar bear museum and go in and out of the gorgeous shops. Sorcha goes to look for a supermarket to stock up on supplies, as my mother and I sit outside a café in our layers having a much-needed, if extortionately priced, coffee.

Even though it's freezing, it's too beautiful to sit inside. Sorcha comes back with supplies, aghast at the prices in the supermarket. 'I can't believe we're here. Aren't we so lucky,' my mother says. It's like her catchphrase for life. I am thinking of getting it printed on a tea towel.

We board the ship the next day and get settled into our rooms. Mammy is tired and so decides to rest for a while before the ship leaves. We spot a pub on the harbour. Sorcha and I decide to go over for a drink. Over two beers (24 euro!) I discover that Sorcha is the worrier amongst us. We have to be really careful with Mammy, she tells me, the changes of temperature from hot inside the boat to the freezing temperatures on deck will really affect her chest.

'We can't let her get sick, she'll get an infection and she'll miss everything.'

Of course she's right. But Mammy will be fine, and we need to be careful not to boss her around too much. We slip back to the ship like two bold teenagers. Mammy is awake and reading in her cabin, all set to have a good look around. My mother has always been an adventurous traveller. She travelled a lot with my father in their early years, including to Russia. As her children went to live in various parts of the world, she came to visit us. In the early nineties she went to visit Sorcha in Nairobi where she was working with an NGO and I travelled with her to St Petersburg to see my sister Kate who was teaching English there. When I was living in Australia, in the mid-nineties, she came over to backpack with me through the Australian desert, up the Gold Coast and on through South East Asia. After I moved home in the late nineties we visited Sorcha and her family in the various countries she has lived throughout Africa and Central America. A year before my mother got sick we did a trip of a lifetime together to the Galapagos Islands, another place she had always wanted to experience.

The rest of our days in the Arctic were filled with amazing

experiences. We were lucky to see the Northern Lights twice, and my mother treated us to some dog sledging.

A week after we returned home, Mammy contracted an infection and was back in hospital. It had begun on the last day of our trip. Her chest was tightening and her breathing was bad. It was two weeks before Christmas. 'I don't care that I got an infection,' my mother said from her hospital bed. 'It was worth it.' She was home by Christmas. It *was* worth it. I am already planning our next trip, a sun-filled Christmas in Lanzarote. I just hope she will be well enough to go.

Thankfully, not every mother's idea of a good time is a trip in sub-zero temperatures to a country where there's only two hours of daylight. My friend, Rosetta, told me about a recent trip to Knock with her mother. Now, for those of you who don't know, Knock is a place of pilgrimage in the west of Ireland where the Virgin Mary is said to have appeared. Her eighty-year-old mother wanted nothing more than to go there for the day and Rosetta, after me driving her mad talking about The Daughterhood, volunteered to bring her. Her father had passed away the year before and she was conscious of spending more time with her mother.

'Shortly after I'd agreed to bring her, Natasha, I became deeply suspicious of her intentions – I think she was trying to bring me back to God or something.' Rosetta's suspicions weren't far off the mark. They said the three traditional rosaries in the car on the way down and three more circling the old church in Knock. 'All was going relatively well, I was even beginning to feel quite virtuous, until my mother insisted we say three more rosaries on the way back. And so there I was, somewhere between the Roscommon bypass and the third sorrowful mystery, uttering my own private mantra, "I value my mother, I value my mother, I value my mother".'

So whether your mother's idea of getting away from it all is a religious pilgrimage, a package holiday in Spain or an overnight in a five-star hotel, travelling with her is a way of spending quality time on neutral territory. There are opportunities for conversations that you otherwise might not have. It takes you out of your mother–daughter routine. I always take lots of photos and talking about the trip afterwards brings almost as much pleasure to both of us as the travel itself.

3. Celebrate Her

'Are you sure thirty chicken breasts are enough?' We're in the supermarket buying provisions for the latest party we are throwing my mother. The trolley is filling up and all I can think about is how many gins and tonics it will take to help me cook all this food. Mammy is walking slowly around the aisle – her beautiful, funky walking stick in one hand and her very long list in the other. 'Can we just stick to the list, a Mhamaí?' I ask, as she studies the price of the olives. We're making smoked mackerel pâté for starters. Our version of keeping it simple. 'But do you think it will be enough? Should we make a chicken liver pâté as well, just in case?' I steer her away from the olives. It's the same palaver every year when we throw a party for my mother.

She hasn't come on these supermarket trips for years. Since lupus, really. Every July we celebrate her birthday with a party in the garden. This year the other helpers, my two sisters, are not here. They're both living abroad. I get up at 7.30am for what is a 2pm invite. The house is quiet, my mother is asleep. I can hear the oxygen machine puffing away. Unfortunately gin is not ideal in the morning, so lots of strong coffees get me through the task ahead instead. It's a beautiful morning, we're having the party in the garden so we're praying for good weather, which will take a bit of divine intervention after the insane rain we've been having.

The preparation hours in the kitchen before a party are some of my favourite times. That beautiful quiet time when I am chopping, mixing, tasting, adding a bit more curry paste, another grate of ginger. I throw a baleful eye at the thirty breasts of chicken piled on the counter waiting to be chopped. Why didn't we pay the extra and get the pre-chopped chicken? Where are my sisters when I need them? I am making a Thai curry so the chicken needs to be cut small. I am on number eleven with only nineteen to go and my mind wanders. A few minutes later, I look down and the size of the chopped chicken has been steadily increasing, as I've stopped concentrating.

Celebrating my mother while I still can is a fundamental one of my Ten Commandments of Daughterhood. I have no clue how long she will be with us but as a family we treat every birthday as if it is her last. I want her to know how much I love her for who she is and who she has become, both as a mother and a woman in her own right. Making a fuss of her on her birthday validates her. It is an expression of our love and admiration for her. She has celebrated us over the years, now it is our turn to celebrate her.

My mother's seventieth was a really special one. We invited old friends she hadn't seen in a long time because she had been too ill. She surprised us by giving each of us a beautiful hardback bound book of photographs taken since we were babies. That day was the happiest I had seen her for years – surrounded by her family, in-laws, grandchildren and new granddaughter, Jessica, she looked so happy. Sorcha gave a speech that encapsulated my mother's story from her early years through to her teaching years, her return to

Jerusalem and then her lupus diagnosis. Sorcha highlighted her great character, her courage, her great sense of humour, her generosity as a friend and her continued love and support as a mother to all of us.

The subject of celebrating our mothers came up a lot during The Daughterhood. How do you even begin celebrating a woman who you don't like or who you simply don't get on with at all? We can hide behind the tradition of celebrating milestone birthdays but it doesn't mean we'll enjoy it or want to do it. However, we'll probably feel less guilty knowing that we've made an effort. I understand that it's not an easy thing to do if you can't stand your mother but maybe you can find some small way that is sincere and hopefully brings both of you joy. That's all you can hope for.

4. Cook with Her (and for Her)

My mother has two copies of a book called *Fifty Great Ways With Mince,* or *Fifty Shades of Mince* as it might be called today. When I told Róisín about this book that I was reared on, she laughed uncontrollably. My mother got it from a German friend Helga in the early 1970s. We had minced beef every way you can think of growing up and some you probably don't want to imagine. Don't knock it. Spaghetti Bolognese, meatballs, home-made burgers, lasagne and shepherd's pie – we lived like kings on that stuff. The only downside of her devotion to that book is that my mother hasn't been able to look at minced beef, cooked or uncooked, since around 1983.

Finding even just one thing that we like to do with our mothers can add so much to the relationship. My mother and I have a shared passion for cooking. Even during the minced-beef years my mother was a creative cook. When she was seventeen she was sent off to finishing school in Germany for a year as she was too young to go to college. She learned to do everything a woman of that time needed to know about running a house, from baking to ironing to cleaning to budgeting and sewing. It may sound archaic today but she claims she would have been clueless on all these fronts if she hadn't got that training. Money was tight so she made all her own clothes for years with a Singer sewing machine, made delicious blackberry jam, apple crumbles, home-made brown bread and all those minced-beef dinners. I also have very fond memories of helping her with the cooking and cleaning for the many dinner parties and house parties she held over the years.

My mother doesn't cook much on her own any more but we love cooking together. My passion for cooking really started when I lived in Australia and Bangkok. I had no choice but to learn and I became quite good at Thai cooking, which is my favourite cuisine. So we often cook together and try out new recipes.

During the years when Sorcha and her family lived away my mother and I had cookathons at the beginning of December where we cooked ten dinners that went into the freezer until Christmas when everyone descended home to my mother's. The cookathons took place over a weekend and, although exhausting, they were great fun. We cooked everything from Thai curries, to chicken and chorizo stew, to fish pies and, of course, the much-loved minced-beef meatballs. The quantities were made to feed at least ten people to save cooking every day during the Christmas holidays. This whole exercise took up loads of time in pre-planning. Long phone calls in the evening were taken up with choosing the dishes to be cooked, the eternal search for containers big enough that would be suitable for freezing, new meatball recipes, maybe adding in some minced pork this year.

The cooking started on the Friday night and normally finished by Sunday lunchtime. My mother's role was very clear: she was chief supervisor, chief advisor, chief taster and provided moral support, as she said herself. She was also responsible for refilling my wine glass or making me a gin and tonic, depending on our mood. These long days together provided good opportunities for great chats and laughter, between the chopping, cutting, mixing and tasting, along with the sips of wine.

The other kind of cooking we do together simply involves trying out a new dish. A few months ago we cooked paella for the first time and another Saturday was spent learning from my mother how to cook the perfect Irish stew. It doesn't sound like much of a bonding activity, but some of the best conversations I've ever had with my mother are when we're waiting for the potatoes to roast or the fish pie to bake.

In the early years of my mother's illness she struggled with letting us take over the cooking in her house when we visited. She would insist on doing the shopping before we came and cooking on the Friday night when we arrived. The next morning was spent in bed recovering the energy that she had exerted the day before. Over the years she has managed gradually to surrender all the responsibilities of cooking to her children. The reality of her limitations set in and she has finally accepted that it's OK to let us do it. Now she even enjoys the fact. But I know how hard that transition has been for her. Having cooked for all of us for so many years, letting go of her role as chief cook has been very difficult. But the beauty of cooking together is that it is a team effort. When we're cooking, she's not my sick mother and I'm not her potentially disempowering daughter. We're both playing our part and together we can create some great food.

5. Keep Her up to Speed

When my mother grew up in 1950s Limerick, her telephone number was Limerick 9. Her family had one of the few phones in the city because her mother, Kathleen, was a doctor and needed to be reached by her patients. Keeping up with modern technology at that time meant knowing how to turn the dials on the wireless and operating the mangle in the backyard.

In the 1980s I remember my mother introducing my grandmother to the magic of a fax machine. Kathleen, my grandmother, couldn't cope with the idea that the message on a piece of paper in one office could materialise on the clunky machine in my mother's kitchen. Learning how to fax meant my grandmother could receive messages from her sister Terry, a missionary nun in Zimbabwe, which gave her a thrill every time. My mother did the same thing with the microwave when that came along and with the video recorder, which apparently blew my grandmother's mind completely. My mother was keeping her mother up to speed with the ways of the modern world so that she wouldn't be left behind.

I find it difficult enough keeping up with the advances in technology. 'It's in the cloud,' my brother Cilian is always saying. I still don't know exactly what he means. My brain isn't wired that way but, thankfully, I have a great staff in their twenties who put up with my Luddite tendencies and help keep me in the loop on a need-to-know basis. At the same time, I am a gadget queen and I am constantly investing in the latest gizmo that will make our lives easier and more enjoyable.

For our mothers, people who remember the days of mangles and one-digit telephone numbers, keeping up can be a nightmare. But technology can also have a hugely positive impact on their lives, so I think we owe it to them to lead the way. In my case it's the blind leading the slightly blinder.

My mother now has an iPad, a mobile phone – she ditched the smartphone because she found it a pain – a Kindle, a Bluetooth speaker, a smart TV with Netflix, a laptop and a digital camera. She uses the iPad to watch Netflix in bed, the mobile phone to keep in touch with us and the Kindle to read books. The TuneIn app on her iPad talks to the Bluetooth speaker so she can listen to radio all over the world. She writes on the laptop, sends emails and Skypes my sister Kate in Turkey. Kate has a one-year-old daughter called Anu. My mother saw her youngest grandchild's first attempt at walking on the computer screen.

It hasn't been easy introducing her to all this new technology but, in terms of her independence and enjoyment of life, it has been worth it. The challenge? We knew there was huge potential for arguments, especially if she didn't get it first time. A smart, sharp woman who has been using various computers for decades, she is probably more advanced than I am in some ways. Still, when I first got her the iPad, the notion of swiping a screen was completely alien to her. When it came to that piece of kit, I must have spent hours repeating the instructions of how to navigate the various apps and showing her how to touch the screen so she could make it work.

But I knew if she got the hang of all these things, she would be more independent and it would allow her not only to keep in touch with us all but it would alleviate the boredom of illness by enabling her to escape into books, movies, writing and the radio. I just had to walk a fine line between not making her feel like an eejit and giving her the confidence she needed to operate all these gadgets.

Of course, some mothers resist the attempts by children to school them in modern technology. While I don't think iPads and Kindles should be forced down anyone's throat, I think it's worth trying to persuade them to give it a go. Even if you don't feel able to teach her, find a niece or nephew who will relish the challenge of teaching the older generation a few new tricks.

6. Be Patient with Her

Of course, introducing new technology to your mother can open up a whole load of fresh possibilities. I don't just mean for how she lives her life – I mean new ways of becoming impatient with your mother. I am talking, of course, about the nine circles of Internet-password hell. My mother has two degrees, was a lecturer at Trinity College, completed an MPhil written in Hebrew and is fluent in five languages. But do you think she can remember her Amazon password? No, she cannot. If you decide to take my advice about the technology, you will also need to steel your resolve when it comes to biting your tongue. Being patient with our mothers, especially as they age, is always challenging. But when you find yourself having to reset a Kindle, email and smart TV password fifty times a year, that's when your mother love will get a full stress test.

But patience is crucial when it comes to our mothers. They have been on the planet decades longer than us. They were in the world long before anybody even had a notion we would ever come along. They have lived and loved and fallen down and gotten back up and now, in the last decades of their lives, the least they should be able to expect from their daughters is a little patience when their ways don't quite fit into how we think the world should run.

And yet we are still impatient. My mother, because of her condition, walks much slower than she did a few years ago. I've had to stop myself hurrying her along, especially if I was carrying two heavy shopping bags. It was an unconscious thing, but I used to walk ahead of her, looking back impatiently every now and then. The unspoken message from me to her was, 'A Mhamaí, could you go a little faster?' Until one day I realised that this was putting her under pressure and I began walking alongside her so we could talk.

I know I can be the Busy Daughter sometimes but I try and take St Francis de Sales' advice when he says have patience with all things; but, first of all, with yourself. I'd add – and with your mother.

7. Don't Be Her Doctor

My mother has an excellent team looking after her: Dr Kavanagh, Dr Waters, Dr Gayne and Dr O'Regan look after all her medical needs. At home she has Olive, known to me and my siblings as Saint Olive. She's really well looked after by her doctors and Olive, so why do I still feel the need to appoint myself Dr Fennell?

That is what I did when she first got sick. It was a whole new world. I was getting used to the reality of having a mother with a debilitating, devastating illness. Dr Fennell here thought that micro-managing everything could somehow alleviate the effects of lupus and pulmonary hypertension.

I was acting out of fear. If my mother had a rattle in her throat, I'd suggest she might need to go to the doctor. If she tried to walk out to the garden, I would object on the grounds that she wasn't able. When I visited her, I'd tell her when to take her tablets and how many. If she wanted a glass of wine with dinner, I'd question whether it was allowed. I thought I was doing the right thing. The daughterly thing. It was only after a couple of weeks that my mother, at a low point and exasperated, told me that my ministrations were not helping. 'I'm trying to figure this out myself, Natasha. Please give me the space to do that.'

It took me a while to get out of the habit and I still have to stop myself. It's our instinct as daughters to try and mind our mothers and help them when they are vulnerable. I've been getting on much better with this lately. I sometimes worry that I've gone too far the other way. A couple of months ago I was in her house when she started having the shakes. I had fired myself from being Dr Fennell for so long that I was at a total loss and presumed this was just one of her regular symptoms. Until Saint Olive appeared. She took one look at my mother and asked whether she had changed her morphine patch recently. My mother's face fell. It should have been changed five days before. Saint Olive found the patch, my mother changed it and the shakes stopped.

Some of my friends have found themselves stuck in doctor mode. It's a hard role for daughters to step away from. One friend Tara has been trying for months to get her mother to move into a bedroom downstairs. She can see that her mother's nightly trek up to her bedroom is becoming increasingly difficult. It takes ten minutes for her to get up the stairs and Tara is scared that one day, when she's not there, her mother will fall. It's a battle that never ends. Tara insists that her mother changes her sleeping arrangements, her mother insists that the sleeping arrangements she has had for thirty-five years are not going to change now. As daughters with ageing mothers we are learning all the time to navigate their new more vulnerable reality. Tara is torn between respecting her mother's wishes and feeling like she should force the issue and install a bed in the front room.

My mother was told that she would have to be on oxygen permanently while I was on holiday recently. She wouldn't take any calls from my siblings or me as she was coming to terms with her new diagnosis. It was very difficult, but I had to stop myself from calling her and respect her need for space.

It can cause huge frustration but, after discussing this with my mother, I think the crucial thing here is to respect our mother's wishes even in their vulnerability. My mother has told me that her biggest fear is that her children will take control of her medical decisions, that she will be disarmed and left without any autonomy or control. We assure her that this won't happen, but seeing the concern she has gives me some insight into Tara's mother, making her way slowly up the stairs night after night.

I'm not my mother's doctor any more but there is still a lot I can do for her. We enjoy going through the bedtime ritual together – the endless to-do list as my mother refers to it. It involves checking the oxygen machine and getting a clean glass of water, and I sit on the bed as she takes her evening medication. I make sure her sleeping tablets and painkillers are close to hand, in case she needs them during the night. We chat, plump up her cushions so her back doesn't get sore and I make sure she is comfortable before I leave. It's about letting my mother take control while I play a supporting role.

8. Let Her Interfere

In all the reading I have done about mother–daughter relationships there was one recurring theme: the constant conflict between intimacy and autonomy. On the one hand, wanting to be close to our mothers; on the other hand, the desperate desire to keep and maintain our independence from them. This Daughterhood business is all about balance. We don't want to let them in too much but at the same time we don't want to shut them out either. If you have an aversion to your mother interfering, my suggestion might sound strange. I say, let her interfere. By that I mean, give her a hearing. Let her state her case, her opinions, her concerns.

'Tell me about it. Persuade me,' is something my mother often says when I tell her about a plan I have that she doesn't agree with. 'I might surprise you.' This can be a difficult thing to do, especially when you know your mother isn't going be 100 per cent behind your latest life plan. When I talked about this to Róisín, she told me that her way is often to shut her mother down immediately when she tries to contribute her tuppence-worth. But afterwards, having climbed down from her high horse, Róisín will often slink back to her mother in search of the advice she initially spurned.

Breaking away on our own and getting to a stage where our mothers accept decisions we make in our lives, even when they don't always approve, can be the biggest challenge of all. Somehow that is what I have managed to do in my relationship with my mother. I did it, I think, by letting her in, even when I didn't feel like hearing what she had to say.

I have had a very fulfilling career since I left college. I worked at RTÉ, Ireland's public service broadcaster, as a reporter for five years after I returned home from my travels. My brother Cilian was also working there at the time producing *The Late Late Show,* Ireland's longest-running chat show. My sister Kate was in the Arts Department, so it was a bit of a family affair. But after five years I was ready to make a move and I applied for Head of Fundraising in Fianna Fáil, the political party that was in power at the time. My mother didn't respond well when I initially told her.

'But you're so happy at RTÉ. I thought you loved your job,' she said. She was right, I did, but I was still only in my early thirties and I wanted to try something else. When I was appointed to the position she still didn't totally approve.

Fianna Fáil had a terrible reputation of corruption and crony-ism, and a lot of it stemmed from the financial donations. 'They only care about staying in power,' she said. 'And they don't care how they do it.' But, as time went on, she got used to the idea as she saw me relish the challenges of the job. And there were chal-lenges.

Despite her quiet and sometimes not-so-quiet disapproval, I stayed in the job for nearly five years and I loved it. I got a real insight into how a political party works. I loved the buzz of the elections and I felt I was working at the heart of where all big decisions were made. Looking back on it now, I was slightly naive as Fianna Fáil fell from grace a few years after I left and are now blamed for the disastrous years that caused Ireland's crash. Of course, my mother was right when she said that they only cared about power. What political party doesn't? And it was for that very reason that I finally left. I don't regret a day that I spent in Fianna Fáil but I do remember my mother's relief when I told her that I was moving on.

In writing this book I have asked my mother lots of questions and have had numerous conversations with her. When at home in her kitchen recently, I asked her how she dealt with the decisions that her five children made over the years that she didn't approve of.

'Acceptance,' she said. 'Seeing you all for who you are, rather than what I think you should be. When any of you ask for advice or my opinion on something, I give you an honest answer, but it is your lives and you will do what you want anyway. I know that and I am OK with that.'

My mother has worked hard all her life on acceptance. Most of all, acceptance of herself. And she says that it was only when she accepted herself that she felt able to let us all go our own ways, too. Maybe your mother is having a hard job accepting a decision you are about to make. Letting her in might feel like the last thing you want to do. But instead of shutting her down, try giving her the space to say what she thinks. She might just surprise you and, even if she doesn't, you've let her have her say.

9. Mind Your Mother Language

The language we use when speaking about our parents as they age is a real bugbear of mine. And my mother's. Even in this book the dodgy mother language has slipped in. We 'bring' them on holiday, we 'send' them away on a break, and we 'take' them shopping. We 'get them' to take their medication. The worst one of all is we 'pack her off' somewhere or another. We have developed the habit of talking about our mothers as though they are children.

Last year my mother was staying with me for the Mother's Day weekend. On the Saturday morning there was a special Mother's Day supplement in one of the national papers giving ideas for Mother's Day. The tone of the supplement read as though it was aimed at under fours. 'Now treat your mother to a day of gentle pampering and book her into an Urban Spa.' 'Why not send Mum away on a relaxing weekend break to Aghadoe Heights? Oh, and for the more adventurous Mum, why not pack her off on a vegan yoga retreat in the mountains? Why not send Mum on an art course where she can explore her hidden creative side?' And on and on it went. My mother read this to me over coffee at the kitchen table. She was expressing horror at the condescending language and she was laughing her head off at the idea of being packed off with the vegans. 'They make mothers sound like imbeciles,' she said. 'Since when do we get packed off, sent off or brought anywhere?'

This patronising tone has crept into all facets of life, from the media to our caring professions. It's all in the tone and language used. 'Are you OK there, pet?' 'Can I get you a cup of tea, darling?' You know what I'm talking about. Since when does everyone over sixty turn stone deaf and revert to childhood? What's with all the raised voices in hospitals and nursing homes? Can we please save all the shouting for those who are actually hard of hearing as opposed to using it on every woman over seventy?

The same applies when *we* are talking about our mothers, though. I remember during my days at school, some of my classmates went home for their lunch. After lunch they compared what their mothers had served up. 'My aul wan [old one] only gave me two spuds and a pork chop for lunch.' 'That's better than what my aul wan gave me,' said another. I know they were only joking but I remember being horrified at the time that they could talk about their mothers in that way. This patronising tone and language strips them of their dignity and is demeaning.

I know how we speak to our mothers and about our mothers is more habit than genuine ill intent. But habits can be broken. As our mothers age, I am asking all of us to be mindful of how we speak about them and to them. Banning the patronising patter around Mother's Day would be an excellent start.

10. Plan her Funeral

It's a Sunday in August. One of those unexpectedly hot Irish summer mornings. It's a stark contrast to the rain and wind that had been forecast. The Irish love talking about the weather and it makes for a big part of the conversations this morning. I'm part of a 100-strong procession walking slowly behind the hearse that is carrying my close friend Joanna's father Sean Gardiner to the church.

'It's a lovely day for a funeral; the weather makes all the difference,' says a neighbour. Joanna links her mother's arm and, with the rest of her family, leads us slowly through the beautiful village of Blackrock in Dundalk. As we make our way to the church, shopkeepers come out and stand on the footpath. Passers-by stand still, blessing themselves. The shops have been shut in his honour. Two men having coffee get to their feet and watch as the hearse passes. As we enter the church grounds a guard of honour lines both sides. Later, Joanna gives a beautiful eulogy for her father. A kind and funny man, president of the rugby club, owner of their family business, father and husband. I sit in the church listening and watching her tell the life story of her father. She gives him a great send-off.

I'm now at an age when funerals have replaced christenings and weddings as the big social events. I am attending more of them than I ever have before. It makes me think about how I want to give my mother the send-off she deserves. I want it all to be done the way she has chosen. My father, who is now eighty-five, calls it 'the big event'. We've discussed what he wants, too.

Joanna's father has been buried and we are back at her house. The crowds of mourners have gone. We are reflecting on the funeral. 'He would have loved today,' she says. 'He would have loved the walking behind him to the church part. I feel we did right by him.'

Over the years, even before she got sick, my mother has asked me and asked herself the question: burial or cremation? The first time was while we were watching *Six Feet Under*. I took one look at her and turned up the volume on the TV.

More recently, I'm the one who has started the conversation about what kind of funeral she wants. But since she's been ill, it's been increasingly important to me that I make sure everything will be as she wants it at the end.

You might think, as many of my friends do, that this is an unthinkable conversation. It's morbid. And it's not a chat anybody really wants to have. I can understand if funeral arrangements are the last thing you want to bring up with your mother. It's not easy. But I've found that having these conversations not only has allowed her to prepare for the inevitable but it's given me a chance to prepare, too.

The most recent chat about her funeral happened as we were walking on the promenade in Salthill, down the road from her house in Galway. I was linking her arm and we were chatting about this and that. I don't know exactly how it started but I asked her, 'Have you decided whether you want to be cremated?'

'Actually, I have,' she said. 'I do want to be cremated. And you are to scatter the ashes in my back garden and the rest in the sea in Maoinis.'

Even though I had asked the question, I was taken aback by her certainty. 'OK,' I said. 'And do you mind if I keep your ashes on my mantelpiece for a while before we scatter them?'

'No, I'd love to be on your mantelpiece,' she said.

I meant it. I want my mother's ashes on my mantelpiece for as long as I can have them. We have discussed how she doesn't want to be laid out in the coffin but in her bedroom in my grand-mother's linen sheets. She wants to be waked at home. With the traditional whisky and snuff.

We have since gone into greater detail. I was shelling prawns in the kitchen and she called down from the sitting room that she's thought of something else. I didn't even have to ask her what she was talking about. 'Queen,' she said. 'What about her?' I said. 'No, Freddie Mercury. "We Are the Champions" I want that song played during the ceremony.'

It brings great comfort to me to know what my mother wants when that time comes. It's not an easy conversation but you can try to broach the subject in little snippets, like asking her what music she'd like or on another occasion, you could ask whether she'd like a cremation or burial.

One day when we were having a gin and tonic in the garden as the sun set, she told me she also wanted 'Carmina Burana' by Carl Orff played. I couldn't recall the tune offhand. 'You know, the one I used to always play when I was doing the hoovering?' I did. She used to keep time to the tune by clattering the nozzle off the skirting boards as she tried to wake us up. She also told me she didn't want any fussy notice in the newspaper. I'm sure she'll let me know more details in time and I'm more than happy to carry out her wishes, including having a big party to celebrate her life.

The Dedicated Daughter writes to her mother

A Mhamaí

When I went down to visit you this weekend, we talked for a long time about what we would be doing if you weren't sick. You had an infection, you were weak, and so, instead of doing those things, we conjured them up by talking through the day we might have had.

We probably would have gone to the craft village in Spiddal, to the shop we both love, where everything is made of glass, from sparkling jewellery to stained-glass lamps. We would have then strolled down to the beach and gone for a swim. From there, we'd have dropped in to Stándún's, that beautiful clothes shop where there is always a big sale on at this time of year. We might have gone into town to Charlie Byrne's Bookshop, had a cup of coffee outside Neachtain's on Cross Street, and watch the world go by.

Instead, we were at home in your lovely house. You slept for most of the day. Later, sitting at the kitchen table, over dinner, we talked about the adventures we might be having. But neither of us felt the loss. It doesn't matter what we're doing because it's the ease we both feel in each other's company that makes our relationship so fabulous. That ease has always been there, from our backpacking days in Australia to sitting in the garden in Galway having a G&T. I know from the millions of mother–daughter conversations I've had that I'm incredibly lucky. We're incredibly lucky. You, Mary Troy, are a woman I love being around. You also happen to be my mother.

Thank you for your infinite belief in me, your constant encouragement and for accepting me for who I am.

Grá mór,

Tasha

8: THE LAST SUPPER

We began on a freezing cold and rainy January night and end on a balmy evening in June. Quite a lot has happened in between and I – Natasha – thought about it as I looked around my house at the daughters: Cathy's sister had died; Maeve was pregnant; Grace had got married; and Sophie's mother had been in hospital and out again. Róisín and I still thought it was so funny and wonderful that our transcriber had ended up stepping away from her keyboard to join The Daughterhood. There was Debbie now, deep in conversation with Anna. And to think she started off as a completely independent, if not so impartial, observer.

As a group we had bonded. I looked around the table for one final time and saw daughters who had, if nothing else, unburdened themselves of some motherly baggage that they'd been carrying for a lifetime.

We weren't strangers any more. Were we friends? It was an odd kind of acquaintanceship. We knew more about these people than we knew about some of our closest friends. And yet their real lives, outside of their capacity as daughters, were still a bit of a mystery. Sunlight shone through the patio door on the women as they laughed and chatted together; the mood much lighter than at our first meeting six months ago.

Previously unspoken secrets had been exchanged. Fears expressed. Unspeakable things uttered, in some cases for the very first time. Now we went around the group, as we always did, but this time we asked whether The Daughterhood had made a difference to our mother relationships.

Maeve sat at the head of the table, rubbing her beautifully pregnant belly. It was funny to think that the life inside her was almost the same age as The Daughterhood. She sipped her water, thoughtfully. 'It's like deciding to do a yoga class or, and this is a bit more extreme, to go to counselling,' she said. Anna poked her head around the patio door; she had flown over from London that morning. She had taken part in most of the previous meetings on Skype – a dislocated voice from the East End. I used to look at the bookshelves behind her and wonder what stuff she read. 'Mind you,' she said, with a laugh. 'I wouldn't go to counselling – this is as extreme as I go!'

There was more laughter and clinking of plates and glasses as Cathy came to join us at the table. She was still grieving for her sister but said she felt closer to her mother than ever before. 'The thing with these meetings is that you are setting aside time to dedicate to an issue you might otherwise not take time for. You look at things that were right in front of your face, but that you'd never seen.'

'If I hadn't done this, I think I might have just ignored it, run away from my responsibilities; instead I feel I've embraced them a bit more,' said Anna. Maeve had another point: 'I would never have considered that the issues with my mother were major issues; I would have just accepted things the way they were, and maybe that would have been fine. But setting aside the time has felt like a positive thing to do. And it has made a difference.'

'Do you still hide behind the couch, Maeve?' someone asked.

'The odd time,' she said. 'I think what that is really about is my mother's selflessness, which can be overwhelming at times. She is coming from a good place but sometimes I see her and I think, "Here she is again." I can't always give her what she needs. I'm really busy.' As she poured herself more elderflower cordial ('Made by my mother. Cravings!'), she said she had been 'mentally checking' herself more lately and that her mother had noticed a difference. 'I've spent more time with her, gone for walks or lunch, and I've noticed that she is landing on my door a bit less. I'm more relaxed around her; maybe it's the pregnancy hormones, who knows?'

Did Sophie have any conclusions? 'I just have to accept my mother the way she is. I don't mean that in a negative sense. I've realised that our relationship is stronger than I thought it was, even if it's very different to most people's. And this whole process has made me think about the fact that this is one of the most treasured relationships of my life, so why would I not take time to consider it, to nurture it?'

Now it was Lily's turn. Had The Daughterhood been useful for her? 'Yes, very,' she said, smiling. 'It has been good to be in an environment where I could share and, while my story might not be the same as the person sitting next to me, it helps just to say it out loud. The fact that I wasn't being judged was wonderful. I felt judged and rejected by my mother my whole life. I've found this a very safe place to be. My situation is not normal. But what situation is? This process helped me *feel* normal, despite the challenges with my mother.'

Lily said she felt very different from most of the daughters in The Daughterhood. 'But I have no regrets about joining. It's like any other group meeting with a common purpose. The book club analogy isn't far off. I've got one member in my book club who never reads the book but she likes the social aspects of the group. Some nights you get more out of it than others. Sometimes the book is the best thing you've ever read, other nights you can't wait to stop talking about it. But, like with this group, at each meeting there is an engagement with others – you talk, you connect, you disagree. It is supportive without being intrusive.'

As she did at almost every meeting, Lily apologised that there was no happy ending to her story. We reassured her that this wasn't about fixing people. 'You have to lead your life,' said Maeve. 'You have to come to terms with all of it. That's all any of us can do.'

'But I just want you to know that you are all so lucky,' Lily said. 'Leave me out of that one,' Anna scolded. 'Well, fine, but the rest of you are definitely luckier than Sophie and I,' Lily continued. 'And I don't care about telling you the truth. I might not have been brave enough to say this at the start but I'm envious of you. I'm jealous that you have a chance to improve things with your mothers. That you even have a chance. For me it's about accepting that it's OK not to like my mother. That it doesn't make a monster out of me. Or out of her either. I feel sad about it but the sadness is closer to acceptance now. As for forgiveness? I don't know.'

Anna was curious. 'Do you need to forgive her? Is that necessary? I feel ambivalent about my mother. I've come to embrace the ambivalence and I don't feel bad about it.' She got up, reached over to the bowl of Thai curry and helped herself to more food. 'The cards I was dealt, motherwise, weren't the best. But the cards she was dealt were worse than mine. She was never really in the game. We've all gone out and taken our chances and made a better game for ourselves. This card-playing analogy is going on a bit longer than I'd have liked, but my point is that I think forgiveness is not essential.'

Lily wiped some invisible crumbs from the table and straightened her napkin. 'You're right, to a point. I suppose maybe acceptance is bigger than forgiveness. She is who she is. Good, bad or indifferent. There is no going back. But I do feel less angry with her. I feel calmer. Counselling has helped with that . . . but forgiveness is still a tricky one.'

Grace said she knew what Lily meant, and that she did feel lucky even though her mother, the mother she knew, was no longer part of her world. The mutual support at the meetings had meant a lot to her. 'We didn't know each other, so it was pure listening. And the acceptance and support surprised me. The mother–daughter relationship is a huge one in our lives, I think; particularly in women's lives. If you are very lucky it's one of the most important relationships in your life, and one of the longest. We don't analyse it that much. We take a lot of the mother–daughter business for granted. I do think that daughters have a lot of guilt about their mammies. You feel the responsibility. You should be her best friend. You should be the person who is there for her. Sons get away with more, I think, in general.'

'It has made me think about my words and actions much more,' Debbie said. 'It made me hope that I can eventually fix things and that my mum and I can be there for each other again in the way that we were during Dad's illness. But, in a way, it has also brought home a certain sadness – I listen to the stories of some of the rest of you and I do wish that I had that relationship with my mum.'

'We know we are lucky,' Róisín said. 'If we didn't before, we know it now.'

Eventually, the talk turned away from our mothers – to work and family and, for Maeve, baby names. The evening was still light when we kissed and hugged goodbye. There were promises to meet up for glasses of wine in a venue that wasn't my house where our mothers would not be mentioned. And that was it. The door closed. Those nights had been some of the most entertaining evenings I'd had for a long time, something that came as a surprise to Róisín and to me. The list of 'things' we ticked off back in January might have been a bit pie in the sky, but in all cases it seemed as though meeting as a group had raised the consciousness of each daughter, forcing us to approach our mothers in a new way.

Last January, I thought I knew that the mother–daughter relationship was complex. Six months later I feel almost overwhelmed by its complexities. And the meetings have confirmed something else I had long suspected: mothers get a very raw deal. In spite of all the other mother clichés, I now believe at least one is true: it really is the hardest job in the world.

In the end, The Daughterhood meetings and their outcome were like most things in life – a mixed success. We were trying to do our best. Our best with our mothers. As we found out, meeting after meeting, when it comes to our mothers our best never felt quite good enough. But what if we were to decide that it was?

As I write, I'm waiting for a new batch of daughters. The next group of women on a mission to stand at their mothers' gravesides with no regrets. Or to minimise those regrets. I imagine there will always be daughters sitting around talking about their mothers. My wish for them, for us, is that they will do that talking with more understanding, insight and intention. That they will do it with other daughters who can share their wisdom and their very different daughter experiences. My wish is that they will laugh and cry and love and appreciate their mothers for the women they were and are. That if they can't love them, my wish is that they will forgive them at the very least; unless, like Anna, they don't feel they need to forgive.

I'm looking forward to spending the time I have left with my own mother. I know it is limited. I have come to accept that; the shock has worn off. I've spent the last few months fobbing my mother off quite a bit. 'I can't talk to you now, a Mhamaí, I'm writing.' 'I can't talk to you now, a Mhamaí, I've a Daughterhood meeting.' Imagine. I can't talk to you, I'm too busy thinking about other mothers, other daughters. Enough. I feel a certain sadness as I close the door on the first Daughterhood group and as I wait for the next one to come together. In the meantime, there is only one thing I want to do – I call my mother.

EPILOGUE

ANN INGLE, RÓISÍN'S MOTHER

This year my children gave me a holiday to Italy for my seventy-fifth birthday. When I told the good news to friends and family they unanimously responded with the mantra 'You deserve it.' I suppose I agreed with them until I began to read *The Daughterhood*.

I deserve it? Yes, of course. Wasn't I widowed at forty and left with eight children to bring up alone? Didn't I rear them, feed them, clothe them, make sure they did their homework and nurtured their talents as much as I could? That's what people mean when they say, 'You deserve it.'

But was it good enough?

I remembered saying goodbye to one of them at the door as they started off from Dublin to a new life in Glasgow. Just a hug and a goodbye and I let her away. She didn't know that I went back into the house and cried, and I didn't know that she felt abandoned.

I remember the time I sent one of them off on their bicycle to the hospital for treatment for a foot injury – 'You'll be fine, just ride slowly.'

And the time I made one daughter cry two days after having a home birth by insisting she didn't call her child Síofra Sorcha Tomásach Aingil (I loved the Síofra Sorcha, even though I find Sorcha a little difficult to pronounce, but the rest . . .). It had to be done, the midwife was to register the birth that day and I thought it for the best. But those tears, that resentment . . . I feel terrible when I think of it now.

The daughter who lost her job at the same time as her husband and when they came home from Donegal I made them chicken pie but gave no sympathy, advice or consolation.

I sold the family home never thinking of the trauma it might cause the last child left adrift.

I could tell you more about the bad decisions I've made over the years, bad mistakes which could have been disastrous. I'm human just like these daughters and their mothers. I always tried to do my best and I have to forgive myself and hope that my daughters will forgive me in return.

Reading the stories of the mothers and daughters in this book was an interesting and rewarding experience. But it saddens me that we expect mothers to be models of excellence and daughters to be compliant and loving.

There are daughters who abandon their mothers without a thought. They justify their actions in whatever way they can. I wasn't even there at the 'mother of all funerals'. I left her for Ireland and a new life when I was twenty-one and our relationship thereafter consisted of fleeting visits, telephone calls and very few letters. I don't think I missed her too much but I never thought about her feelings. I wish now I had thought more about our relationship and that I might have had the benefit of a book like *The Daughterhood* before it was too late.

The daughters in these pages are courageous. Having responded to Róisín and Natasha they have shown that they care and want to make things better despite everything.

I have four daughters but the truth is my relationship with each of them is unique. I am a different mother to each of them because they are individuals with their own distinctive personalities.

I always say my eldest was brought up by Dr Spock because he was my only point of reference at the time. If I had to give her a label it would be the 'Anything You Can Do, I Can Do Just as Well' Daughter. We have a great relationship on equal terms, I like to think, although who makes the best marmalade is still a point of contention. Academically and in many other ways she has surpassed me. I remember very well the first time she found out I wasn't perfect. The teacher in school had for some reason used the word 'disremember'. 'There's no such word,' I told her emphatically and of course an enquiry took place and it was found that there was. In fairness to me, it was a word that the Americans had made up but it was acceptable apparently. It was downhill from then and I was no longer 'she who knows everything'.

There is an Independent Daughter among them. They are all that way because that was what I was aiming for but she is more than most. She doesn't really need me for anything much and that's OK, too. I know she loves me because, as they say, actions, earrings and foreign holidays speak louder than words.

Then there is Róisín but she's told you everything, hasn't she? Not quite. She takes me to special events because of her work and I feel privileged. We argue quite a lot, heatedly sometimes, but then we make it up as quickly. She thinks I treat her differently and says things like 'You wouldn't say that to the others' and she's probably right. Recently after a few days away with her and her family she sent me a text: 'Being with you makes every occasion better.' Yesterday she telephoned to check that I was all right after my eye injection. How did she remember that? I think this book is helping both of us.

I live with my youngest daughter and her husband Killian and that is just right for me. Katie was what other people might have called a clingy child. I never saw it that way. I liked her wanting me around all the time. Now she is married with children of her own and we have made a home together.

I have four daughters (and four wonderful sons) with whom I am well pleased but should I expect or ask for more? Natasha says, *'It's about doings things with and for our mothers . . . It's about bringing them pleasure and at the same time making life pleasurable for ourselves . . .'*

Natasha's idea of discussing death and funeral arrangements is something that I will attend to. Funerals are for the living and, whilst I have strong views about cremation and inexpensive coffins, I must ask my children how they would like my burial service to be conducted.

I have said I expect nothing from my daughters. They didn't ask to be born, as I was reminded by them in their teenage years when things didn't go their way. But if I'm pushed there are a few things I might wish for from them.

I would like to be accepted just as I am with all my faults and foibles. My daughters laugh at me sometimes and I don't mind, well, not too much.

What else do I want? Respect for me and my views. I love it when my opinion is asked for, even though most of the time it isn't acted upon (unless it coincides with theirs). I do wish they would wait for me to finish speaking because, if they don't, inevitably I will forget the wondrous words I was about to utter.

I love being alone with my daughters individually but that doesn't happen too often because of the grandchildren and their busy lives. Recently one daughter and I spent a whole day together at a series of talks at Smock Alley Theatre in Dublin. It was very special for me as we were able to talk about the topics raised and she introduced me to her colleagues. Róisín has already mentioned the day she interviewed me in a restaurant, just the two of us. We were more like two giggling friends than mother and daughter.

I love to laugh with them. One daughter and I were mistaken for Spanish women in a museum in Madrid once. The curator was telling us in Spanish an amusing story about one of the paintings. We knew it was amusing because he was chuckling all the way through but we never understood a word. We laughed so much that day that even remembering it brings tears to our eyes. Róisín has already told you about the nightdress and how we lay on our backs on the floor, our sides aching, like characters from Peppa Pig.

I love when they think of what I might need when I don't even know it myself. One daughter on a very tight budget walked into my bedroom one day with a television she had bought in Tesco and set it up for me as a surprise.

I'm grateful for their love and understanding and fervently hope that I will never be a burden to them. I trust if I am, they will be able to hide it from me. They all have a theatrical flair so it shouldn't be too difficult. I can only take so much honesty.

I came across *The Four Agreements* by Miguel Don Ruiz some years ago and gave a copy to each of my daughters and we often quote it back to one another. One of the agreements reads:

Always do your best. Your best is going to change from moment to moment; it will be different when you are healthy as opposed to sick. Under any circumstance, simply do your best and you will avoid self-judgement, self-abuse and regret.

There are times in our lives when we are not able to muster the strength, patience and understanding that is required of us. We are only human. All we can do is our best and as we learn more we will become better daughters and mothers. Sometimes our best may not be good enough, other times it will be stupendous. I am thankful for the love and companionship of my daughters. Their best has been and always will be good enough for me.

MARY TROY, NATASHA'S MOTHER

When Natasha asked me to write about 'motherhood' I found that the word did not sit easily with me. 'Daughterhood' I had become used to as she and I had had many discussions about her book, but neither were words that would have been part of my normal vocabulary. I realised that it was not a term that I and my friends, also mothers, ever used. Yes, we talked about our children but rarely about ourselves as mothers. With very close friends I might express some of the guilt I feel about times when I failed as a parent. But most of our talk centres on our children, usually attributing their good points and strengths to them and their faults to ourselves.

'If only' is a phrase commonly used: if only I had listened more; if only I had been more there for them; if only I had praised them more. The list of 'if onlys' may differ but one thing we are all agreed on is that being a mother presents an ongoing challenge that lasts a lifetime. Reading the stories of the daughters brought back memories of my own relationship with my mother. I could empathise with their guilt, their impatience to the point of anger at times, and their inability to communicate meaningfully. Most moving are the accounts of loving her but not being able to show it and not being sure that their mother loves them; all emotions I went through with my own mother.

As contraceptives were not easily available at the time, I remember saying to my future husband that if we were going to get married then we were probably going to have a baby. He was rather taken aback and, even though I had no great feeling about babies, never having had anything to do with them, somehow I knew that having one would change my life forever. And it did. I was a student at the time, attending two universities. And, sure enough, after two months of marriage, I discovered I was pregnant. My feelings on hearing the news were a mixture of shock and delight but, honestly, I was more concerned with finishing my degrees. Exams finished in October and the baby was due in November so I had just six weeks to look forward to the birth of my first child. I can still see myself on the bus in a duffel coat going to the hospital both excited and apprehensive. Two days of labour and a C section later, I was presented with my son Oisín, 9 lbs 10 ounces. As I held him in my arms and he looked at me with his piercing blue eyes, I was filled with very mixed emotions. My heart filled with a love that brought tears to my eyes; it was as if his ten little fingers wrapped themselves around my heart never to let go and yet and yet . . . he was a being separate from me, his own person.

As the months went by, the feeling that Oisín did not 'belong' to me grew stronger and, when I mentioned this to friends, they told me that I had no maternal instinct. So for months I suffered all sorts of fears and anxieties about my ability to be a 'good' mother. Did I lack the right maternal feelings and instincts to guide me on this unchartered journey (sorry Natasha) of motherhood? Then my sister, Margaret, gave me a present – *The Prophet* by Kahlil Gibran – and there I found the answer to all my worries, fears and apprehensions.

In his section on your children he opens with: 'Your children are not your children . . . And though they are with you yet they belong not to you.' We may give them our love and try to be like them, but must never try to make them like us. He goes on to compare them to arrows let fly to go where no parent can go as they belong to the future. It's our job to be the best archer we can so that the children we send forth are the best that they can be. On reading this gone was all the guilt and I felt confirmed as a natural mother.

And it was the same when Cilian, Natasha, Sorcha and Kate were born. I realised they, too, were given into my care to nurture and love as individuals and not mine to possess or own.

When Natasha was born I knew very early on that something wasn't right. And my maternal instinct was correct. As she mentioned, there were many visits to doctors and I agonised as to how I would cope with a potentially blind and brain-damaged child. Luckily, Natasha has overcome her visual impairment so well that, meeting her today, you would never suspect she is legally blind, as she goes about her work as any full-sighted person.

I have vivid memories of the time the children got chicken pox or measles in their teens and I rushed home from work to give them hot lemon and pineapple juice with honey and I felt their pain as if it were my own. And, as with all their illnesses, I suffered with them and would have taken on all their pain myself if I could. I became very defensive and when they were bullied or badly treated, I found myself immediately jumping to their defence. Indeed, there were instances when I felt such a rage that at times I felt I would have killed for them.

Each of my children has a strong character and expresses themselves accordingly. During their teenage years this led to raised voices and rows, so that I had to ask some not to come home for dinner and handed out £1, which I could ill afford, to pay for them to eat out. I did try to support them in whatever path they wanted to follow, though, and honestly did not try to impose any expectations of my own.

As the years went by, there were failures and successes, triumphs and disappointments as each pursued their chosen paths. Bumps along the way included one failing exams in college (though with some study he would have passed no problem); having to drive to Derry from Galway to bring back a daughter to re-sit her maths in the leaving cert; and a manic weekend trying to bring back a daughter from France in time to re-apply for college. The list could go on. There were also sad, sad days, for example as my two sons, in spite of excellent qualifications, left to go to England for work. There was a time when all five were out of the country and I was alone here. As there was no Skype, phone bills were enormous but phone I did because it was important to me to know how they were.

When I was growing up we never had friends in to play and I wanted my house to be one where all the children could bring theirs. And they did, in droves! My own relationship with my mother had been strained but with her grandchildren it was quite different. She showed them affection, chatted to them and was very supportive in all that they were involved with: paying for courses, giving them gifts and listening to them. They were very good to her, too, going in to see her, doing messages and reading to her as her sight deteriorated. She enriched their lives and is remembered with love by them all, especially by the youngest, Kate, who was particularly close to her.

And how are things today, you might ask? My health complications have meant that my children have had to look out for me, particularly in the last six years. One does all the practical things around the house, gets the big shopping and organises my pills (quite a task). With one I have discussions on political and philosophical topics; with another discussions about being a mother;

and with another on how best to bring up a child as a single parent. Natasha has written about how they got together to build the en suite in Sorcha's house, but what she didn't say was how overwhelmed I was by it. I had tears of joy and gratitude streaming down my face. For this was not an act of duty to a parent. No, this was an act of love for me, their mother – as was the trip to the Arctic with Natasha and Sorcha, which I will never forget. I treasure the laughs and fun we have when together, especially the evenings spent eating in the garden when laughter can get so raucous I worry the neighbours might complain! We are great party givers and love nothing better than a reason to celebrate: birthdays, anniversaries, successes – any excuse and we party, something I really appreciate about us all.

I've always loved to travel and I have been very lucky to have had Natasha as a travelling companion over many years and to many places. In Australia we travelled for a week with two boys who were only in their early twenties and we all got on very well ... the only hiccup happened when I refused to eat in McDonald's and the generation gap suddenly became apparent!

My relationship with Natasha is very close. In many ways she is the rock of the family and has become my touchstone. Her energy is palpable and she has an abundance of common sense. I talk to her about decisions or choices I have to make in regard to everything from choosing paint colours and recipes, to how I should react to certain circumstances. Advice is there but never judgements; I am left to make my own final decisions which she accepts. She doesn't take my power from me. She organises holidays for us, rings virtually every day and I'm always welcome in her house in Dublin.

I feel very blessed. I love my children unconditionally and have seen them grow into adults who are ethical, hardworking and what I like to call 'decent' human beings. I haven't had to see them go to war, become drug addicts or jailed for any crime. My relationship with each is different, naturally, but I know they are always there for me. I finally accept that they love me.

And let me finish with Kahlil Gibran: 'Love possesses not nor would it be possessed; for love is sufficient unto love.'

POSTSCRIPT

Maeve had a daughter and Lily's expecting!

ACKNOWLEDGEMENTS

We would like to thank Kerri Sharp of Simon and Schuster UK for believing in this project from the start and for all her support during the writing of this book. We're also very grateful to our editor Jo Roberts-Miller for her eagle eyes and warmth towards the book. We really appreciate the time taken by all the women who responded to our callout for daughters at the very beginning of this project. But, above all, we are eternally grateful to the women who joined The Daughterhood and shared their stories with such honesty, courage and great humour along the way.

I – Natasha – would like to thank Róisín for being the perfect collaborator on The Daughterhood. I'll always remember the often moving, more often hilarious, and deeply fulfilling evenings we spent in my kitchen obsessing over all things mother/daughter. Thank you to Ivan Mulcahy of Mulcahy Associates for backing this idea from the very beginning. I owe a deep gratitude to my many friends, in particular, Fiona Slevin, Joanna Gardiner, Rosetta Herr, Susan Heraghty, Sadhbh McCarthy, Adelaide Nic Charthaigh, Cathy Higgins, Claire Molloy and Veronica Cosgrove. They allowed our regular coffee and dinner dates to morph into mini Daughterhood forums and their stories were a constant source of inspiration.

I couldn't have written this book without the support of my family. My father, Desmond, was a constant source of encouragement while my sister, Kate, gave loads of support over Skype from her home in Turkey. My eldest brother Oisín, the backbone of the family, made sure I didn't leave this idea on the back burner. A very special thank you to my sister, Sorcha, whose clarity of thought and insights were particularly valuable during the occasional wobbler. I'm deeply indebted to my brother and business partner, Cilian, for his infinite belief and confidence in me and this book. His unique perspective is a constant inspiration to me. A Mhamaí, buíochas ó chroí as do thacaíocht, do gháire agus do ghrá.

Thank you to all at Stillwater Communications who helped at various stages of The Daughterhood: Rebecca Bury, Lisa Madden, Úna Ní Chárthaigh and Sinéad Ní Bhraoin.

And, finally, I want to thank all the women I spoke to on planes, trains and anywhere I could start a mother conversation. Hearing what you all had to say about your mothers and the willingness with which you spoke confirmed for me that the world needs The Daughterhood.

I – Róisín – would like to thank Natasha – for your friendship, for the laughs and for coming to me with this brilliant idea. Thanks also to my colleagues at the *The Irish Times*, especially Kevin O'Sullivan. I am so lucky to have Faith O'Grady, agent extraordinaire, of the Lisa Richards Agency in my corner. Thanks Faith. Thanks to all my great friends who have supported me in so many different ways, especially Amanda Brady, Patsey Murphy, Paul Howard, Trevor White, The Pot Luckers, Rosita Boland, Alison O'Connor, Una Mullaly, Sarah Francis,

Fiona O'Malley, Aisling McDermott and Lisa Kehoe. Thanks to all my brothers and sisters for your love and tolerance. Special thanks to Joya and Priya for being the kindest, funniest, most loving and bestest daughters a mother could have – I want to shake it off with you forever. Biggest thanks go to my lovely Jonny for making sure I had the time and space to work on this project and for loving me, which can be hard sometimes. Finally to my mother Ann Ingle for everything – I owe you lunch, Ma (yeah, I know, AND the rest).